SECOND EDITION 0

Teacher's Book

CB126800

SUPER MINDS

Lily Pane
with Herbert Puchta · Peter Lewis-Jones

CAMBRIDGE
UNIVERSITY PRESS

Thanks and Acknowledgments

Acknowledgments

The authors and publishers acknowledge the following sources of copyright material and are grateful for the permissions granted. While every effort has been made, it has not always been possible to identify the sources of all the material used, or to trace all copyright holders. If any omissions are brought to our notice, we will be happy to include the appropriate acknowledgments on reprinting and in the next update to the digital edition, as applicable.

Photography and Illustrations

The photographs and illustrations in the teaching notes are reused from the Student's Book.

The photographs and illustrations in the Introduction are reused from the Student's Book, Workbook, Practice Book, Flashcards, Presentation Plus, and Practice Extra.

Contents

Map of the Book

Say *Hello!* (pages 4–9)

Vocabulary	Language Focus	Story
Colors: *blue, green, yellow, orange, red, pink* Numbers 1–10	• *Hello! What's your name?* • *I'm …* • *What color is it?*	*Friends* **Value** Making Friends

▶ Song: Let's Be Friends

1 My Classroom (pages 10–19)

What's in my classroom?

Vocabulary	Language Focus	Story	Think and Learn
Classroom Objects: *window, chair, book, pencil, table, door*	• *Imperatives* • *What is it? It's …*	*The Butterfly* **Value** Appreciating Nature	**Math:** Patterns **Project:** Create a pattern.
▶ Song: Look! It's My Classroom		▶ Creativity: Create That!	▶ Review: Think Back

2 My Body (pages 20–29)

How do we move?

Vocabulary	Language Focus	Story	Think and Learn
The Body: *eyes, ears, arms, legs, mouth, nose, head*	• *I have …* • *How many … ?*	*Great Costumes!* **Value** Using Your Imagination	**Science:** Our Skeleton **Project:** Draw three stick people.
▶ Song: Run, Run, Run!		▶ Creativity: Do That!	▶ Review: Think Back

3 My Family (pages 30–39)

What's a family?

Vocabulary	Language Focus	Story	Think and Learn
Family: *mom, dad, sister, brother, grandpa, grandma*	• *This is my …* • *Is this your … ?* • *Yes, it is. / No, it isn't.*	*Cool Grandma* **Value** Appreciating Family	**Social Science:** An Animal Family **Project:** Make an animal family.
▶ Song: A Nice Family		▶ Creativity: Create That!	▶ Review: Think Back

4 At the Zoo (pages 40–49)

Where can we find animals?

Vocabulary	Language Focus	Story	Think and Learn
Animals: *parrot, fish, zebra, lion, big, small*	• Adjectives • *What's your favorite … ?*	*My Favorite Animal* **Value** Friendship	**Science:** Animal Habitats **Project:** Make a puzzle.
▶ Song: Where Are the Animals?		▶ Creativity: Do That!	▶ Review: Think Back

5 My Food (pages 50–59)

What food do we eat?

Vocabulary	Language Focus	Story	Think and Learn
Food: *milk, oranges, cupcakes, tomatoes, chocolate, pears*	• *I like / I don't like …* • *Do you like … ?* • *Yes, I do. / No, I don't.*	*The Cupcakes* **Value** Sharing	**Science:** Fruit and Vegetables **Project:** Make a food picture.
▶ Song: I Like *You*		▶ Creativity: Create That!	▶ Review: Think Back

6 My Town (pages 60–69)

What's in your town?

Vocabulary	Language Focus	Story	Think and Learn
Places in a Town: *bus stop, school, movie theater, hospital, toy store, park*	• *There's / There are …* • *Where's the … ? It's there.*	*The Toy Store* **Value** Being Kind	**Geography:** Maps and Towns **Project:** Make a map of your dream town.
▶ Song: A Really Cool Town		▶ Creativity: Do That!	▶ Review: Think Back

7 Jobs (pages 70–79)

What's a job?

Vocabulary	Language Focus	Story	Think and Learn
Jobs: *teacher, firefighter, gardener, police officer, vet, doctor*	• *He's/She's a …* • *Is he/she a … ?* • *Yes, he/she is. / No, he/she isn't.*	*The Teacher* **Value** Appreciating Others	**Social Science:** Inside and Outside Jobs **Project:** Make a class poster.
▶ Song: Helping Me, Helping You		▶ Creativity: Create That!	▶ Review: Think Back

8 My Clothes (pages 80–89)

What clothes do we need?

Vocabulary	Language Focus	Story	Think and Learn
Clothes: *hat, coat, scarf, boots, sweater, gloves, jeans, T-shirt*	• *I'm wearing …* • *Is he/she wearing … ?*	*Hot or Cold?* **Value** Being Prepared	**Science:** Different Clothes **Project:** Draw items of clothing.
▶ Song: It's Cold!		▶ Creativity: Do That!	▶ Review: Think Back

9 My Hobbies (pages 90–99)

What are hobbies?

Vocabulary	Language Focus	Story	Think and Learn
Hobbies: *play soccer, run, paint a picture, swim, read, dance*	• *I'm + ing* • *Are you + ing?* • *Yes, I am. / No, I'm not.*	*Guess What I'm Doing?* **Value** Saying Sorry	**Math:** Bar Charts **Project:** Make a bar chart about your friends.
▶ Song: I'm Having Fun		▶ Creativity: Create That!	▶ Review: Think Back

Key to Teaching Notes Icons

- Cambridge Life Competencies Framework
- Cognitive Control Functions
- Stickers
- Story
- Values

In the teaching notes, these two icons use the colors shown here in order to help contrast the two areas for teachers. For students, both kinds of icon use one color.

Welcome to SUPER MINDS SECOND EDITION

Rediscover *Super Minds!*

Welcome to *Super Minds 2nd Edition*, a thoroughly updated and enhanced new edition of a much-loved English course from this renowned author team.

Accompany your students on exciting adventures with the intrepid characters, as they enjoy creative projects, authentic CLIL content, and the flexibility of the extensive skills practice, while working toward B1 level on the Common European Framework of Reference for Languages (CEFR).

Aligned to the Cambridge Life Competencies Framework, *Super Minds 2nd Edition* has a particular focus on developing critical and creative thinking skills. In addition, throughout the course, students will develop their working memory, inhibitory control, and cognitive flexibility, three key cognitive control functions for young learners. Together with the universal values introduced in each story, these skills help create curious and successful lifelong learners and socially responsible individuals.

Super Minds 2nd Edition is supported by a comprehensive digital package in *Cambridge One*, a new-generation learning environment, including big-screen quality animated videos for the classroom and Practice Extra, with digital activities for home or lab learning. In addition, Practice Extra includes comprehensive data views, rewards, and the capacity to assign homework digitally.

Super Minds 2nd Edition is a course that combines the very best of rich classroom experience with current pedagogical research.

Super Minds Starter level brings completely new content and has a comprehensive, literacy-based approach, providing students with essential language support integral to literacy training that will ensure they become fully literate in English.

Super Minds 2nd Edition: The Thinking Course, Revisited

***Super Minds* is loved by millions of learners of English in over 70 countries. Since its publication, we have conducted extensive research to find out what teachers and learners love about *Super Minds* and what could be updated and made even better.**

While this new and improved 2nd Edition of *Super Minds* maintains its easy-to-use, comprehensive language syllabus and unit structure, the experience of teaching and learning with the course is thoroughly refreshed and contemporary.

What have we kept?

The things teachers and learners love:

- relatable characters who enjoy exciting adventures
- fun and catchy songs and chants that aid engagement in the classroom and at home
- interactive and engaging projects and activities
- authentic CLIL content and extensive skills practice
- a comprehensive language syllabus.

What have we improved?

***Super Minds 2nd Edition* represents a significant update. Here's how *Super Minds 2nd Edition* has changed:**

1 New Design

- The characters and stories throughout the course have been transformed with new contemporary illustrations: today's students will find them as relatable as ever and be delighted by their adventures.
- Higher levels have been designed to reflect the increased sophistication of today's pre-teens.
- A full-color Workbook gives learners further practice and consolidates learning.

2 Fresh and Updated Content

- Exciting new animated story videos and song videos from Starter to Level 4, as well as animated *Language Focus* videos at all levels.
- New *Think and Learn* CLIL content and videos linked to topics students will be studying in their first language.
- Creative and critical thinking strands have been updated and developed in line with the Cambridge Life Competencies Framework. Activities are mapped to the Framework and explained in the Teacher's Book.
- Activities designed to enhance cognitive control functions, which will lead to more successful language learning.
- New *Big Questions* at the beginning of every unit give students a gradual introduction to inquiry-based learning.

3 Enhanced Digital Support

- Extensive digital support for teachers and students is accessed through our new learning environment, *Cambridge One*.
- Presentation Plus gives easy access to resources in the classroom, including the new animated videos.
- Practice Extra provides extra digital activities for students in a carefully tailored environment designed specifically for primary learners. It includes interactive games to review language and *Brain Break* activities to aid motivation and help recharge the brain.

Presentation Plus

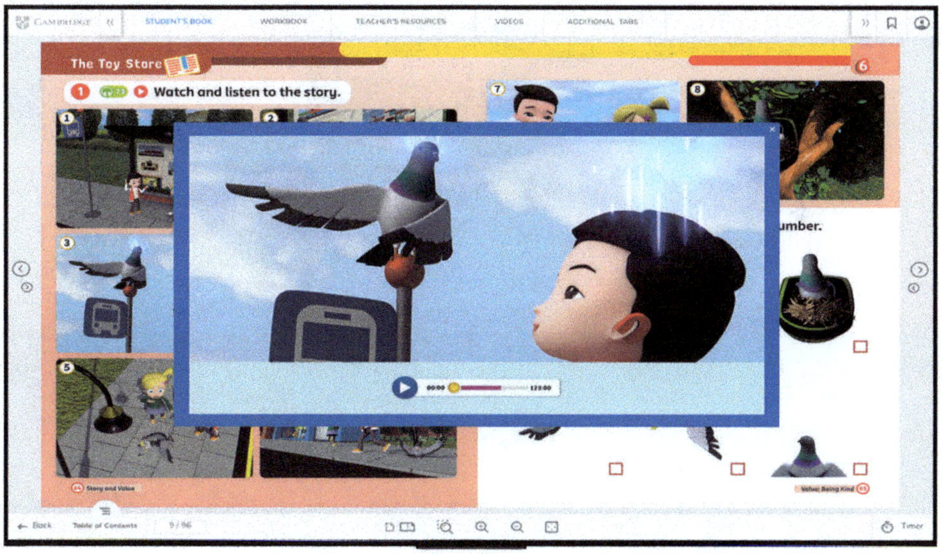

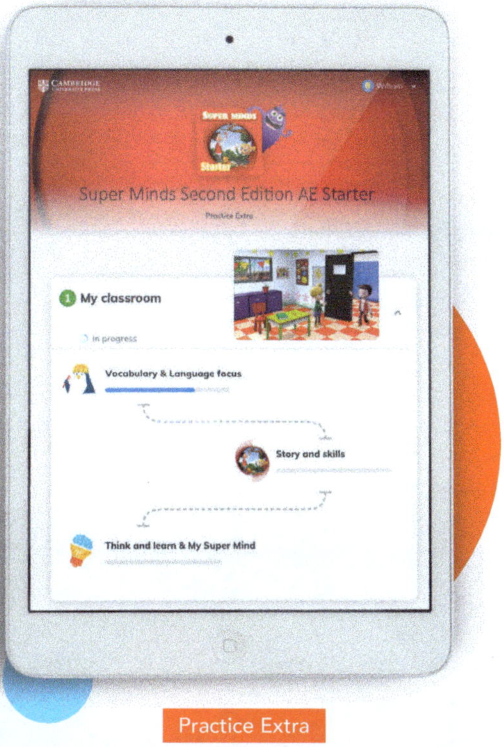

Practice Extra

The Cambridge Life Competencies Framework

Our world is changing fast, and we need to prepare our students with the skills and experiences that go beyond learning an additional language.

Our job as primary educators is complex. How do we prepare our students for a future that may be dramatically different from the present? Experts say there are some key skills that will be essential for the citizens of tomorrow: working together with people from around the world, thinking creatively to solve problems, analyzing sources more critically, communicating our views effectively, and maintaining a positive mindset in an increasingly complex world.

The Cambridge Life Competencies Framework supports teachers in this challenging area – we understand that the engaging and collaborative nature of the language classroom is the perfect place to develop and embed these key qualities.

Competency

- Communication
- Collaboration
- Learning to Learn
- Creative Thinking
- Critical Thinking
- Social Responsibilities
- Emotional Development

Core Areas

- Preparing for creativity
- Generating ideas
- Implementing ideas and solving problems

Components

- Generating multiple ideas
- Elaborating on and combining ideas
- Imagining alternatives and possibilities

Example "Can Do" statements

- Finds new uses for objects and explains these ideas in detail

Super Minds 2nd Edition and the Cambridge Life Competencies Framework

The Cambridge Life Competencies Framework underpins the Critical and Creative Thinking strands of *Super Minds 2nd Edition*, helping to create curious and successful lifelong learners.

Critical Thinking

This activity from Unit 4 of the Student's Book helps learners understand and analyze links between ideas by sorting and classifying according to key features.

Creative Thinking

This activity from Unit 1 of the Student's Book helps learners develop creative thinking skills by participating in creative activities such as drawing pictures to represent vocabulary and familiar concepts.

For more information about the *Cambridge Life Competencies Framework*, go to languageresearch.cambridge.org/clc

Cognitive Control Functions

Successful language learning requires our learners to be in control of their own learning and of themselves. To do this, they need to:

- set goals
- organize learning over time
- focus attention to be able to stay on task
- adapt behavior in order to overcome challenges and reach goals.

To manage these behaviors successfully, the brain uses **cognitive control functions,** which determine students' success in learning and have a significant influence on their future success and well-being.

Activities in *Super Minds 2nd Edition* have been designed to enhance the **three core areas** of learners' cognitive control functions:

Working memory

is the ability to remember information so that certain tasks can be completed.

This activity in Unit 6 of the Workbook helps to improve learners' working memory.

1 51 Listen. What can you remember? Draw.

2 Finish the picture. Draw what a good friend does.

Inhibitory control

refers to the abilities to focus attention and to control our emotional and behavioral responses.

This activity in Unit 6 of the Workbook helps to improve learners' inhibitory control.

Cognitive flexibility

is needed for solving problems and enables students to look at issues from different viewpoints, to think "outside the box," and to adapt to changing conditions.

This activity in Unit 2 of the Student's Book helps to improve learners' cognitive flexibility.

3 Draw a monster. Play *Ask the Monster*.

Unit Walkthrough

Key vocabulary

is presented in an opening illustration that features the *Super Minds* characters and sets the scene for the main story of the unit. Full-color digital or printed flashcard sets help learners practice vocabulary.

The Big Question

is a new feature that gives a gradual introduction to inquiry-based learning. Each *Big Question* is directly related to the unit topic and is explored throughout the unit with further ideas for exploitation available in the Teacher's Book.

Fun and informative songs

practicing and extending the vocabulary and language of the unit are featured throughout *Super Minds 2nd Edition.* Karaoke song videos can be found in Presentation Plus and the teacher and learner resource areas in *Cambridge One.*

Contextualized language

is presented in new 2nd Edition story-based animated *Language Focus* videos, featuring the entertaining character Penny the Penguin. Each Starter level unit has one animated video that can be accessed through Presentation Plus and the teacher and learner resource areas in *Cambridge One.*

Episodic adventure stories

linked to the unit theme run throughout each level and feature the classic *Super Minds* characters.

Brand new big-screen quality animated story videos

are a new feature of the 2nd Edition and can be accessed through Presentation Plus and the teacher and learner resource areas in *Cambridge One*.

Universal values

are introduced with each story and supported with extension activities in the Teacher's Book. Thinking about values and applying them when interacting with others is a key life competency and helps build socially responsible individuals.

Think and Learn CLIL projects

integrate content and language, with students learning about other curriculum subjects in English so that their English is expansive. The CLIL syllabus has been specially designed to cover similar topics as those that students will be encountering in their first language at the same stage.

Brand new documentary-style videos

present the topic and the vocabulary of the CLIL pages.

Project

Each *Think and Learn* spread culminates in a project that can be done in class or assigned as homework.

Create That! and *Do That!*

offer further opportunities for students to develop their creativity as well as practice their listening skills.

Think Back

review pages help to consolidate learning.

How do we approach literacy in *Super Minds*?

The Starter level *Super Minds* Student's Book provides a gradual introduction to literacy, while Workbook activities enhance and develop literacy skills as learners progress through the course.

In Units 0 to 3, learners complete matching, tracing, and coloring activities as they learn to recognize and write numerals. Learners have repeated exposure to words on the page, supported by pictures and sounds, but are not expected to read or write words at this stage.

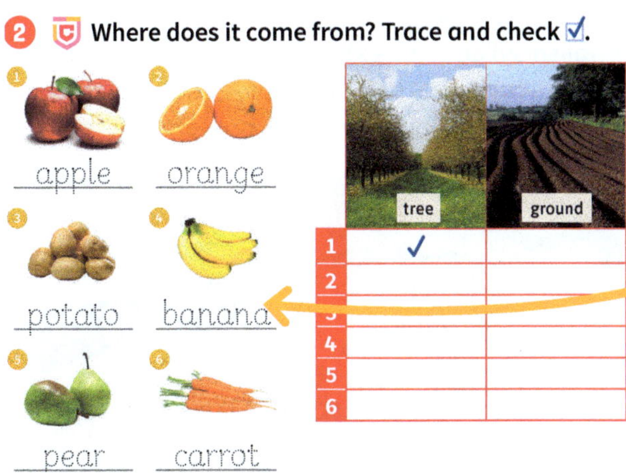

In Units 4 to 6, learners begin reading and tracing single words and matching them to objects as well as learning to write single letters.

In Units 7 to 9, learners start to read sentences with key vocabulary and to write words with models or pictures as prompts to complete sentences with key language from the units.

Components Overview

Student's Components

The **Student's Book** contains 10 units, each with a fun and relevant topic for learners and its own vocabulary and language focus. The back of the Student's Book also contains an additional *Language Focus* section for each unit and two pages of colorful stickers to practice language and skills in corresponding activities throughout the book.

The **Workbook**, now full-color for the 2nd Edition, correlates page by page with the Student's Book, making it easy to use both books in class. The Workbook also includes a code for students to access the Digital Pack, including Practice Extra.

Student's Book

Workbook

For Levels 1–6, the **Super Practice Book** is an additional and optional component for students that practices both language and skills, with teacher and parent notes also available. This component has been updated for the 2nd Edition to include speaking and listening in addition to reading and writing pages.

Teacher's Components

The **Teacher's Book** features the Student's Book pages interleaved on each spread, ensuring that your classroom experience is as smooth as possible. It includes activity-by-activity mapping to Critical and Creative Thinking in the Cambridge Life Competencies Framework, as well as to cognitive control functions.

Flashcards help learners practice key vocabulary from the unit, with an illustration or photo on one side and target language on the other. Digital flashcards are available for all levels, with the option of a set of printed flashcards for each level from Starter to Level 4.

Flashcards

Poster packs are available, with five vibrant posters for each level, providing teachers with an eye-catching, engaging resource for language practice. The posters focus on key language from the Student's Book and include extra words from the corresponding Young Learners English syllabus to extend students' vocabulary. Accompanying activity notes offer a variety of interactive, engaging activities to fully exploit the posters.

Level 1 Super Practice Book

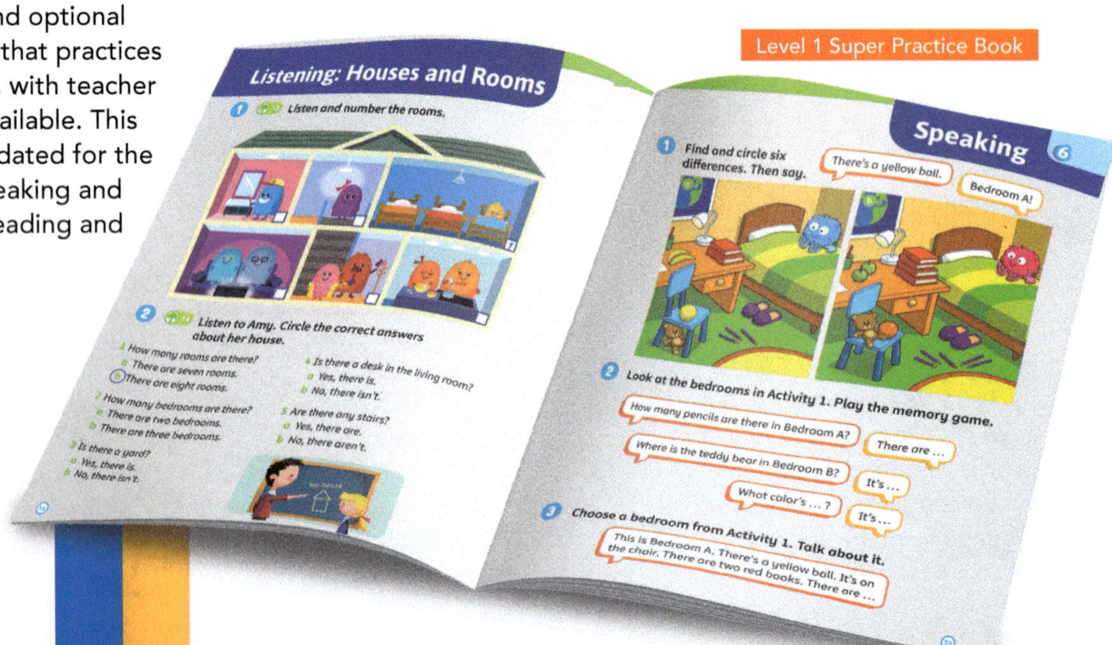

Digital Components

***Super Minds 2nd Edition* is supported by a comprehensive digital package for the teacher and the student. It is designed to be flexible and offers rich support for the classroom, while offering age-appropriate additional support for students, whether in the classroom or at home.**

The digital package can be found all in one place in our new learning environment *Cambridge One*, ensuring the digital experience is smooth and intuitive. Teachers can access the content using the unique code found on the inside front cover of this Teacher's Book. Students will find their access code on the inside front cover of their Workbook.

The *Super Minds 2nd Edition* digital package contains the following components.

For teachers:

Presentation Plus provides page-faithful reproductions of the Student's Book and Workbook, and includes:

- hotspots to audio and video content and interactive reproductions of activities
- interactive games and digital flashcards
- quick and easy access to the Teacher's Book notes corresponding to the Student's Book or Workbook page.

Teacher Resources include:

- a wide range of downloadable photocopiable activities
- teacher's notes, parent's notes, and answer keys for the Super Practice Book
- downloadable, printable tests for Starter Level
- access to all the course audio and video.

Test Generator provides the option of ready-made or customizable tests at different levels of challenge for Levels 1 to 6.

For students:

Practice Extra includes:

- online activities that consolidate classroom learning, including animations and interactive games to engage students
- *Brain Breaks*, activities designed to aid motivation and help recharge the brain.

Learner Resources provide students with access to the wealth of audio-visual content that *Super Minds 2nd Edition* has to offer.

Portfolio provides students with the opportunity to document and present their project work.

Presentation Plus

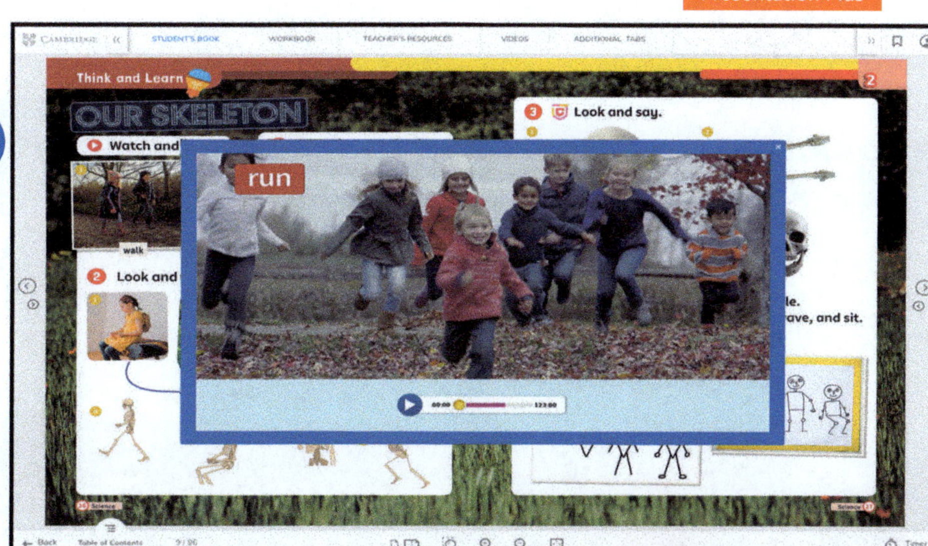

Practice Extra

Say *Hello!*

1 01 Listen and sing.

Learning outcomes:
- to learn greetings
- to sing a song

New language: *Hello!, What's your name?, I'm (Whisper)., Let's be friends., Bye., Goodbye.*

Materials: flashcards 1–6 (colors) and 7–16 (numbers *one* to *ten*), one strip of paper per student, construction paper, glue

Warm-up

Aim: to get to know each other
- Write your name on the board, and introduce yourself, e.g., *I'm (Lauren).*
- Hand out strips of paper (see Materials), and ask students to write their names on them.
- Invite students to come to the board, show their names, and introduce themselves, e.g., *I'm (Chris.)*
- Place students' names on the board.
- Leave the names on the board for the Ending the lesson activity.

Presentation

Aim: to introduce the series characters
- Ask students to look at page 4, and introduce the characters Misty (the girl on the left) and Whisper (the boy on the right).
- Tell students both Whisper and Misty have special powers they will discover soon.

1 01 ▶ 02 SB p4 Listen and sing.

Aim: to sing a song
- Students look at the illustration on page 4 again.
- They identify the two characters, Misty and Whisper.
- Play the audio (01). Point to the characters as they are mentioned.

For song lyrics, see TB p100.

- Play the audio again, and sing with the class.
- Play the song video, pausing after each verse for students to repeat.
- When students have learned the song, use the karaoke version of the video or audio (02) to practice the song again.
- Invite pairs of students to perform as Misty and Whisper while singing the song.

1 01 WB p4 Listen and say the names. Color.

Aim: to identify characters

For song lyrics, see TB p100.

Key: Misty, Whisper

Ending the lesson

Aim: to practice new language
- Point to two names on the board, and invite those two students to the front.
- Students introduce themselves.
- Repeat with other students.
- Take out the construction paper (see Materials), and glue students' names on it. Display the poster in the classroom.

Extension activity

Aim: to practice new language
- Teach students how to say goodbye to you when the lesson is over.
- Pretend you are leaving the classroom, and say goodbye. Close the door after you. Then knock at the door, open it, and say hello.
- Volunteer students perform following your example.
- Remind students to say goodbye to you at the end of the class.

Learning outcomes:
- to review new language

Recycled language: *Hello. What's your name?, I'm (Misty).*

Materials: puppets, soft ball

Warm-up

Aim: to review new language
- Take out the puppets. (see Materials)
- Act out a conversation between the two puppets using the language from the song from page 4.
- Volunteer students use the puppets to perform in front of the class. They give the puppets new names.

1 03 SB p5 Listen and point. Say the names.

Aim: to review new language
- Play the recording.

For script, see TB p100.

- Students listen and point to each character as they hear their names.
- Students say the characters' names as they point to them.

2 SB p5 Ask and answer.

- Students perform the dialogue from the recording with a partner.
- One of the students performs as Whisper and the other as Misty.

1 WB p5 Match and say.

Aim: to identify characters

Key: 1 a, 2 b

2 02 WB p5 Listen and match.

Aim: to identify characters

For script, see TB p100.

Key: One bell – Whisper, Two bells – Misty

Ending the lesson

Aim: to practice new language
- Students stand in a circle.
- Take out the soft ball (see Materials).
- Give the ball to one student. This student says his/her name, e.g., *I'm Pedro.*, and throws the ball to another student as he/she asks *What's your name?*
- Continue until everyone has participated.
- An alternative is to ask students to sit in a circle and ask them to roll the ball on the floor.

Extension activity

Aim: to practice new language
- Students invent and draw a new character in their notebooks: an animal or a person.
- They think of a name for their character.
- Students go around the classroom with their notebooks.
- They pretend they are the character they have invented and introduce themselves.

1 03 Listen and point. Say the names.

2 Ask and answer.

1 04 Listen and point. Listen and say the words.

2 Look and find. Say.

Learning outcomes:
- to learn colors

New language: *blue, green, yellow, orange, red, pink, What color is it?*

Materials: plastic bottle, flashcards 1–6 (colors), strip of paper with six empty circles in a row (one per student) (optional)

Warm-up

Aim: to review language
- Students sit in a circle.
- Put a bottle (see Materials) in the middle of the circle and spin it.
- Whoever the bottle points to must introduce himself/herself.

Presentation

Aim: to teach colors
- Show one colored pencil at a time, and elicit the colors students may already know.
- Correct pronunciation by saying the colors yourself.
- Ask students to show you a pencil that is the color you say.

1 04 SB p6 Listen and point. Listen and say the words.

Aim: to teach new vocabulary
- Play the recording. Students point as they listen.

For script, see TB p100.

- Play the recording again for students to repeat.
- Say colors in random order for students to point to them.
- Ask *What color is it?* while pointing to any of the pencils on the page.
- Encourage students to ask you questions.

2 SB p6 Look and find. Say.

Aim: to practice new language
- Show students how to do the activity.
- Point to something in the classroom and ask *What color is it?*
- Students answer.
- Students work in pairs. One of them points and asks, and the other says the color.
- Change pairs.

1 03 WB p6 Listen and color.

Aim: to practice colors

For script, see TB p100.

Key: 1 red, 2 yellow, 3 green, 4 blue, 5 orange, 6 pink

2 WB p6 Match and say.

Aim: to practice new language

Key: 1 ⚀, 2 ⚁, 3 ⚂, 4 ⚃, 5 ⚄, 6 ⚅

Ending the lesson

Aim: to review new language
- Take out the *colors* flashcards. (see Materials)
- Place the cards face down in a pile on your desk.
- Make two or three teams.
- Take the first card in the pile, and do not show it to the class.
- Call out the name of a student per team.
- Those students must guess what color you are holding.
- The students who guess first get a point for their team.

Extension activity

Aim: to practice new language
- Hand out the strips of paper. (see Materials)
- Tell students you will say colors, and they have to color the circles in the order you mention them from left to right.
- Students take out six colored pencils of the colors they have learned, i.e., blue, green, yellow, orange, red, and pink.
- Say a color, and give students time to color the first circle. Continue with the rest of the colors.
- Go around the classroom to check performance.

Extra support: You may want to reduce the quantity of circles to three instead of six, and let students color the circles in random order, as long as they use the colors you mention.

Learning outcomes:
- to teach numbers

New language: numbers 1 to 10

Recycled language: colors

Materials: flashcards 7–16 (numbers *one* to *ten*)

Warm-up

Aim: to review colors
- Play *I Spy with My Little Eye* to review colors.
- Make groups.
- Make sure students take turns guessing.

1 05 SB p7 Listen and point. Listen and say the numbers.

Aim: to teach numbers
- Ask ten students to stand up in front of the class.
- Start counting them out loud.
- Start all over again. Students repeat after you.
- Students sit down.
- Play the recording while student point to the kites on page 7.

For script, see TB p100.

- Play the recording again for students to say the numbers out loud.

2 SB p7 Point and say. Count.

Aim: to practice new language
- Point and say the numbers out loud.
- Students repeat as a class.
- Make pairs.
- Students count the numbers together.
- Go around the classroom to check pronunciation.

Key: one, two, three, four, five, six, seven, eight, nine, ten

1 04 WB p7 Listen and point. Say the numbers.

Aim: to practice numbers

For script, see TB p100.

2 WB p7 Point and say. Count.

Aim: to practice numbers

Ending the lesson

Aim: to practice new language
- Take out the *numbers* flashcards. (see Materials)
- Show them, one by one, in chronological order, and say the numbers out loud.
- Then show the cards in random order for students to say the number.
- Put the numbers in a pile face down.
- Volunteer students go the front, take one card, and say the number.

Extension activity

Aim: to practice new language
- Take out the *numbers* flashcards.
- Students take out ten colored pencils.
- Show one flashcard.
- Students show the corresponding number of pencils on their tables.
- Go around the classroom to check performance.

1 05 **Listen and point. Listen and say the numbers.**

2 **Point and say. Count.**

Friends

1 06 Watch and listen to the story.

Learning outcomes:
- to listen to, watch, and act out a picture story
- to review language from the unit

New language: *Poor rabbit., cool, Watch this!, Close your eyes., Where are you?, Here!, Wow!*

Recycled language: colors, numbers

Value: making friends

Materials: blindfold, a toy rabbit (optional)

Warm-up

Aim: to make students familiar with the story
- Students open their books to pages 8 and 9.
- Point to the characters and elicit their names.
- Students tell you the colors of different elements in the story you point to.
- Pre-teach the word *rabbit*.

Friends

1 06 SB pp8–9 Watch and listen to the story.

Aim: to present a picture story
- Play the audio as students follow the story in their books.
- Play the audio again. Pause after each frame. Students listen and repeat.

For script, see TB page 100.

- Play the *Friends* video to the end.
- Talk about the story value: making friends.
- Students tell you what they do with their friends.

  Note: The discussion will need to be in your students' first language (L1).

1 05 WB p8 Listen and match.

Aim: to review the picture story

For script, see TB p100.

Key: a 3, (b 1), c 4, d 2

2 06 WB p8 Listen and point.

Aim: to review the picture story

For script, see TB p100.

Ending the lesson

Aim: to practice vocabulary from the story
- Put a blindfold on. Tell students you will try to discover where a student is.
- Say the name of a student. The student stands somewhere in the classroom and does not move from there.
- Ask *Where are you?*
- The student should always answer *Here!* for you to guess where he/she is.
- When you find him/her, it is another student's turn to take your role.

Extension activity

Aim: to act out the story
- Play the *Friends* video again.
- Take out the toy rabbit to use it as a prop, and call two students to play Whisper and Misty.
- Help students to perform in front of the class.
- Let other students act out the story.

Learning outcomes:
- to review language from the story and the unit

Recycled language: vocabulary and grammar from the unit

Value: making friends

Critical thinking: Solves simple puzzles

Critical thinking (WB): Identifies characters, setting, plots, and theme in a story

Cognitive control functions (SB & WB): Cognitive flexibility

Materials: board markers/chalk that are the colors taught in this lesson, flashcards 1–6 (colors) and 7–16 (numbers *one* to *ten*)

Warm-up

Aim: to review language
- Take out the *colors* and *numbers* flashcards.
- Play a memory game with them.
- Make two teams, A and B.
- Place the flashcards in random order on your desk.
- Students memorize where each one is.
- Choose one student from team A.
- He/She turns around and you take a card from the desk.
- When the student turns around, he/she must guess the flashcard that is missing.
- Continue with team B.
- Scramble the flashcards from time to time.
- The team with the most correct guesses is the winner.

Extra support: Instead of using the *colors* and *numbers* flashcards at the same time, use them separately.

2 SB p9 Find and color. Say the colors.

Aim: to review language from the unit
- Students find the objects in the story scenes and color them their original color.
- To check performance, point to each object and ask *What color is it?*
- Student say the colors.

Key: 1 red, 2 green, 3 blue, 4 yellow

1 WB p9 What's good? Draw ☺.

Aim: to understand the value of making friends

Key: 1

2 WB p9 Complete the picture. Draw yourself making friends.

Aim: to understand the value of making friends

Ending the lesson

Aim: to review language from the unit
- Take out the markers/chalk. (see Materials)
- Place the markers/chalk on your desk.
- Invite one student to the board.
- Say a number and color, e.g., 5, blue.
- The student draws five simple objects or shapes that are blue, e.g., five blue lines.
- Continue with other students.

Extension activity

Aim: to focus on the value of making friends
- Students tell you what they would like to share with new friends, e.g., a toy they have.
- Remind students that Whisper and Misty have superpowers that they showed to each other. Ask students to think of things they like or know how to do that they would like to tell a new friend about, e.g., that they know how to play a musical instrument.

Note: This discussion will need to take place in L1.

2 Find and color. Say the colors.

1 My Classroom

1 07 Listen and point. Say the words.

BIG QUESTION What's in my classroom?

2 08 Listen and chant.

Learning outcomes:
- to name and talk about things in the classroom
- to say a chant

BIG QUESTION to start to think about the Big Question *What's in my classroom?*

New language: *table, chair, book, pencil, door, window*

Recycled language: colors, numbers

Cognitive control functions: Working memory

Flashcards: 17–22 (classroom objects)

Warm-up

Aim: to review numbers
- Write the numbers 1 to 10 on the board.
- Say the numbers as you write each of them. Students repeat after you.
- Circle a number at random for students to say it out loud. Continue with the rest of the numbers.
- Ask volunteers to come to the front, point to a number, and choose another student to say the number out loud.

Presentation

Aim: to present classroom objects
- Take out the *classroom objects* flashcards.
- Hold up each flashcard one at a time, and say the word for the class to repeat.
- Place the flashcards face down on your desk.
- Ask volunteers to come to the front, choose one flashcard, and show it to the class.
- Students say the word. Correct pronunciation, if necessary.

1 07 SB 10 Listen and point. Say the words.

Aim: to practice classroom objects
- Students look at the pictures in their Student's Book.
- Point to the two characters and introduce them: *This is Whisper, and this is Misty.*
- Point to the scene, and say *This is a classroom.*
- Play the recording. Students listen and point to the corresponding objects.

For script, see TB p100.

- Play the recording again for students to repeat the words.
- Stick the flashcards on the board in random order.
- Students listen to the recording once more. Volunteers put the flashcards in order of occurrence.

BIG QUESTION What's in my classroom?

Aim: to encourage students to identify what is in a classroom
- Read the Big Question. Ask students to say the names of all the classroom objects they already know in English.
- Ask students to think about which of the classroom objects on the flashcards they consider the most important.

Note: Some of the discussion will need to be in L1.

2 08 SB p10 Listen and chant.

Aim: to give students further practice saying the classroom words
- Play the recording. Students listen and follow the chant in their Student's Books.

For chant script, see TB p100.

- Play the recording again, pausing after each verse for students to repeat. Do the chant as a class and then in groups.

Practice

Aim: to personalize and practice the new language
- Encourage students to show you or point to the classroom object you mention.
- Say *Pencil.* Students show you a pencil, etc. Speed up the pace when you say the words.

1 07 WB 10 Listen and match. Say.

Aim: to practice new language from the lesson

For script, see TB p101.

Key: 2 table, 3 window, 4 book, 5 door, 6 chair

2 08 WB 10 Listen and color.

Aim: to practice new language from the lesson

For script, see TB p101.

Key: window: orange and blue, chair: green and yellow, book: red and blue, pencil: yellow and blue

Ending the lesson

Aim: to review classroom objects and numbers
- Encourage volunteer students to reproduce the chant on the board by using numbers and drawing, e.g., 1, 2, 3, 4, (drawing of a table), (drawing of a chair), etc.

Extension activity

Aim: to review classroom objects, colors, and numbers
- Ask students to open their notebooks.
- Dictate classroom objects for students to draw, e.g., *one window, three pencils,* etc.
- Start another dictation including colors, e.g., *two green books.*
- Go around the classroom and check performance.

Learning outcomes:
- to give and follow instructions in the classroom

New language: *Stand up., Sit down., Open/Close your book.*

Recycled language: classroom objects

Materials: flashcards (classroom objects), 30 paper squares (1 for each letter of the classroom objects: *table, pencil, chair, door, book, window*. Write each letter in uppercase on the squares, e.g., a *T* on a square for the word *table*.), Unit 1 stickers, scissors

Warm-up

Aim: to review classroom objects

- Make six groups, one for each of the classroom object words taught on page 10.
- Distribute the paper squares corresponding to a classroom object to each group, e.g., the letters *T, A, B, L, E* to one group.
- Students make the word with the paper squares.
- Ask groups to stick the words on the board.

1 09 SB 11 Listen and point. Listen and stick.

Aim: to present classroom instructions

Note: In order to carry out *Listen and stick* activities, students will first need to cut out their stickers with the backs attached.

- Give students time to look at the pictures in their Student's Books.
- Ask students to point to the corresponding picture as you play the recording. Do the activity with your students by holding up your book and pointing to the pictures.

For script, see TB p101.

- Students prepare their stickers.
- Play the recording again. Students listen and stick them in the corresponding place in Activity 1.

Key: 1 open your book, 2 close your book, 3 stand up, 4 sit down

2 10 SB 11 Look, listen, and say.

Aim: to give students practice with classroom instructions

- Play the recording for a third time for students to repeat.
- Correct pronunciation, if necessary.

3 SB 11 Work with a partner. Say and do.

Aim: to give students practice with giving and following instructions

- Students work in pairs to give and follow instructions.
- After three instructions, students swap roles.

1 09 WB 11 Listen and color.

Aim: to identify instructions

- Check that students know what they are going to color. (the edge of the picture)

For script, see TB p101.

Key: 1 green, (2 blue), 3 red, 4 yellow

2 10 WB 11 Listen. Point and say.

Aim: to practice instructions

For script, see TB p101.

Key: 2 Open your book.
3 Stand up. 4 Close your book.

Ending the lesson

Aim: to review giving and following instructions

- Play *Simon Says* with the class.
- Students follow your instructions only if you say *Simon says …* before the instruction, e.g., Say *Simon says … sit down*. If you give an instruction without saying *Simon says …* and a student follows it, he/she has to leave the game. The winner is the student who stays in the game up to the end.

Extension activity

Aim: to expand on the new language from the lesson

- Go to the door and open it. Say *Open the door.* Close it and say *Close the door.*
- Ask a volunteer to open a window and another to close it.
- Encourage students to show you other things in the classroom that can be opened or closed, e.g., a pencil case, a backpack, your eyes, hands, etc.
- Give directions to close and open the things mentioned by the students. Teach new vocabulary.
- Students work in pairs to give and follow directions.

1 09 Listen and point. Listen and stick.

1

2

3

4

2 10 Look, listen, and say.

3 Work with a partner. Say and do.

1 11 Listen and sing.

2 Count the classroom objects and the children.

Learning outcomes:
- to sing a song
- to talk about things in the classroom

New language: *Look!, Come (along) and see!, children, teacher, girl, boy*

Recycled language: classroom objects, numbers, colors

Creative thinking (WB): Creates texts that express personal interests, emotions, or identity

Materials: 3 pieces of construction paper (optional)

Warm-up

Aim: to review language
- Play the recording of the chant on page 10.
- Students chant with you. Use a gesture to communicate *Take a look.*

1 11 ▶ 12 SB 12 Listen and sing.

Aim: to sing a song with the class, and listen for details
- Students look at the picture. Elicit what they can see.
- Say *This is a girl, and this is a boy* as you point to the children in the picture.
- Draw a picture of a girl, and another of a boy on the board.
- Count how many girls and how many boys there are in your class with the help of the students.
- Ask a volunteer to write the correct number under each of the drawings on the board.
- Draw a teacher and say *I'm a teacher, one teacher* and write number one under the drawing.
- Count the students in your class out loud with the help of the students and say *(Twenty) children, (ten) girls and (ten) boys.*
- Play the audio (11).
- Use gestures for *Look!* and *Come and see!* to communicate their meaning.

For song lyrics, see TB p101.

- Play the audio again, and sing with the class.
- Play the song video, pausing after each verse for students to repeat.
- When students have learned the song, use the karaoke version of the video or audio (12) to practice the song with the whole class.

Practice

Aim: to practice the song
- Make three groups, one for each of the three verses in the song.
- Play the karaoke version (12) again. Groups sing their part.
- Swap verses among groups and sing again.

2 SB p12 Count the classroom objects and the children.

Aim: to review numbers
- Invite volunteers to come to the front and draw a table, chair, book, pencil, door, window, girl, and boy.
- Students copy the drawings in their notebooks.
- In pairs, students count the classroom objects and children in the picture and write the numbers under their drawings.
- Check results as a class.

Key: 5 tables, 10 chairs, 6 books, 9 pencils, 1 door, 3 windows, 5 girls, 4 boys

1 11 WB p12 Listen. Point and sing.

Aim: to sing a song

For song lyrics, see TB p101.

2 WB p12 Draw yourself in your classroom. Point and say.

Aim: to personalize language

Ending the lesson

Aim: to practice new language in the lesson
- Assign different objects mentioned in the song to different groups: table, chair, door, window, pencil, book.
- Students hold the object or get near it.
- Students sing the song and when a group hears the object they were assigned, they show it, tap on it, touch it, etc. For example, when the word *door* is mentioned, students could knock on the door.

Extension activity

Aim: to review classroom objects and numbers
- Make three groups.
- Students draw a new classroom scene from the one on page 12. They should include tables, chairs, books, pencils, doors, windows, girls, and boys, but not more than ten per category.
- Encourage students to paint the objects different colors.
- Groups exchange drawings.
- A group comes to the front and a student at a time counts the number of objects or people of each category.
- Check results as a class.

Stronger Students: Ask students to say the number of objects, but taking the colors into consideration, e.g., two blue pencils, four red tables, etc.

Learning outcomes:
- to sing a rap
- to play a game

New Language: *What is it?, It's a (book).*

Recycled language: classroom objects, numbers

Creative thinking: Draws pictures to represent vocabulary and familiar concepts

Materials: flashcards 17–22 (classroom objects), blindfold (optional), tape, drawings of: a girl, boy, teacher

Warm-up

Aim: to introduce new language
- Take out the classroom object flashcards.
- Show one at a time, and say *What is it? It's a (book).*
- Show the flashcards again, and ask students what each object is.
- Encourage students to use *It's a …*

1 13 SB p13 Listen and circle.

Aim: to focus students on grammatical form
- Students look at the pictures in their Student's Books.
- Point to objects in the pictures and ask *What is it?*
- Play the recording. Students circle the corresponding option.

For song lyrics, see TB p101.

- Check answers as a class.

Key: 2 table, 3 book, 4 chair

2 SB p13 Watch and listen.

Aim: to focus students on grammatical form
- Play the *Penny the Penguin* video.
- Show the last scene of the video when Paul holds the icicle. Ask *What is it?* Elicit the answer from students.
- Play the recording again. Students join in with the rap. Encourage students to shake their heads when they say *No, no, no.*

For script, see TB p101.

3 SB p13 Play the game.

Aim: to practice new language from the lesson
- Students look at the picture in their Student's Books.
- Draw part of a classroom object and ask *What is it?*
- The first student who answers your question correctly is the next one to draw.
- Allow students to draw incomplete numbers as well to practice numbers.

1 12 WB p13 Listen and circle.

Aim: to identify classroom objects

For script, see TB p101.

Key: 2 chair, 3 window, 4 chair

2 13 WB p13 Listen and point. Say.

Aim: to practice new language

For script, see TB p101.

Ending the lesson

Aim: to practice key language from the lesson
- Take out the *classroom objects* flashcards and the three drawings mentioned in the Materials. Show them to the class and ask them to name them.
- Ask a volunteer to come to the front and face the board.
- Stick a flashcard on the volunteer's back, and ask him/her to turn around.
- The volunteer guesses what the object is by saying *It's a …*
- The class says *yes* or *no.*
- Repeat with other volunteers.

Extension activity

Aim: to practice key language from the lesson
- Blindfold a volunteer and turn him/her around and around until he/she loses direction.
- Lead him/her to an object to touch it. Ask *What is it?* and let the volunteer guess by saying *It's a …*
- Repeat the activity with other volunteers.

1 13 Listen and circle.

1

2

3

4

2 Watch and listen.

3 Play the game.

The Butterfly

1 14 Watch and listen to the story.

Learning outcomes:
- to listen to, read, watch and act out a picture story
- to review language from the unit

New language: *(open/close your) eyes*, *(sit) here*, *butterfly*, *beautiful*

Recycled language: giving and following instructions

Value: appreciating nature

Materials: a small picture of a butterfly (the size of a child's nose), tape, animal toys in a bag (optional)

Warm-up

Aim: to review the characters
- Remind students of the names of the two characters they were introduced to in the first episode of the story, Misty and Whisper.
- Students identify the two characters in the new episode on page 14.
- Students tell you what their superpowers are.

The Butterfly

1 14 SB pp14-15 Watch and listen to the story.

Aim: to present a picture story
- Give students time to look at the story frames.
- Point to the butterfly, and ask *What is it?* If nobody knows the word, pre-teach it.
- Students tell you what color the butterfly is.
- Play the recording as students follow the story in their books.

For script, see TB page 101.

- Go through the story frames, and ask about the objects, e.g., Point to the window, and say *What is this?* Repeat with *butterfly*, *table*, *chair*, *classroom*, *pencil*, etc.
- Play *The Butterfly* video to the end.
- Talk about the story value: the importance of appreciating nature.
  Note: Some of the discussion will need to be in L1.
- Play the video again. Students watch, listen, and repeat.

For script, see TB p101.

1 14 WB p14 Listen and match.

Aim: to identify the story scenes

For script, see TB p101.

Key: 2 c, 3 a, 4 b

2 WB p14 Look and match.

Aim: to identify the story scenes

Key: 1 b, 2 a

Ending the lesson

Aim: to practice the story
- Put students into groups of five: two will play Whisper and Misty, and the other three the children who enter the classroom at the end of the story.
- Give the butterfly picture with a piece of tape to one of the groups, and guide them to perform using the butterfly as a prop, e.g., they put the butterfly on the window sill, they tape the butterfly on the nose of the student who plays Misty.
- Other groups perform for the class.

Extension activity

Aim: to review language from the lesson
- Take out the bag with animal toys. (see Materials)
- Ask a volunteer to come to the front. Say *Sit here, please. Close your eyes.*
- The student touches one of the toy animals inside the bag.
- Ask *What is it?* The volunteer takes a guess *It's a …*
- Say *Open your eyes.* Take the toy from the bag, and show it to the class.
- Ask pairs of students to come to the front and repeat the activity using *Sit here, close your eyes, open your eyes, What is it?, It's …*

Learning outcomes:
- to interpret deeper meaning from the story
- to review language from the story and the unit

Recycled language: instructions, classroom objects, colors, numbers

Value: appreciating nature

Critical thinking: Solves simple puzzles

Critical thinking (WB): Identifies characters, setting, plots, and theme in a story

Cognitive control functions (SB & WB): Cognitive flexibility

Materials: 1 piece of construction paper and glue (optional)

Warm-up

Aim: to review instructions
- Elicit from students all the instructions they have learned in the unit, i.e., *stand up, sit down, open/close* (*book/eyes*), and perform them as a class.

Stronger students: Ask volunteers to come to the front, and give instructions for the class to follow.

2 SB p15 What's different? Look and circle.

Aim: to focus on detail in the story
- Give students time to look at the new story frames.
- Students circle the differences they see between these new frames and the ones in the picture story.
- Students do the activity individually and then check in pairs.
- They then share their discoveries orally with you.

Key: 1 The table is pink. 2 There are two butterflies. The chair is blue. 3 Misty's eyes are open. There are three pencils. 4 The book is orange. There are six children.

1 WB p15 What's good? Draw ☺.

Aim: to understand the value of appreciating nature

Key: 1

2 WB p15 Look and find your favorite picture. Draw ☺.

Aim: to understand the value of appreciating nature

Ending the lesson

Aim: to improve critical thinking skills
- Give students time to look around the classroom in silence. Encourage them to pay special attention to where things are.
- Invite three volunteers to go outside.
- Change the position of three things in the classroom.
- Invite students to come in again and guess what has been changed.
- Repeat the activity.

Extension activity

Aim: to focus on the value of appreciating nature
- Students bring a picture or a drawing of an animal or plant they consider beautiful.
- Encourage students to tell you why they have chosen it.
- Students glue their pictures onto the piece of construction paper. (see Materials)
- Display the poster on a classroom wall.

Note: Some of this discussion will need to take place in L1.

2 What's different? Look and circle.

Think and Learn

PATTERNS

Watch and listen.

1 15 Listen and point.

1

crayon

2

pen

3

eraser

2 Point and say the numbers.

1 2 3 4 5 ? 7 8 ? 10

1 2 3 ? 5 6 7 ? 9 10

3 16 Say what's next. Listen and check.

1

?

2

?

3

?

Learning outcomes:
- to integrate other areas of the curriculum through English: math
- to identify patterns

New language: *crayon, pen, eraser, pattern*

Recycled language: numbers, colors, classroom objects

Critical thinking: Makes predictions and estimations from given information

Critical thinking (WB): Sorts and arranges things by shape, size, color, weight, texture, and position.

Flashcards: 17–22 (classroom objects)

Warm-up

Aim: to review numbers, colors, and classroom objects

- Show one colored pencil. Say *One (red) pencil.* Show two colored pencils that are the same color and say *Two (red) pencils.*
- Continue practicing with more pencils and different colors.
- Encourage students to provide examples.

SB p16 Watch and listen. What is a pattern?

Aim: to raise awareness of what patterns are

- With Student's Books closed, play the *Think and Learn* video.

For videoscript, see TB p102.

- Ask students what they think a pattern is. They can use L1 to give an explanation.
- Explain that patterns are series or sequences of repeats. Elicit from students examples of everyday life where patterns are followed, e.g., the way goods are organized on the shelves in stores, lyrics in songs, etc.
- Play the video again and elicit the pattern in the video. Volunteers come to the board and draw and color this repeated pattern.

1 15 SB p16 Listen and point.

Aim: to practice identifying words used in the patterns

- Students open their books.
- Point to the classroom objects and ask *What is it?* to elicit each of the new words: *crayon, pen, eraser*. Students may already know these words.
- Play the recording. Students listen and point.

For script, see TB p102.

2 SB p16 Point and say the numbers.

Aim: to recognize patterns

- Start reading the first pattern of numbers, and stop where numbers are missing. Let students complete the first pattern out loud. Repeat with the second pattern.
- Encourage students to count the two patterns backward.

3 16 SB p16 Say what's next. Listen and check.

Aim: to practice solving patterns

- Students work in pairs to solve the patterns.
- They draw the next item in the patterns in their notebooks.
- Go around the classroom to check results.
- Play the recording. Students say the patterns out loud as they listen to the audio.

For script, see TB p102.

Key: 1 a blue pencil, 2 a yellow crayon, 3 a red pen

1 15 WB p16 Listen and color.

Aim: to review colors

For script, see TB p102.

Key: 1 a green book, 2 a yellow pencil, 3 a red and blue eraser

2 WB p16 Point and say the numbers.

Aim: to identify a pattern

3 WB p16 Look and say what's next.

Aim: to complete patterns

Key: 1 blue door, 2 table

Ending the lesson

Aim: to create patterns

- Stick the flashcards on the board.
- Students work in small groups and create a pattern by drawing classroom objects from the flashcards.
- Students draw the pattern in their notebooks and add a question mark at the end, as in Activity 3.
- Groups swap notebooks for the other groups to decipher the pattern by drawing the item that is missing.

Extension activity

Aim: to reinforce awareness of patterns

- Students work in pairs.
- They use their colored pencils, crayons, erasers, pens, or any other classroom object they want to use to make a pattern on their tables.
- Pairs swap places with another pair. They take their pencil cases with them and complete the pattern with their classroom objects.
- Pairs check each other's results.

Learning outcomes:
- to extend the focus on math through English
- to complete a project

Recycled language: *butterfly*, *boy*, *girl*, classroom objects

Creative thinking: Creates content for peers to use in class activities

Critical thinking (WB): Sorts and classifies objects and activities according to key features

Materials: letter-size paper (1 per student)

Warm-up

Aim: to review language from the lesson
- Students look at the pictures on page 17. Point to each item and ask *What is it?*
- Review the words *butterfly*, *boy*, and *girl*.
- Students play *Telephone* in small groups.
- When you say *Go!* an appointed member of the group whispers a word from the pictures to the student on his/her right. The game continues until the last student says the whispered word out loud.
- Go around the classroom and check performance.

4 SB p17 Choose and circle the next picture.

Aim: to practice patterns
- Students do the activity in pairs.
- Once they have finished the activity, ask a volunteer to read the first pattern out loud. Check results.
- Continue with the rest of the patterns.

Key: 2 the green door, 3 the blue pencil, 4 the orange butterfly

5 Project SB p17 Create your own pattern. Say.

Aim: to enable students to apply what they have learned about patterns
- Go through the vocabulary from previous lessons in the Student's Book by asking *What is it?* Elicit colors and classroom objects.
- Hand out paper and ask students to draw a repeated pattern using the vocabulary you have reviewed.
- Students can create their patterns at school or at home.
- Encourage students to use different colors and quantities in their patterns.
- Say: *Check the pattern.*
- Hold up some patterns and say, e.g., *Look! A pattern – pink eraser, blue pencil, green pen, pink eraser, blue pencil,* etc.
- Students say their patterns out loud to a partner. Praise students for their different patterns.
- Display the patterns around the classroom. Take photos of them, and save them to students' digital portfolios.

Extra support: For less-confident students, suggest they choose only two classroom objects and two colors.

Stronger students: Ask students to choose any of the patterns displayed in the classroom and say it out loud.

4 WB p17 Find the wrong picture. X it out.

Aim: to identify patterns

Key: 2 yellow butterfly, 3 orange book, 4 final yellow butterfly, 5 blue butterfly

5 WB p17 Complete the pattern. Say.

Aim: to complete a pattern

Key: green chair, red pen, green chair

Lesson review

- With students, review what they have learned in the lesson and if they liked the project.
- Hold a class vote for the most difficult pattern from the ones displayed in the classroom.

Extension activity

Aim: to solve patterns
- Point to one of the patterns displayed around the classroom.
- Ask a volunteer to tell you what would come next in the pattern.
- Repeat with other patterns and students.

Stronger students: Encourage students to draw more challenging patterns on the board for the class to solve.

4 Choose and circle the next picture.

5 Project Create your own pattern. Say.

Create That!

1 17 Listen and imagine.
Then draw your picture.

2 Show your picture to your friend. Say.

Learning outcomes:
- to listen, imagine, and draw to demonstrate meaning
- to describe a classroom

New language: *desk*

Recycled language: colors, numbers, classroom objects

BIG QUESTION to answer the Big Question *What's in my classroom?*

Creative thinking: Chooses options to create something new

Cognitive control functions (WB): Inhibitory control

Materials: relaxing music, a drawing of a classroom, construction paper (optional)

Warm-up

Aim: to trigger imagination
- Pre-teach the verb *imagine.*
- Say *Close your eyes. Imagine a butterfly.* Give students time before you continue. Ask *What color is it? Blue, red, orange, yellow?* Pause. *The butterfly is beautiful. Open your eyes.*
- Students draw the butterfly they have imagined in their notebooks and color it.
- Ask a volunteer to come to the front with his/her drawing. Ask *What color is your butterfly?*
- The rest of the class compares their butterflies with the volunteer's butterfly. If they are the same color, they put up their drawings.
- Continue with other volunteers.

1 17 SB p18 **Listen and imagine. Then draw your picture.**

Aim: to give students practice in listening and following instructions
- Explain the activity. Make sure students have colored pencils.
- If possible, play relaxing music and ask students to rest their heads on their tables for some time before the activity.
- Pre-teach *desk*. Play the recording. Students open their eyes and draw their pictures.

For script, see TB p102.

- Play the recording again before students draw, if necessary.
- Circulate as students draw their pictures. Praise students for their imagination and for their originality.

2 SB p18 **Show your picture to your friend. Say.**

Aim: to practice oral skills
- Revisit the Big Question *What's in my classroom?* before students show their pictures.
- Write the Big Question on the board and read it out loud.
- Review structures students have learned to orally describe their drawings. Provide a sample by showing a picture of a classroom. (see Materials)
- Say *Look! It's my classroom.* Point to classroom objects in your drawing and describe them: *A (red) desk, a (yellow) chair …*

1 16 WB p18 **Where does the butterfly go? Listen and draw.**

Aim: to practice listening skills and boost creativity

For script, see TB p102.

Key: Butterfly's route: 1 red and blue desk, 2 the green book, 3 the pink and green pen, 4 the orange and yellow window, 5 the yellow and green door

Ending the lesson

Aim: to sing for pleasure
- Play the recording of the song on page 12.
- Students sing as they listen.
- Encourage students to sing the song differently—more slowly, faster, whispering, etc.

Extension activity

Aim: to trigger creativity
- Students cut out pictures of chairs, windows, doors, and classroom objects from magazines or search for them on the internet and print them.
- Hand out construction paper to small groups.
- Groups take out their pictures and stick them on the paper to create a fun classroom.
- Students draw extra details.
- Groups present their collages to the rest of the class.
- Display the posters on the classroom walls.

Learning outcomes:
- to review language from the unit by taking a quiz
- to reflect on learning

BIG QUESTION to think about how the unit has helped them answer the Big Question *What's in my classroom?*

Recycled language: vocabulary and grammar from the unit

Cognitive control functions (WB): Cognitive flexibility

Materials: 28 paper squares made of construction paper. They should be the same size.

Warm-up

Aim: to review colors, instructions, and classroom objects
- Students work in pairs.
- Distribute 1 paper square (see Materials) per student or pair, depending on the number of students in the class.
- Assign one of the following to each pair: *stand up, sit down, open the book, close the book, boy, girl, table, pencil, chair, door, window, book, crayon, eraser*
- Students draw what was assigned to them twice, e.g., 2 drawings representing the instruction *stand up.*
- Students take turns showing their drawings to the class for them to say the word or phrase, e.g., *Stand up.*
- Play a memory game. Put paper squares face down on your desk.
- Make three groups of students. A group at a time turns a pair of squares face up and sees if they match. If they do, the group keeps the pair; if not, it is the next group's turn.
- The winner is the group with the most pairs of cards.

1 18 SB p19 Listen and point. Then say.

Aim: to review instructions
- Play the recording. Students listen and point to the corresponding picture and say the instruction.

For script, see TB p102.

- Ask individual students to say the instruction.

2 19 SB p19 Listen and circle.

Aim: to enable students to review language from the unit by taking a quiz
- Make sure students understand how to answer by circling one of the picture options in 1–4.
- Play the recording. Students work individually.
- Students compare answers in pairs.

For script, see TB p102.

- Check answers with the class.

Key: 2 an orange door, 3 a red window, 4 a yellow book

3 SB p19 Draw the last picture.

Aim: to review patterns
- Explain how the activity works.
- Students draw the last picture of each pattern.
- Choose students to read the patterns out loud for the rest of the class to check results.

Key: 1 a green crayon, 2 a pink eraser

1 WB p19 Look and say. Circle ☺, 😐, or ☹.

Aim: to enable students to assess their own learning

2 WB p19 What's in your classroom? Circle ☑ or ☒.

BIG QUESTION Aim: to enable students to revisit the Big Question and consolidate learning

3 WB p19 Color the objects.

Aim: to improve fine motor skills

Ending the lesson

Aim: to enable students to express their preferences
- Ask students what their favorite activity is from the unit (e.g., the song, chant, or one of the games), and hold a class vote.
- Repeat the most popular activity with the class.

Extension activity

Aim: to enable students to share what they have learned
- Put students into groups of three.
- Students open their Workbook to page 19.
- A student points at one of the pictures in Activity 3 and asks the student on his/her right about it, e.g., *What is it?*
- The other student answers by mentioning the object and its color, e.g., *It's a yellow pen.*
- The group continues asking and answering questions about the rest of the objects.

1 18 Listen and point. Then say.

2 19 Listen and circle.

3 Draw the last picture.

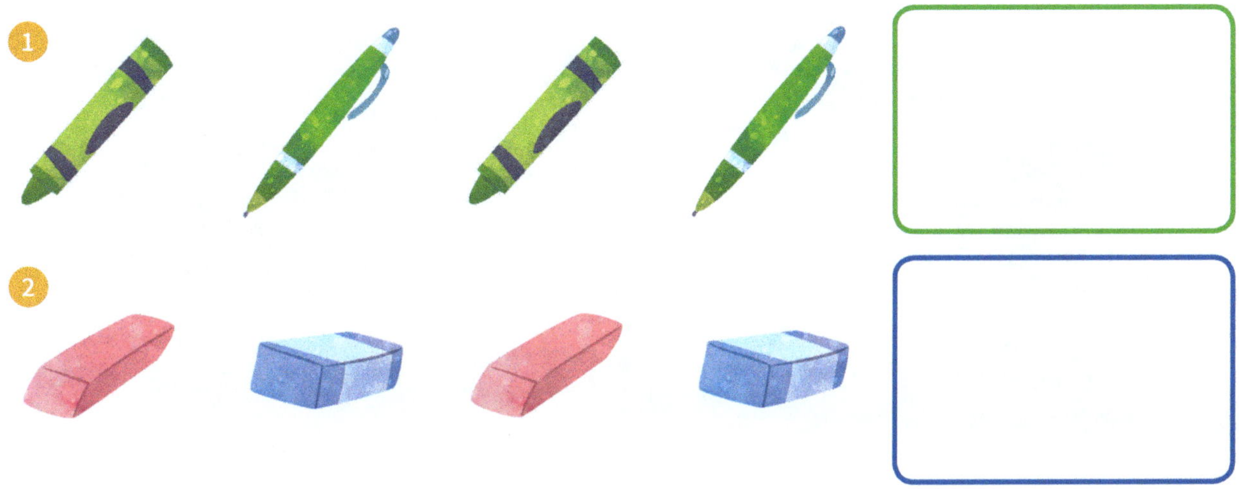

2 My Body

1 20 Listen and point. Say the words.

BIG QUESTION How do we move?

2 21 Listen and chant.

Learning outcomes:
- to name and talk about parts of the body
- to say a chant

BIG QUESTION to start to think about the Big Question *How do we move?*

New language: *arms, legs, head, eyes, ears, nose, mouth, run*

Recycled language: numbers, instructions

Cognitive control functions: Working memory

Flashcards: 23–29 (the body)

Warm-up

Aim: to review numbers
- Write an incomplete pattern of numbers 1 to 10 on the board.
- Encourage students to say the numbers that are on the board, and complete the pattern.

Presentation

Aim: to present parts of the body
- Take out *the body* flashcards.
- Hold up the *arms* flashcard and place it on top of one of your arms.
- Say the word. Students repeat after you.
- Continue with the rest of the flashcards.

1 20 SB p20 Listen and point. Say the words.

Aim: to practice parts of the body
- Students look at the pictures in their Student's Book.
- Point to the two characters and introduce the new one, Oscar.
- Point to the scene and ask students where the characters are. (At a costume party.)
- Elicit what costumes the characters are wearing.
- Play the recording. Students listen and point to the corresponding parts of the body.

For script, see TB p102.

- Play the recording again for students to repeat the words.
- Touch your eyes and say *Two eyes*. Do the same for the rest of the parts of the body.
- Students count the parts of the body of the monster costume Whisper is wearing.

BIG QUESTION How do we move?

Aim: to make students aware of how our body moves
- Read the Big Question. Ask students what they use to move. (their legs)
- Ask students how they moved as babies. (by crawling)
- Elicit what the skeleton is and how important it is for us to move.

Note: Some of the discussion will need to be in L1.

2 21 SB p20 Listen and chant.

Aim: to give students further practice saying the parts of the body
- Elicit from students what they see in the scene and the quantity of parts of the body the monster has.
- Play the recording.
- Students listen to the chant.

For chant script, see TB p102.

- Play the recording again, pausing for students to repeat.
- Say the chant as a class and then in groups.

Practice

Aim: to personalize and practice the new language
- Give instructions students already know, e.g., *stand up, sit down, close/open your books.*
- Add more instructions using the parts of the body, e.g., *Close your eyes. Touch your nose. Open your mouth. Look at your leg.*
- Volunteers give instructions to the rest of the class.

1 17 WB p20 Listen and match. Say.

Aim: to practice new language

For script, see TB p102.

Key: 2 arms, 3 mouth, 4 legs, 5 ears, 6 head, 7 eyes

2 18 WB p20 Listen and color.

Aim: to practice new language

For script, see TB p102.

Key: arms – blue, nose – green, eyes – blue, mouth – pink, head – yellow, legs – orange

Ending the lesson

Aim: to review numbers and parts of the body
- Students draw a monster in their notebooks and give it a name.
- Ask students not to color their monsters.
- Volunteers show their creations to the class and say how many parts of the body it has.

Extension activity

Aim: to review numbers and parts of the body
- Ask four students to hand in their monster drawings to you.
- Students get into four groups.
- Hand out one of the notebooks to each group.
- Students create a new version of the chant from Activity 2 by describing the new monster, e.g., *Two noses, one mouth, four legs, two heads.*
- Groups say the chant to the class.

Learning outcomes:
- to identify differences
- to play a game

New language: *I have …*

Recycled language: parts of the body, numbers, colors

Cognitive control functions (WB): Cognitive flexibility

Materials: a mask the size of your face with three eyes, four ears, and two mouths; fluffy toys or action figures (students bring one from home) (optional)

Warm-up

Aim: to review parts of the body and colors
- Students use the drawing of a monster in their notebooks.
- Give students instructions to color their monsters, e.g., *Color the eyes green. Color the legs blue.*
- Go around the classroom to check performance.

1 22 SB p21 Listen to the monsters. Color.

Aim: to introduce *I have …*
- Give students time to look at the pictures in their Student's Books.
- Students get their colored pencils ready.
- Play the recording for students to listen and color.
- Check results by pointing at each monster and saying *Number 1. What color is it?*

For script, see TB p102.

Key: 1 red, 2 blue, 3 orange, (4 green)

2 23 SB p21 Look, listen and say.

Aim: to teach *I have …*
- Say *I have two* (brown) *eyes, a nose, two ears …*
- Take out the mask (see Materials), and put it on your face.
- Say *I'm a monster! I have three eyes, four ears, and two mouths.*
- Students look at the monsters in their books.
- Play the recording for students to listen and repeat.

For script, see TB p102.

3 SB p21 Play the monster game.

Aim: to give students practice with *I have*
- Students work in pairs.
- They look at the monsters in their Student's Books.
- Partners take turns describing a monster for the other student to guess it. They use *I have* to describe the monsters.
- Go around the classroom to check performance.

Note: One student selects a monster, and writes the number on a piece of paper so nobody can see it. Then the student says three sentences about the monster they have chosen, e.g., *I have three ears. I have one nose. I have three legs.* The others look at the picture and guess: *You are monster* (5). The student responds *Yes/No.*

1 19 WB p21 Listen to the monsters. Match.

Aim: to practice new language

For script, see TB p102.

Key: 2 a, 3 d, 4 c

2 WB p21 Point. What does the monster say?

Aim: to practice new language

Key: I have 3 ears. I have 4 legs. I have 3 eyes. I have 2 arms.

Ending the lesson

Aim: to review using *I have*
- Students play in small groups.
- They open their notebooks where their drawing of a monster is.
- One student per group stands up, goes around the tables, and chooses one monster without telling the group.
- He/She describes the monster to the group, e.g., *I have two blue eyes …*
- The student whose monster is described says *It's a monster!*, as in the chant.
- Continue with other volunteers.

Extension activity

Aim: to expand on the new language from the lesson
- Students work in small groups.
- They take out their toys and show them to their partners.
- Ask students to pretend they are their toys.
- They describe their toys to their group by saying *I have two green eyes, four legs, …*
- Go around the classroom to check performance.

1 22 Listen to the monsters. Color.

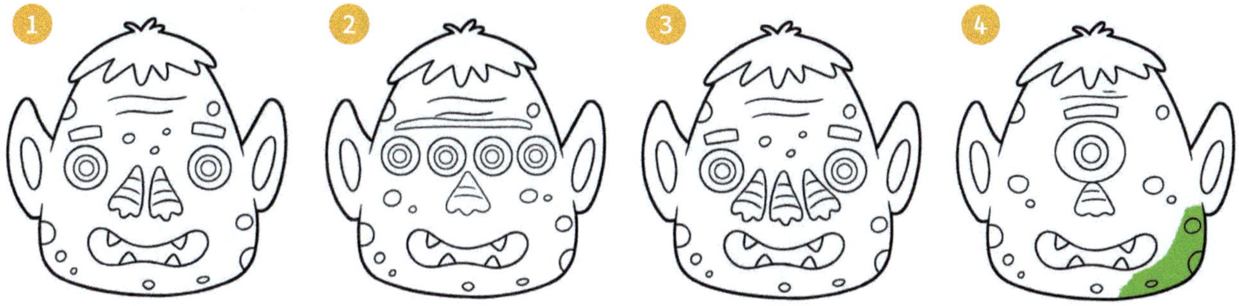

2 23 Look, listen, and say.

3 Play the monster game.

1 24 Listen and sing.

2 Which monster? Say *chocolate* or *ice cream*.

1

2

3

4

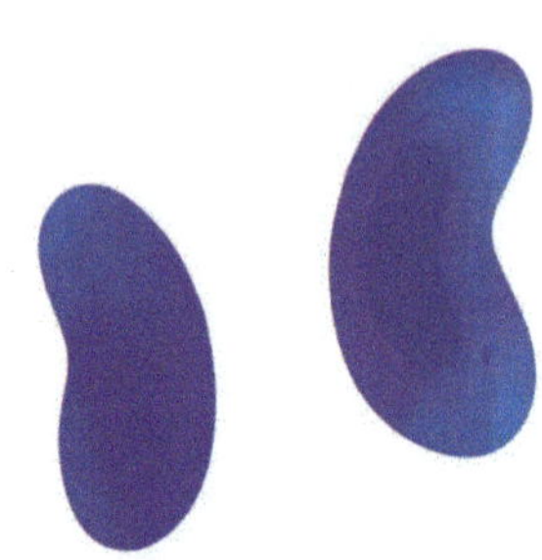

Learning outcomes:
- to sing a song
- to talk about parts of the body

New language: *horrible, chocolate, fiery, bold, ice cream, body, cold*

Recycled language: parts of the body, numbers

Cognitive control functions: Cognitive flexibility

Cognitive control functions (WB): Working memory

Materials: flashcards 23–29 (the body), paper (1 piece per student), tape, pictures of parts of the body cut out from magazines (ask students for them) (optional)

Warm-up

Aim: to review language
- Distribute paper, 1 piece per student.
- Students draw the face of a monster. They choose the quantity of features they want to draw on the face, e.g., two mouths.
- Collect the drawings and put them face down on your desk.
- A volunteer comes to the front.
- Tape a face on his/her back.
- The volunteer makes guesses, e.g., *I have two mouths.*
- The class says *Yes* or *No.*
- He/She can only make six guesses.
- Continue with other volunteers. Keep the faces for the next lesson.

1 24 ▶ 25 SB p22 Listen and sing.

Aim: to sing a song with the class
- Students look at the picture. Elicit what they can see.
- Pre-teach *chocolate* and *ice cream.*
- Play the audio (24).
- Teach new vocabulary from the song. For example, to teach *horrible*, say *Are the monsters beautiful? No, they are horrible.* Use gestures to teach new words such as *cold.*

For song lyrics, see TB p102.

- Play the audio again and sing with the class.
- Play the song video, pausing after each verse for students to repeat.
- When students have learned the song, use the karaoke version of the video or audio (25) to practice the song with the whole class.

Practice

Aim: to practice the song
- Make three groups, one sings the chorus and the other two a monster each.
- Play the karaoke version (25) again. Groups sing their part.
- Swap roles among groups.

2 SB p22 Which monster? Say *chocolate* or *ice cream.*

Aim: to practice new language
- Students look at the pictures in their Student's Books.
- Point to the pictures for students to identify the monster the parts of the body belong to.

Key: 1 ice cream, 2 chocolate, 3 chocolate, 4 ice cream

1 20 WB p22 Listen. Trace and color.

Aim: to practice new language

For song lyrics, see TB p102.

2 WB p22 Look and match. Color.

Aim: to understand new language

Key: 1 b, 2 a

Ending the lesson

Aim: to practice new language
- Take out *the body* flashcards.
- Make a table of three columns on the board.
- Paste the flashcards vertically in the first column.
- Draw an ice cream cone (for the ice cream monster) on top of the second column and a chocolate bar (for the chocolate monster) on top of the third.
- Volunteer students complete the table by adding numbers to it, e.g., number 3, next to the *arms* flashcard under the column for the chocolate monster.
- Once they have added the corresponding number, they say *I have* (*3 arms*).

Extension activity

Aim: to practice new language
- Students take out the parts of the body they have cut out from magazines.
- They create monsters with their cut outs and paste them in their notebooks.
- Students work in pairs.
- They pretend they are the monsters and say what they have, e.g., *I have three green eyes.*

Learning outcomes:
- to improve listening skills
- to play a game

New language: *How many?*, *You have …* , *Help!*

Recycled language: parts of the body, colors, numbers

Creative thinking: Creates content for peers to use in class activities

Cognitive control functions: Cognitive flexibility

Materials: monster faces students drew in previous lesson, music (if possible, scary music), paper, 3 bags (optional)

Warm-up

Aim: to introduce *how many*
- Take out the monster masks students drew in previous lessons.
- Place them face down on your desk.
- Invite a volunteer to come to your desk and choose one.
- Ask *How many (ears)?*
- Distribute masks randomly.
- Students work in pairs asking questions with *how many* about the masks.

1 26 SB p23 Listen and draw.

Aim: to improve students' listening skills
- Make sure students know what to do.
- Play the recording once for students to listen to the entire audio.

For script, see TB p103.

- Play the recording again and pause to give students time to draw their monsters.
- Students compare their monsters.

Key: Students draw two noses, four ears, three arms, and four legs.

2 SB p23 Watch and listen.

Aim: to focus students on grammatical form
- Play the *Penny the Penguin* video.
- Students watch and listen.
- Check understanding of grammar.
- Elicit what the monster in the video is like. Ask *How many (ears)?*

For script, see TB p103.

- Play the recording again.
- Encourage students to say *Oh, no, a monster. Help!*

3 SB p23 Draw a monster. Play *Ask the Monster.*

Aim: to practice new language
- Students draw a monster in their notebooks.
- They give it a name. Encourage students to use names such as the one in the song, e.g., *the chocolate monster.*
- Students work in pairs. Tell students they should pretend they are the monsters.
- Partners ask questions using *How many (legs) do you have?*

Note: Children work in pairs and take turns being A or B. A has created a monster and B asks the monster questions, e.g., *How many ears do you have?*, etc.

1 21 WB p23 Listen to the monster. Circle ✓ or ☒.

Aim: to practice new language

For script, see TB p103.

Key: 2 ✓, 3 ☒, 4 ☒, 5 ✓, 6 ☒

2 WB p23 Look and remember. Cover. Ask and answer.

Aim: to practice oral skills

Ending the lesson

Aim: to practice new language
- Distribute paper.
- Students draw six parts of the body on separate pieces of paper.
- Make three small groups, and hand out a bag per group.
- Assign a student per group who will act as the "judge."
- Students put their drawings inside a bag.
- Groups pass the bag around.
- Students take out six drawings from the bag and place them face up on their tables.
- The judge asks *How many ears do you have?* and each member of the group answers *I have …*
- The students who have the most (ears) get a point.
- The judge continues with the rest of the parts of the body.
- The students who get the most points are the winners.
- Keep the drawings in a bag for another lesson.

Extension activity

Aim: to play a game
- Play *Musical Chairs.*
- Set up chairs in two rows back to back (one chair less than the number of students in the class).
- Play music.
- Students walk around the chairs.
- When you stop the music, say *Run, run, run. Here I come!*, as in the song from page 22.
- Students run to sit on a chair.
- The student who is left standing is out of the game.

1 26 **Listen and draw.**

2 **Watch and listen.**

3 **Draw a monster. Play *Ask the Monster*.**

Great Costumes!

1 27 Watch and listen to the story.

Learning outcomes:
- to listen to, read, watch and act out a picture story
- to review language from the unit

New language: *costume*

Recycled language: parts of the body, numbers, *I have ... , How many ... ?*

Value: using your imagination

Materials: costume (your size), drawings of 2 eyes, 1 nose, 1 ear, 2 arms (the same size as the parts of the body of a child), tape, paper (optional)

Warm-up

Aim: to introduce the picture story topic
- Ask students to close their eyes.
- Put on your costume. (see Materials)
- Students open their eyes.
- Teach the word *costume*.
- Ask what students' favorite costumes are and if they have ever been to a costume party.

Note: Some of the discussion will need to be in L1.

Great Costumes!

1 27 SB pp24–25 Watch and listen to the story.

Aim: to present a picture story
- Remind students of the names of the two characters they were introduced to in previous units, i.e., Misty and Whisper.
- Give students time to look at the story frames.
- Play the audio as students follow the story in their books.

For script, see TB page 103.

- Go through the story frames and ask what parts of the body they can see in Misty's costume.
- Play the *Great Costumes!* video to the end.
- Talk about the story value: using your imagination. Say that imagination makes life more fun and helps you become creative.

Note: Some of the discussion will need to be in L1.

- Play the video again. Students watch, listen, and repeat.

1 22 WB p24 Listen and match.

Aim: to revisit the unit story

For script, see TB p103.

Key: a 2, (b 1), c 3

2 23 WB p24 Listen and circle.

Aim: to revisit the unit story

For script, see TB p103.

Key: 4 a, 5 b

Ending the lesson

Aim: to practice the story
- Ask a volunteer to come to the front. Tape the parts of the body (see Materials) on him/her so that the student has four eyes, two noses, three ears, and four arms.
- Play Whisper's part of the story and guide the volunteer to play Misty's part.
- Repeat with another student.
- Ask a student to play Whisper's part.
- Students practice the story in pairs.
- Go around the classroom to check performance.

Extension activity

Aim: to organize a costume party
- Organize a costume party.
- Hand out paper. Students make costume party invitations.
- Provide a very simple sample of an invitation.
- Students exchange invitations.
- Students dress up in their favorite costumes for the next lesson.
- Teach students how to describe what they are dressed up as, e.g., *I'm a doctor.*

Learning outcomes:
- to review language from the story and the unit

Recycled language: parts of the body, numbers, classroom objects

Value: using your imagination

Critical thinking (WB): Identifies characters, setting, plots, and theme in a story

Critical thinking (WB): Sorts and arranges things by shapes, size, color, weight, texture, and positions

Materials: Unit 2 stickers, scissors, cards with letters (1 per each letter of the parts of the body vocabulary), tape, students' drawings from the lesson on page 23

Warm-up

Aim: to review parts of the body
- Take out the cards (see Materials) and put them face up on your desk.
- Stick the first letter of one of the parts of the body, e.g., *L* for *leg*, on the board.
- Invite a volunteer student to add another letter to make a word, e.g., *E*.
- Continue until the word *LEG* is complete.
- Do the same for other parts of the body.
- Volunteer students draw the parts of the body next to the corresponding words.

Extra support: Instead of starting the warm-up by using the letters, use *the body* flashcards first. Students tell you the word and then use the cards with letters to spell them.

2 SB p25 Find, count, and stick.

Aim: to practice new language
- Students take out their stickers.
- Give students time to look at the frames and identify Misty's parts of the body.
- Point to a picture and ask *What is it? (It's a nose.)*
- Students count the parts of the body in the picture story frames and stick the corresponding number next to the correct picture.

Key: 1 4 arms, 2 4 eyes, 3 3 ears, 4 2 noses

1 WB p25 What's good? Draw ☺.

Aim: to focus on the unit value

Key: 1

2 WB p25 Look and circle ☺ or ☹.

Aim: to focus on the unit value

Key: Students' own answers

Ending the lesson

Aim: to review language
- Draw a window, a door, a chair, and a table on the board.
- Elicit the name of each school object from students.
- Students copy the drawings in their notebooks.
- Point to one of the drawings and ask *How many are there in the classroom?*
- Students write the corresponding number next to each drawing in their notebooks.
- Distribute six of students' drawings per person. (see Materials)
- Students paste them in their notebooks and write the quantity of each part of the body they have.
- Students work in pairs and say how many parts of the body they have in their notebooks by using *I have.*

Extension activity

Aim: to focus on the value of using your imagination
- Ask students when they use their imagination.
- Elicit examples such as: when you listen to a story, watch a movie, draw a picture, play with friends, etc.
- Ask how they think Whisper uses his imagination in the story.

Note: Some of this discussion will need to take place in L1.

2 Find, count, and stick.

1

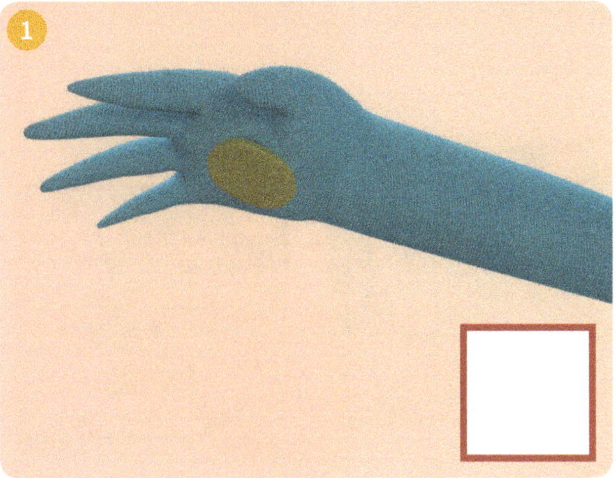

2

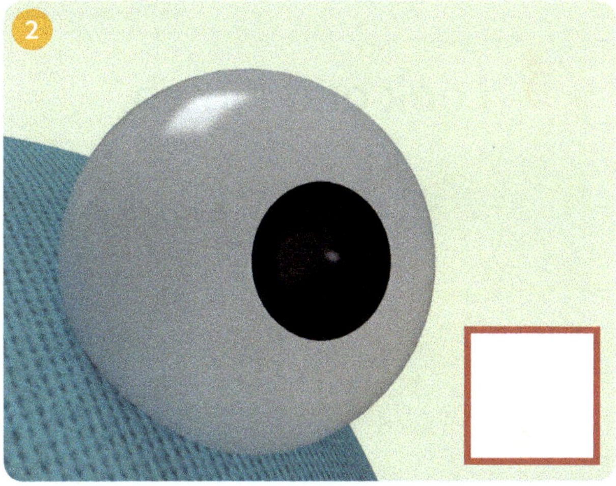

3

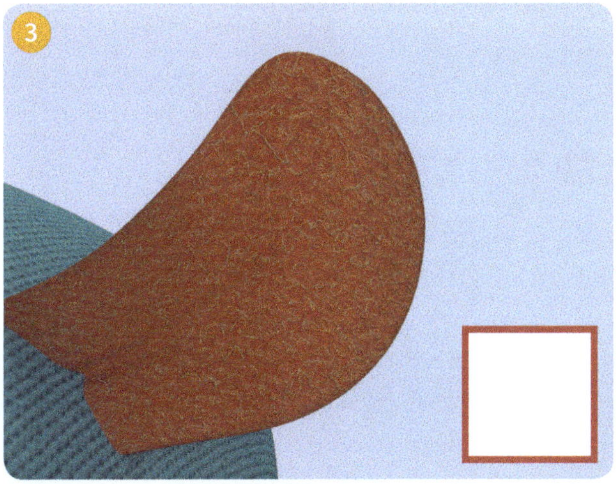

4

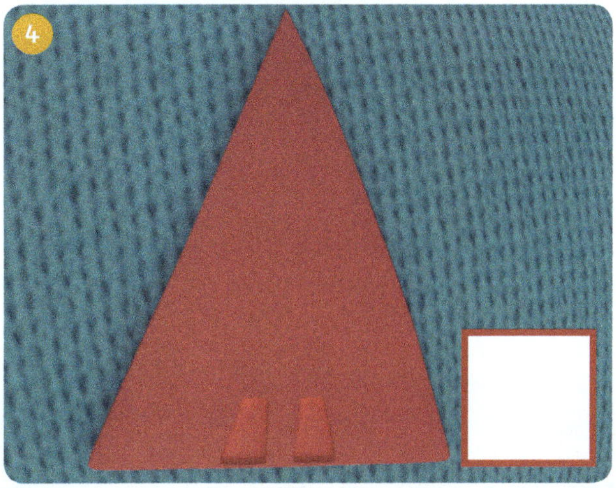

Think and Learn

OUR SKELETON

Watch and listen.

1 28 Listen and point.

1 walk

2 run

3 wave

2 Look and match.

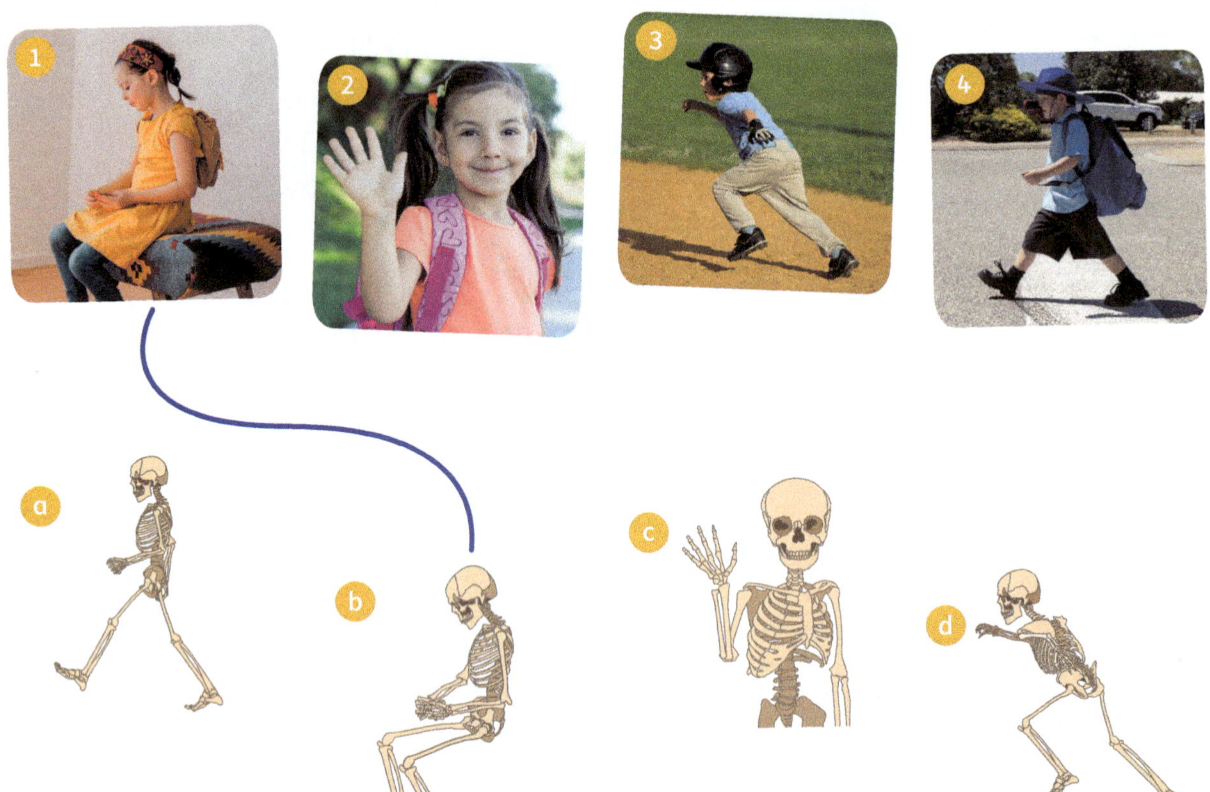

Learning outcomes:
- to integrate other areas of the curriculum through English: science

BIG QUESTION to answer the Big Question *How do we move?*

New language: *walk, wave, bone, skeleton*

Recycled language: *Sit down., Stand up., open/close, run*

Materials: picture of a hand skeleton (optional)

Warm-up

Aim: to review language and introduce the topic of the lesson
- Play *Simon Says* to review instructions: *sit down, stand up, close/open (book).*
- Ask students what parts of the body they used when they followed your instructions.
- Introduce the word *bone* and talk about what a bone is.
- Teach the word *skeleton* and talk about the importance of it to be able to move.

SB p26 Watch and listen. How does our skeleton move?

Aim: to deepen understanding of the unit Big Question
- With the Student's Books closed, play the *Think and Learn* video.

For videoscript, see TB p103.

- Elicit from students what movements are shown in the video by asking them to perform them.
- Help students identify what part of the body is used for each movement.
- Perform each of the actions from the video: shake your head, walk, run, sit, bend down, jump, stretch your arms, wave.
- Students say *head, legs,* or *arms* based on the part of the body you are using for each movement.

1 28 SB p26 Listen and point.

Aim: to present words to describe how we move
- Students open their books.
- Play the recording.
- Students listen and point to the corresponding action.

2 SB p26 Look and match.

Aim: to identify parts of the body
- Elicit the actions of the pictures 1 to 4.
- Students match the actions with the corresponding skeletons.
- Check results as a class.

Key: 2 c, 3 d, 4 a

1 24 WB p26 Listen and match. Say.

Aim: to identify movements

For script, see TB p103.

Key: a 3, (b 1), c 2, d 5, e 4

2 25 WB p26 Listen and circle ☑ or ☒.

Aim: to practice listening skills

For script, see TB p103.

Key: 2 ☒, 3 ☑, 4 ☒, 5 ☒

Ending the lesson

Aim: to practice new language
- Tell students they will have a lesson about exercise.
- Use the verbs learned in the lesson (shake your head, walk, run, sit, bend down, jump, stretch your arms, wave) to make an exercise routine.
- Give instructions for students to follow the routine.

Extension activity

Aim: to identify parts of the body
- Show a picture of a hand skeleton and stick it on the board.
- Tell students that there are 27 bones in a hand.
- Ask students to touch their hands and feel their bones.
- Students make an outline of one of their hands in their notebooks and write 27 inside it.

Stronger students: Students look at the sample of the hand skeleton and draw the bones inside the outline of their hand.

Learning outcomes:
- to extend the focus on science through English
- to complete a project

Recycled language: actions, parts of the body

Critical thinking: Makes predictions and estimations from given information

Creative thinking: Uses different media to make and describe his/her own designs

Cognitive control function: Cognitive flexibility

Materials: letter-size paper

Warm-up

Aim: to review language from the lesson
- Repeat the exercise routines you followed in the previous lesson.
- Use these verbs: shake your head, walk, run, sit, bend down, jump, stretch your arms, and wave.

Stronger students: Invite students to give a gym lesson to the class.

3 SB p27 Look and say.

Aim: to practice parts of the body
- Students work in pairs.
- Pairs look at the pictures and identify the part of the body the skeleton bones belong to.
- Encourage students to ask each other questions about the bones by using *What is it? (It's a leg.)*.

Key: 1 head, 2 arms, 3 leg, 4 mouth

4 Project SB p27 Draw three stick people. Show how they run, wave, and sit.

Aim: to enable students to apply what they have learned about a skeleton
- Draw students' attention to the drawing of the stick people in their books.
- Draw a stick figure on the board. Say: *Look at my stick figure!* Point to the legs, arms, and head and elicit the body words.
- Ask a group of students to come to the front and together draw a stick person following the sample in the book.
- Mime "run," "wave," and "sit" and elicit action words after each mime.
- Students draw lines, rectangles, circles, and triangles to complete a stick person.
- They draw a male and female stick person.
- Hand out paper.
- Students work in groups of three.
- They draw three stick people, each doing something different, i.e., running, sitting, and waving. Ask: *What's different?* Students say: *legs, arms,* or *head*.
- Nominate students to mime their three stick figures in any order. The others say the order of the mimes once they see all three, e.g., *wave, run, sit*.
- Students keep them for the Extension activity.
- Take photos of the drawings, and save them to students' digital portfolios.

3 26 WB p27 Listen and color.

Aim: to practice new language
- Check that students know what they are going to color. (the edge of the picture)

For script, see TB p103.

Key: 1 red, 2 blue, (3 green), 4 yellow

4 27 WB p27 Listen and match.

Aim: to practice new language

For script, see TB p103.

Key: 2 c, 3 b, 4 a
- Ask the students to look at the skeletons, and hypothesize which of the objects goes with which skeleton posture, e.g., sit – chair.
- Students then listen and check their hypotheses.

Lesson review

- With students, review what they have learned in the lesson and if they liked the project.
- Students vote for the stick person that most accurately shows an action.

Extension activity

Aim: to review new language
- Each student chooses a drawing out of the three stick people they drew in Activity 4.
- Say one verb, e.g., *run*.
- Those students who have a stick person that is running hold up the drawing.
- Continue with the rest of the verbs.
- Display the drawings around the classroom.
- Students stand in a circle and move around.
- Say a verb, e.g., *wave*.
- Students run to the closest drawing showing the action you mentioned and touch it.
- Repeat several times.

3 Look and say.

1
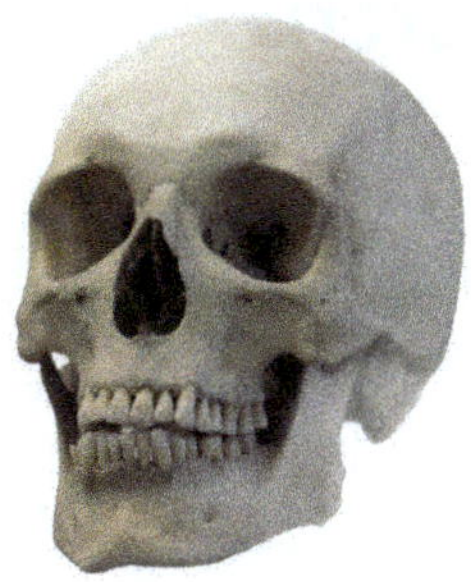

2

3

4
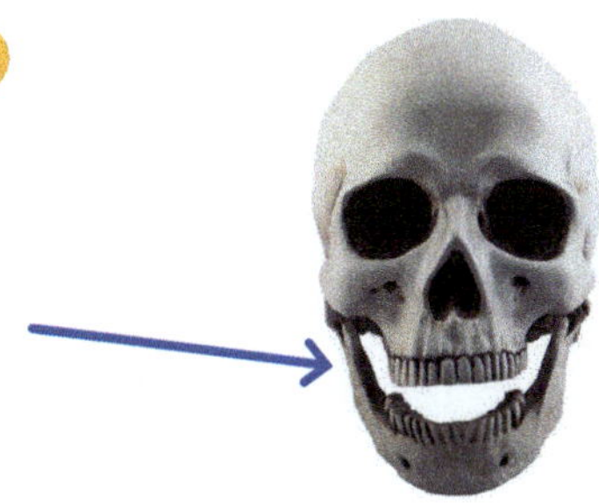

4 Project Draw three stick people. Show how they run, wave, and sit.

Do That!

1 29 Listen and act it out with your teacher. Then listen again and match.

1 2 3 4 5 6

Learning outcomes:
- to follow instructions
- to identify sequences

Recycled language: actions

Creative thinking: Listens and responds physically to songs, rhymes, chants

Materials: paper

Warm-up

Aim: to review language
- Ask volunteers to come to the front and draw stick people doing the following actions: stretching arms, jumping, and bending down.
- Students draw them in their notebooks.

1 29 SB p28 Listen and act it out with your teacher. Then listen again and match.

Aim: to give students practice in listening and following instructions
- Students open their books and identify the actions in the pictures.
- Ask students to stand up.
- Play the recording for students to act it out with you.

For script, see TB p104.

- Play the recording again for students to put the pictures in their books in order (1–6).
- Check results as a class.

Key: 2 orange, 3 green, 4 yellow, 5 red, 6 pink

1 28 WB p28 Listen and color.

- Check that students know what they are going to color. (the edge of the picture)

Aim: to practice new language

For script, see TB p103.

Key: 1 blue, 2 orange, 3 green, (4 yellow), 5 pink, 6 red

2 WB p28 Look at the pictures again. Circle a face for you.

Aim: to practice new language

Key: Students' own answers

Ending the lesson

Aim: to review actions
- Students work in small groups.
- Hand out paper.
- Students draw an exercise routine with stick people.
- They write a number next to each stick person to show how many times the action should be performed, e.g., a stick person that is stretching arms and the number 3 next to it.
- One group goes to the front and reads their routine for the rest of the class to follow.
- Keep the exercise routines for future lessons.

Extension activity

Aim: to play a game
- Take six of the drawings of stick people that are displayed in the classroom, two for each of the actions.
- Stick them on the board.
- Make two groups of students and ask them to stand in two lines.
- Say an action.
- The first student in each line runs to the board and touches the corresponding picture.
- The student who touches the correct picture first gets a point for his/her group.
- Continue with the rest of the students in the line.

Learning outcomes:

- to review language from the unit by taking a quiz
- to reflect on learning

BIG QUESTION to think about how the unit has helped them answer the Big Question *How do we move?*

Recycled language: vocabulary and grammar from the unit

Creative thinking: Creates texts that express personal interests, emotions, or identity

Cognitive control functions: Cognitive flexibility

Warm-up

Aim: to review colors

- Students work in small groups.
- Play *I Spy with My Little Eye* to review colors.

1 30 SB p29 Listen and point. Then say.

Aim: to review parts of the body

- Play the recording.
- Students listen, point to the corresponding picture, and say it.

For script, see TB p104.

Key: eyes, ears, legs, mouth, arms

2 31 SB p29 Listen and color.

Aim: to review parts of the body

- Give students time to identify the differences among the dragons.
- Play the recording.
- Check that students know what they are going to color. (the edge of the picture)
- Students work individually.
- Check results as a class.

For script, see TB p104.

Key: a blue, b green, (c red), d pink

Stronger students: Students work in pairs. One student describes a dragon using *I have* for the other student to guess the dragon.

3 SB p29 Look and circle. Then say.

Aim: to review actions

- Explain how the activity works.
- Students match the pictures individually.
- They check results in pairs.

Key: b

1 WB p29 Look and say. Circle ☺, 😐, or ☹.

BIG QUESTION Aim: to enable students to revisit the Big Question and to consolidate learning; to enable students to assess their own learning

2 WB p29 Draw your favorite monster.

Aim: to enable students to personalize the topic

Ending the lesson

Aim: to enable students to express their preferences

- Ask students what their favorite activity is from the unit (e.g., the song, chant, or one of the games) and hold a class vote.
- Repeat the most popular activity with the class.

Extension activity

Aim: to enable students to share what they have learned

- Put students into groups of three.
- Each student opens their Workbook to page 29.
- Students take turns showing the monsters they have drawn for Activity 2.
- Students pretend they are the monsters and describe themselves, e.g., *I have a big nose.*

1 30 Listen and point. Then say.

2 31 Listen and color.

3 Look and circle. Then say.

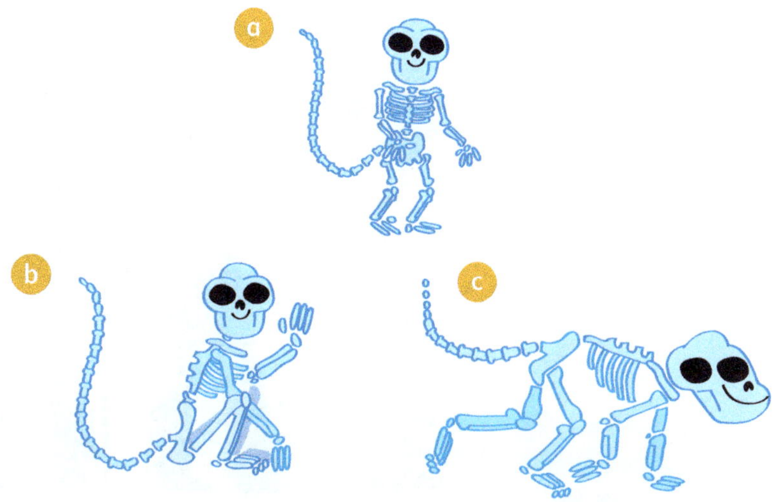

3 My Family

1 🎧32 Listen and point. Say the words.

BIG QUESTION What's a family?

2 🎧33 Listen and chant.

Learning outcomes:
- to name and talk about members of the family
- to say a chant

BIG QUESTION to start to think about the Big Question *What's a family?*

New language: *mom, dad, sister, brother, grandpa, grandma, crazy*

Recycled language: numbers

Cognitive control functions: Working memory

Materials: flashcards 30–35 (family), pictures of families that are different sizes and types

Warm-up

Aim: to introduce the unit topic
- Show a picture of a family. (see Materials)
- Say *This is a family.*
- Ask *How many are they?*
- Count with the class.
- Continue with the pictures of other families.
- Stick the pictures on the board.

Presentation

Aim: to present members of the family
- Take out the *family* flashcards.
- Hold up the *mom* flashcard and say the word.
- Students repeat after you.
- Point to a mom in one of the pictures on the board and say: *This is a mom.*
- Continue with the rest of the flashcards and pictures on the board.
- Leave the family pictures on the board for the Ending the lesson activity.

1 32 SB p30 Listen and point. Say the words.

Aim: to practice members of the family
- Students look at the pictures in their Student's Book.
- Point to the two characters and ask who they are.
- Point to Misty's family and say *This is Misty's family. How many are they?*
- Play the recording. Students listen and point to the corresponding member of the family.

For script, see TB p104.

- Play the recording again for students to repeat the words.

BIG QUESTION What's a family?

Aim: to make students aware of what a family is
- Read the Big Question. Ask students how many are in their family.
- Ask why they think a family is important.

Note: Some of the discussion will need to be in L1.

2 33 SB p30 Listen and chant.

Aim: to give students practice with new language
- Elicit from students what they see in the scene.
- Students count the members of the family with you and say who they think each of them is, e.g., *mom.*
- Play the recording.
- Students listen and follow the chant in their Student's Books.
- Teach the word *crazy.*

For chant script, see TB p104.

- Play the recording again, pausing for students to repeat.
- Say the chant as a class and then in groups.

Practice

Aim: to personalize and practice the new language
- Volunteer students talk about their families using *I have …*
- Other students tell you about their families. They say the members of their family and how many there are in their families.

1 29 WB p30 Listen and color.

Aim: to practice new vocabulary
- Check that students know what they are going to color. (the edge of the picture)

For script, see TB p104.

Key: 1 mom: yellow, 2 dad: orange, 3 sister: green, (4 brother: pink), 5 grandpa: red, 6 grandma: blue

2 WB p30 Look and match. Say.

Aim: to practice new vocabulary

Key: 1 b, (2 a), 3 d, 4 c, 5 f, 6 e

Ending the lesson

Aim: to review members of the family
- Stick the flashcards in random order around the pictures of the families. (see *Presentation* activity)
- Volunteer students come to the front and draw lines from the flashcards to the corresponding member of the family in any of the pictures.

Extension activity

Aim: to review language from the unit
- Students create a new version of the chant from Activity 2 by describing their family, e.g., *Do you want to see my crazy family? There's my mom, there's my …*
- Invite some students to say their chant.

Learning outcomes:
- to talk about your family

New language: *This is my …*

Recycled language: members of the family

Creative thinking: Creates texts that express personal interests, emotions, or identity

Creative thinking (WB): Draws pictures to represent vocabulary and familiar concepts

Materials: photos of your family members, paper

Warm-up

Aim: to review numbers and members of the family
- Write the members of the family on the board.
- Students draw a picture of each one in their notebooks and write the quantity of each member of the family they have next to the corresponding picture, e.g., (drawing of grandma) 2.

1 34 SB p31 Listen and circle the correct person.

Aim: to identify family members
- Give students time to look at the pictures in their Student's Books.
- Play the recording for students to circle the correct member of the family in each picture.
- Check results as a class.

For script, see TB p104.

Key: 2 dad, 3 grandpa, 4 sister

2 35 SB p31 Look, listen, and say.

Aim: to practice new language
- Students look at the pictures in Activity 1.
- Play the recording for students to listen and repeat.

For script, see TB p104.

3 SB p31 Draw your family. Point and say.

Aim: to give students practice with *This is my …*
- Show a photo of one of the members of your family and introduce him/her, e.g., *This is my brother.*
- Continue with the rest of your family.
- Hand out paper.
- Students draw their family and color it.
- Students work in pairs.
- They use *This is my …* to introduce their family members.
- Change pairs and continue with the activity.
- Students keep the drawing for the Ending the lesson activity.

1 30 WB p31 Listen and circle.

Aim: to practice new language

For script, see TB p104.

Key: 2 brother, 3 sister, 4 grandma, 5 grandpa, 6 mom

2 WB p31 Draw someone from your family. Circle.

Aim: to practice new language

Ending the lesson

Aim: to review new language
- Students work in new pairs.
- They introduce their family, but they make some mistakes, e.g., they point to their mom and say *This is my sister.*
- Partners say *Yes* when they think the sentence is true or *No* when the sentence is false.
- Keep the drawings.

Stronger students: Encourage stronger students to say *No, this isn't your mom. This is your sister.* when they consider a sentence is false.

Extension activity

Aim: to expand on the new language from the lesson
- Students work in small groups.
- Hand out paper.
- Students draw a crazy family that could be made up of animals, monsters, etc.
- Groups introduce their crazy families to the class.

1 34 Listen and circle the correct person.

2 35 Look, listen, and say.

3 Draw your family. Point and say.

1 36 Listen and sing.

2 How many in each family? Look and count.

Learning outcomes:
- to sing a song
- to play a memory game

New language: *nice*

Recycled language: members of the family

Creative thinking (WB): Creates texts that express personal interests, emotions, or identity

Materials: flashcards 30–35 (family), students' drawings of their families from the previous lesson, letter-size paper (optional)

Warm-up

Aim: to review new language
- Play a memory game.
- Stick the flashcards in a row on the board in random order.
- Make three teams.
- Ask a student from one group to memorize the sequence of the members of the family on the board.
- He/She turns back and has to say the members in the order they appear, e.g., mom, dad, sister.
- Continue with the other groups.
- Repeat the activity.
- Give a point to the groups when they make no mistakes.
- The winning group is the one that gets the most points.

1 36 ▶ 37 SB p32 **Listen and sing.**

Aim: to sing a song with the class
- Students look at the picture. Elicit how many families they can see.
- Pre-teach *nice*.
- Play the audio (36).
- Students listen and point to the corresponding family in the picture.

For song lyrics, see TB p104.

- Play the audio again and sing with the class.
- Play the song video, pausing after each verse for students to repeat.
- When students have learned the song, use the karaoke version of the video or audio (37) to practice the song with the whole class.

Practice

Aim: to practice the song
- Group students to make the four families mentioned in the song, e.g., a family made up of a mom and a son.
- There will be a member of each family who will sing to introduce his/her family to the class. For example, for the family made up of a mom and son, the "son" will sing this part of the song: *This is mom and me. This is mom and me. This is a family. A nice family.*
- Play the karaoke version (37) again. Groups sing their part.

2 SB p32 **How many in each family? Look and count.**

Aim: to practice new language
- Students look at the pictures in their books.
- They do the activity in pairs.

Key: 2, 2, 5, 7

1 31 WB p32 **Listen. Write numbers.**

Aim: to improve listening skills

For song lyrics, see TB p104.

Key: 1 dad, 2 grandpa, 3 grandma, (4 mom)

2 WB p32 **Draw your family.**

Aim: to improve drawing skills

Ending the lesson

Aim: to practice new language
- Take out the students' drawings of their families.
- Hand out one per student in random order.
- Students count how many members there are in the family.
- Say a number, e.g., three.
- Students who have a drawing of a family made up of three members hold their drawings up.
- Continue with other numbers and other members of the family, e.g., two brothers.
- Keep the drawings for another lesson.

Extension activity

Aim: to practice new language
- Ask volunteer students to come to the front.
- Say the names of family members.
- Students write them on the board.

Extra support: Help volunteers by providing the consonants of the names of the family members. They complete the vowels with their classmates' help.
- Remove the words from the board and write scrambled versions of these words instead. Ask students in small groups to unscramble the words writing them on a piece of paper. The first team to hold up their piece with all words correctly unscrambled wins.

Learning outcomes:
- to improve listening and oral skills

New language: *Is this your … ?, Yes, it is., No, it isn't.*

Recycled language: family members

Materials: bag, students' drawings of their family, Unit 3 stickers, students bring one photo of a family member (sister, brother, mom, dad, or grandparent), big envelope

Warm-up

Aim: to introduce *Is this … ?*
- Go around the classroom and borrow some school supplies from different students.
- Put them in a bag.
- Go back to one of the students that lent you an object.
- Take any object from the bag and ask *Is this your* (*pencil*)*?*
- Encourage students to answer using *Yes, it is. No, it isn't.*
- Ask a volunteer to take your role.

1 38 SB p33 Listen and stick.

Aim: to improve students' listening skills
- Students take out their stickers.
- Give students time to look at the silhouettes in their books.
- Play the recording.
- Students place the stickers on the silhouettes.

For script, see TB p104.

- Play the recording again for students to check their work.
- Students stick the members of the family in the corresponding place on the page.

Key: 1 the sister, 2 the grandpa, 3 the dad, 4 the mom, 5 the grandma, 6 the brother

2 SB p33 Watch and listen.

Aim: to focus students on grammatical form
- Play the *Penny the Penguin* video.
- Students watch and listen.
- Play the video again, and pause to ask questions, e.g., *Is this Penny's sister?*
- Students answer using *Yes, it is. / No, it isn't.*

For script, see TB p105.

- Play the recording again.
- Students repeat.

3 SB p33 Ask and answer.

Aim: to practice new language
- Hand out the students' drawings of their families to their owners.
- Students work in pairs.
- Students ask and answer questions with their partners about the members of their families using *Is this your … ? Yes, it is. / No, it isn't.*
- Encourage students to say who the member of the family is when there is a negative answer, e.g., *No, it isn't. This is my* (*sister*).

1 32 WB p33 Listen. Circle ☑ or ☒.

Aim: to expose students to new language

For script, see TB p105.

Key: 2 ☑, 3 ☒, 4 ☑, 5 ☑, 6 ☒

Ending the lesson

Aim: to practice new language
- Students take out their photos. (see Materials)
- Ask them not to show them to their classmates.
- Go around the classroom and collect the photos in an envelope. (see Materials)
- Make three teams.
- A member of a team takes one photo from the envelope and guesses who the photo belongs to by asking *Is this your (sister)?*
- If the answer is positive, the team gets one point.
- Continue with the rest of the groups.
- The winner is the team that gets the most points.

Extension activity

Aim: to practice members of the family
- Show students how to draw a simple family tree.
- Explain the layers that are usually followed when we draw a family tree.
- Students draw their family trees and write the names of each family member.
- Display the trees around the classroom.

1 38 Listen and stick.

2 Watch and listen.

3 Ask and answer.

Cool Grandma

1 39 Watch and listen to the story.

Learning outcomes:
- to listen to, read, watch, and act out a picture story
- to review language from the unit

New language: *nuts, squirrel, flower, helmet, goggles*

Recycled language: colors, classroom objects, members of the family, *cool, tree, how many, have*

Value: appreciating family

Materials: 10 nuts (preferably acorn nuts), goggles, and a helmet (or any of the two)

Warm-up

Aim: to review *how many, have*
- Students work in pairs.
- Pairs sit back to back.
- One student (student 1) uses his/her pencil case, while the other (student 2) uses his/her notebook and colored pencils to draw.
- Student 1 has to choose five colored pencils. Colors can be repeated.
- Student 2 asks *How many (red) pencils do you have?*
- Student 1 answers, and student 2 draws the amount of pencils and their color in his/ her notebook.
- Students turn around to check their work.
- Pairs swap roles.
- Go around the classroom to check performance.

Stronger students: Encourage students to provide the name of other classroom objects, e.g., eraser, ruler, sharpener.

Cool Grandma

1 39 SB pp34–35 Watch and listen to the story.

Aim: to present a picture story
- Remind students of the names of the two characters they were introduced to in previous units, i.e., Misty and Whisper.
- Give students time to look at the story frames.
- Play the audio as students follow the story in their books.

For script, see TB p105.

- Go through the story frames and teach these words: *park, squirrel, flower, helmet, goggles,* and *nuts.*
- Ask simple comprehension questions, e.g., Who is this? (*Misty./Whisper.*) Where are they? (*At the park.*) What's the first squirrel's name? (*Sammy.*) Where is Sammy? (*In a tree.*) How many squirrels are there? (*Three.*)
- Play the *Cool Grandma* video to the end.
- Talk about the story value: appreciating family. Ask students why they think having a family is important.

Note: Some of the discussion will need to be in L1.
- Play the video again. Students watch, listen, and repeat.

1 33 WB p34 Listen and match.

Aim: to identify story scenes

For script, see TB p105.

Key: a 3, b 4, c 2, (d 1)

2 WB p34 Look and match.

Aim: to identify story scenes

Key: 1 b, 2 a

Ending the lesson

Aim: to act out the story
- Invite four students to the front. Assign roles to each of them, i.e., Misty, Sammy, Jumpy, Grandma.
- You will act out Whisper.
- Hand out the props, i.e., nuts to Sammy, goggles and helmet to Grandma.
- The three squirrels sit on your desk, which will be the tree.
- Play the video and pause for students to play their roles.
- Invite other groups to act out the story without your help.

Extension activity

Aim: to act out a new version of the story
- Students work in groups of five.
- Encourage groups to think of a new version of the story. They can be a different animal, change the characters' names, and use other objects instead of nuts.
- Groups practice their new version of the story and then perform in front of the class.

Learning outcomes:
- to review language from the story and the unit

Value: appreciating family

Critical thinking: Solves simple puzzles

Critical thinking (WB): Identifies characters, setting, plots, and theme in a story

Critical thinking (WB): Sorts and arranges things by shapes, size, color, weight, texture, and positions

Warm-up

Aim: to review new language from the story

- Dictate new vocabulary from the story for students to draw in their notebooks.
- Students draw a nut, a squirrel, a flower, a helmet, and goggles.

2 SB p35 Find and count. Draw how many.

Aim: to practice new language

- Students go through the story frames and count how many of the things in Activity 2 they see.
- They draw them in their books.
- Students compare results with their partners.

Extra support: Instead of asking students to draw, ask them to write the corresponding quantity in numbers.

Key: 3 squirrels, 10 acorns, 2 flowers

1 WB p35 What's good? Draw ☺.

Aim: to understand the meaning of appreciating the family

Key: 1

2 WB p35 Look at the family activities. Write 1, 2, and 3.

Aim: to understand the meaning of appreciating the family

Key: Students' own answers

- Ask the students to look at the pictures in the book. Ask: *Which activity is your number one?* Help them to write 1 under the picture they like most.

Stronger students: Students point and say: *My number 1.* for example.

Ending the lesson

Aim: to review language

- Draw a butterfly, a squirrel, a nut, and a flower on the board.
- Students draw them in their notebooks.
- Then ask students to draw a park scene.
- Students draw butterflies, squirrels, nuts, and flowers in their park scene.
- They swap notebooks with a partner.
- Partners count how many of each category there are in the park scene and write the numbers, e.g., 5 (drawing of a butterfly).

Extension activity

Aim: to focus on the value of appreciating family

- Ask students what they do with their families.
- Students tell you what the members of their families do to help each other when they have a problem.

Note: Some of this discussion will need to take place in L1.

2 Find and count. Draw how many.

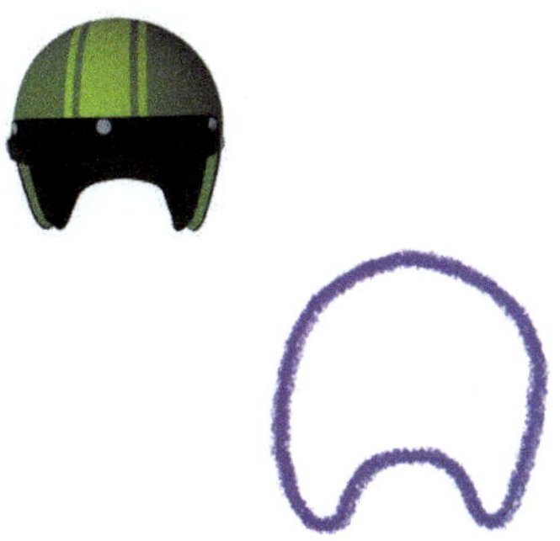

Think and Learn

An Animal Family

Watch and listen.

1 (40) Listen and point.

1

chicken

2

dog

3

duck

4

cat

2 Look and match.

1

2

3

4

Learning outcomes:
- to integrate other areas of the curriculum through English: social science

BIG QUESTION to answer the Big Question *What's a family?*

New language: *chicken, dog, duck, cat, baby, kitten, puppy, chick, duckling*, animal sounds

Recycled language: family members, colors

Critical thinking (WB): Matches objects, people, letters, pronunciations, and words

Materials: six pictures of animal families cut into six puzzle pieces (e.g., a picture of a dog family cut into 6 puzzle pieces), bag, paper

Warm-up

Aim: to teach animal sounds in English
- Say the name of animals in your native language and ask students to produce the sounds they make.
- Say *Woof, woof* and elicit what animal students think this sound is produced by.
- Continue with *meow, cluck,* and *quack.*
- Ask volunteer students to draw the animals on the board.
- Touch one animal at a time for students to produce its sound.
- Touch the drawings in random order and change speed.

SB p36 Watch and listen. What is an animal family?

Aim: to identify animal families
- With the Student's Books closed, play the *Think and Learn* video.

For videoscript, see TB p105.

- Elicit from students what animals they have seen in the video.
- Ask *What color are the chicken's babies? How many are there in the duck family? What's your favorite family in the video?*

1 40 SB p36 Listen and point.

Aim: to present words to describe animal families
- Students open their books.
- Play the recording.
- Students listen and point to the corresponding animal.

2 SB p36 Look and match.

Aim: to identify animal families
- Point to the adult animals and ask *What are they?* (*Dogs.*)
- Point to a puppy and say *This is a puppy, a baby dog.*
- Students match the parents to their babies.
- Check performance as a class.

Stronger students: Teach the name of the other baby animals that appear on the page, i.e., *kitten, chick,* and *duckling*. Encourage students to say the name of the adult animals and the name of their babies.

Key: 2 green, 3 blue, 4 orange

1 34 WB p36 Listen and color.

Aim: to identify animals
- Check that students know what they are going to color. (the edge of the picture)

For script, see TB p105.

Key: 2 dog: red, 3 duck: green, 4 cat: blue

2 WB p36 Draw lines to make families.

Aim: to identify families

Key: 2 b, 3 a, 4 c

Ending the lesson

Aim: to identify animal families
- Take out the animal family puzzles. (see Materials)
- Make six groups.
- Give one piece of an animal family puzzle per group.
- Put the other pieces in a bag.
- Groups take turns taking a piece from the bag and seeing if it belongs to their animal family.
- If it doesn't, they put the piece inside the bag again.
- Continue until a group completes its puzzle.

Extension activity

Aim: to draw an animal family
- Hand out pieces of paper.
- Students draw an animal family.
- Encourage students to give them a specific feature that makes it clear that they are part of the same family, e.g., same color, an ear that is another color, same eye size, etc.
- Display the animal families around the classroom. (Keep them on the walls for the Extension activity on page 37.)

Learning outcomes:
- to extend the focus on social science through English
- to complete a project

Recycled language: animals, family members

Critical thinking: Sorts and arranges things by shapes, size, color, weight, texture, and positions

Creative thinking: Based on a model, develops new content

Cognitive control functions: Cognitive flexibility

Materials: finger puppet templates, students' animal family drawings that are displayed around the classroom

Warm-up

Aim: to introduce the lesson topic
- Remind students of the well-known story "The Ugly Duckling."
- Elicit what made the "ugly duckling" different. (the size of the egg, the "ugly duckling" didn't quack, its neck, etc.)
- Ask what the "ugly duckling" really was. (A swan.)

Note: Some of this discussion will need to take place in L1.

3 SB p37 Look and circle the different animal.

Aim: to identify families
- Students work in pairs.
- Pairs look at the pictures in their books and identify the animals that don't belong.
- They circle the animal that does not belong in each case.
- Elicit what family each one is, e.g., a dog family.
- Ask what animal does not belong to the family.

Key: 1 the kitten, 2 the duckling, 3 the dog

4 Project SB p37 Make an animal family. Say.

Aim: to enable students to apply what they have learned about what a family is
- Student choose a template of a cat or dog animal family.
- They color, cut out, and make their finger puppets.
- Students work in pairs.
- They pretend they are one of the members of the family, e.g., a kitten.
- They wear it on one hand, while they wear the rest of the family on the opposite hand.
- Students use their chosen puppet to introduce its family: *This is my family.*
- Then pairs ask questions about each other's family members, e.g., *Is this your (brother)?*
- Family members introduce themselves by saying *Hello, what's your name? I'm …*
- Encourage students to use animal sounds as well.
- Invite pairs to perform in front of the class.
- Take photos of the finger puppets and save them to students' digital portfolios.

3 35 WB p37 Listen and draw.

Aim: to identify families

For script, see TB p105.

Key: cats > ducks > dogs > chickens

4 WB p37 Look and find your favorite family. Draw ☺.

Aim: to show preferences
- Students go back to number 1. They look at the pet families and draw smiley faces according to their preferences. They draw four smileys for their favorite family, three for the second most popular, etc.

Key: Students' own answers

Lesson review

- With students, review what they have learned in the lesson and if they liked the project.
- Hold a class vote for the best puppet family performance.

Extension activity

Aim: to review the unit topic
- Hand out the animal family drawings displayed around the classroom to their owners. (see Materials)
- Students draw an animal that does not belong to the family in their drawings somewhere in the scene.
- Students exchange their drawings with a partner.
- They circle the animal that does not belong.

3 Look and circle the different animal.

1

2

3

4 Project Make an animal family. Say.

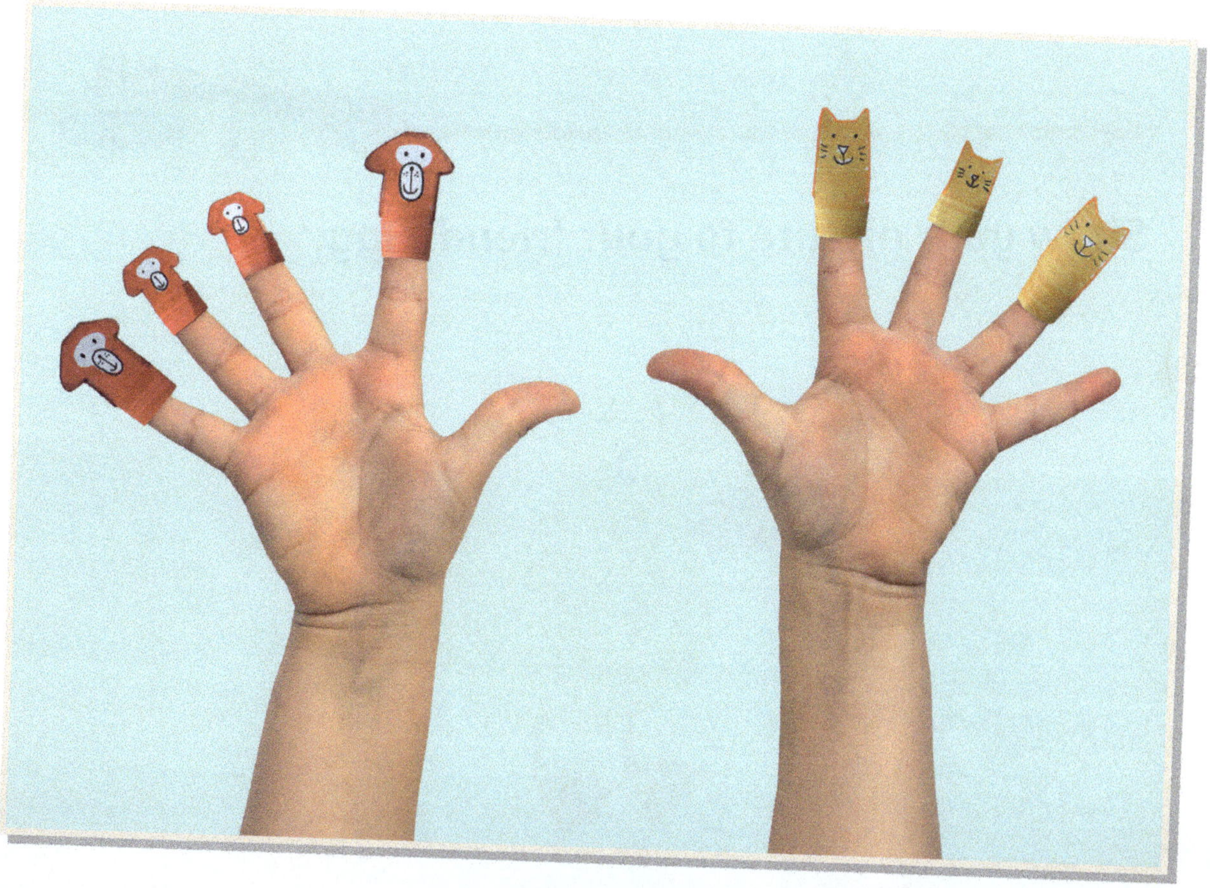

Create That!

1 41 Listen and imagine.
Then draw your picture.

2 Show your picture to your friend. Say.

Learning outcomes:
- to follow instructions
- to listen, imagine, and draw to demonstrate meaning

Recycled language: animals

Creative thinking: Chooses options to create something new

Cognitive control functions: Inhibitory control

Materials: soft music, letters for each of these words: Short words: *cat, dog, chicken, nut, dad, mom, duck, park*; Long words: *kitten, duckling, puppy, chick, sister, brother, flower, grandma, grandpa*

Warm-up

Aim: to get students ready for Activity 1
- Ask students to sit comfortably, put their heads on their tables, and close their eyes.
- Play soft music for several minutes for the class to relax.
- Students open their eyes.
- Give instructions for them to stretch their arms, legs, and backs.

1 41 SB p38 **Listen and imagine. Then draw your picture.**

Aim: to activate students' creativity
- Play the recording.
- After students open their eyes, they draw a picture in their books and color it.

For script, see TB p105.

2 SB p38 **Show your picture to your friend. Say.**

Aim: to practice new language
- Students walk around the classroom and show their drawings to their partners.
- Students who drew the same baby animal or sister/brother get together in a group.
- Check which baby is the most popular.

1 36 WB p38 **Listen and color. Say.**

Aim: to improve listening skills
- Check that students know what they are going to color. (the edge of the picture)

For script, see TB p105.

Key: 1 red, 2 green, 3 blue, 4 yellow, (5 orange)

2 WB p38 **Look at the pictures again. Circle ☺, 😐, or ☹.**

Aim: to show preferences

Key: Students' own answers

Ending the lesson

Aim: to review vocabulary spelling
- Make two groups.
- Two students per group come to your desk.
- Give the letters of a short word (see Materials) to each group face down.
- When you say *Go!* students turn the letters over and make a word.
- The group that makes the word the quickest gets a point.
- Continue with other students.

Stronger students: Hand out the letters for longer words if you consider students confident enough to make the words.

Extension activity

Aim: to activate creativity
- Draw a circle, a square, a triangle, and a rectangle on the board.
- Students choose an animal they like.
- They draw the animal using those four shapes only.
- Make pairs.
- Students show their animals to each other and guess what they are: *Is this a … ? Yes, it is./ No, it isn't.*
- Teach the name of new animals, if necessary.
- Students walk around and show their drawings to their classmates.
- Hold a class vote for the drawing that was the most creative.

Learning outcomes:
- to review language from the unit by taking a quiz
- to reflect on learning

BIG QUESTION to think about how the unit has helped them answer the Big Question *What's a family?*

Recycled language: vocabulary and grammar from the unit

Cognitive control functions (WB): Cognitive flexibility

Warm-up

Aim: to review vocabulary
- Students work in two groups.
- Choose a category, e.g., family.
- Three students from group A say one member of the family each, e.g., mom, dad, sister.
- Three students from group B have to repeat the series in the same order without making a mistake.
- Continue with other categories, e.g., colors, animals.

1 42 SB p39 Listen and point. Then say.

Aim: to review members of the family
- Play the recording.
- Students listen, point to the corresponding picture, and say it.

For script, see TB p105.

Key: brother, sister, mom, dad, grandpa, grandma

2 43 SB p39 Listen and color.

Aim: to review members of the family
- Give students time to identify the members of the family.
- Play the recording.
- Check that students know what they are going to color. (the edge of the picture)
- Students work individually.
- Check results as a class.

For script, see TB p105.

Key: 1 blue, (2 red), 3 yellow, 4 green, 5 orange, 6 pink

3 SB p39 Look and circle the different animal.

Aim: to identify the one that doesn't belong
- Students look at the pictures and circle the animal that does not belong to the family.
- Teach new vocabulary.

Key: 1 the octopus, 2 the chick, 3 the kitten

1 WB p39 Look and say. Circle ☺, 😐, or ☹.

Aim: to enable students to assess their own learning

2 WB p39 Complete the family and color. Say.

BIG QUESTION Aim: to enable students to revisit the unit Big Question and consolidate learning

Ending the lesson

Aim: to enable students to express their preferences
- Ask students what their favorite activity is from the unit (e.g., the song, chant, or one of the games) and hold a class vote.
- Repeat the most popular activity with the class.

Extension activity

Aim: to enable students to share what they have learned
- Put students into pairs.
- Students open their Workbook to page 39.
- Students take turns talking about the animal family in Activity 2. Students can talk in terms of mom, dad, babies, etc.

1 42 Listen and point. Then say.

2 43 Listen and color.

3 Look and circle the different animal.

4 At the Zoo

1 44 Listen and point. Say the words.

BIG QUESTION Where can we find animals?

2 45 Listen and chant.

Learning outcomes:
- to name and talk about animals
- to say a chant

BIG QUESTION to start to think about the Big Question *Where can we find animals?*

New language: *parrot, lion, fish, zebra, big, small, welcome, black, white, pet*

Recycled language: *baby*

Critical thinking (WB): Sorts and arranges things by shapes, size, color, weight, texture, and positions

Cognitive control functions: Working memory

Flashcards: 36–41 (animals)

Warm-up

Aim: to introduce the unit topic
- Write the word *Welcome* on the board.
- Elicit the meaning of the word, and ask students if they have seen this word before.
- Write the word *zoo* on the board, and ask students if they have ever been to a zoo.

Presentation

Aim: to present new vocabulary
- Take out the *animal* flashcards.
- Students repeat after you.
- Show the *big* and *small* flashcards and make questions about the animals: *Is this animal big or small?*

1 44 SB p40 Listen and point. Say the words.

Aim: to practice animal names
- Students look at the pictures in their Student's Book.
- Point to the two characters and ask who they are.
- Ask *Where are they?* (*At the zoo.*) *What animals can you see on the poster? How many are there?*
- Point to the baby and elicit the word *baby*. Ask *Is the baby big or small?*
- Point to the tree, elicit the word, and ask if it is big or small.
- Play the recording. Students listen and point to the corresponding picture.

For script, see TB p106.

- Play the recording again for students to repeat the words.

BIG QUESTION Where can we find animals?

Aim: to make students aware of where animals live
- Read the Big Question. Ask students where animals live.
- Ask about indigenous animals and if they have ever seen them.

Note: Some of the discussion will need to be in L1.

2 45 SB p40 Listen and chant.

Aim: to give students practice with new language
- Elicit from students what they can see in the pictures.
- Ask what color the animals are. Teach *black* and *white*.
- Play the recording.
- Students listen and follow the chant in their Student's Books.

For chant script, see TB p106.

- Play the recording again, pausing for students to repeat.
- Say the chant as a class and then in groups.

Practice

Aim: to personalize and practice the new language
- Teach the word *pet*.
- Ask *Do you have a pet?*
- Students talk about their pets, whether they are big or small and what color they are.

1 37 WB p40 Listen and number. Say.

Aim: to practice new language

For script, see TB p106.

Key: a 2, b 4, c 3, (d 1)

2 WB p40 Look and draw. Say.

Aim: to identify animals

Key: 1 fish, 2 parrot, 3 fish

Ending the lesson

Aim: to review animals
- Stick the flashcards on the board.
- Volunteer students come to the board, point to one flashcard, and say the word.

Stronger students: Volunteer students come to the board and write the first letter of each animal on the flashcards.

Extension activity

Aim: to review language from the unit
- Students describe their favorite animal by chanting *It's a dog. It's small. It's small. It's black and white.*
- Invite volunteers to chant in front of the class in small groups.

Learning outcomes:
- to talk about animals

New language: *It's a (big) …, shark*

Recycled language: animals, *big, small, beautiful, nice*

Critical thinking (WB): Solves simple puzzles

Cognitive control functions: Working flexibility

Materials: picture of an animal from any habitat (students bring it from home; they look up the name of the animal in English), flashcards 1–6 (colors), paper, Unit 4 stickers

Warm-up

Aim: to review colors
- Place the *color* flashcards on the board and review them.
- Elicit other colors that students know and the new ones.
- Hand out paper to some students, and ask them to color a circle for each of the colors that are missing in the flashcards.
- Place the new colors on the board, next to the *color* flashcards.
- Leave the flashcards on the board to aid students with Activity 1.

1 46 SB p41 Listen and stick.

Aim: to improve students' listening skills
- Students take out their stickers.
- Give students time to look at the silhouettes in their books.
- Play the recording.
- Students place the stickers on the silhouettes.

For script, see TB p106.

- Play the recording again for students to check their work.
- Students stick the animals in the corresponding place on the page.

Key: 1 a big lion, 2 a black and white zebra, 3 a small fish, 4 a small lion, 5 a big fish, 6 a green parrot

2 47 SB p41 Look, listen, and say.

Aim: to practice new language
- Students look at the pictures in Activity 1.
- Play the recording for students to listen and repeat.

For script, see TB p106.

3 SB p41 Complete the pictures. Point and say.

Aim: to give students practice with *It's a* (adjective) …
- Focus on the first picture. Point at the incomplete cub, and guide students to guess what it is. (A baby lion.) Encourage students to use: *It's a (big/small) …*
- Give students time to complete the pictures.
- Point to the pictures, and encourage students to say what they see, e.g., *It's a black and white zebra.*
- Teach the word *shark.*

Key: 1 small, 2 black and white, 3 big, 4 [Students say the color.]

1 38 WB p41 Listen and check ☑.

Aim: to improve visual recognition

For script, see TB p106.

Key: 2b: small lion, 3b: big zebra, 4b: big lion, 5b: small fish, 6a: blue and red parrot

2 WB p41 Match and draw lines. Say.

Aim: to practice new language

Key: 2 d, 3 e, 4 c, 5 b

Ending the lesson

Aim: to review new language
- Ask students to take out their pictures of animals. (see Materials)
- They tell you the names of the animals in English. Correct pronunciation.
- Place the pictures on the board.
- Point at any animal and say *It's a (big) horse.* Use colors and other adjectives students already know, e.g., *nice, beautiful.*
- Encourage students to describe the animals.
- Leave the pictures on the board for the Extension activity.

Extension activity

Aim: to expand on the new language from the lesson
- Divide the class into three groups.
- Give clues about an animal, e.g., *It's green and red.*
- A member of the group comes to the board and touches an animal.
- If he/she guesses correctly, the group gets a point. If he/she doesn't, it's the next group's turn.
- Continue with a set amount of clues.

Stronger students: Call students from each group to give clues instead of giving them yourself.

1 46 Listen and stick.

1

2

3

4

5

6

2 47 Look, listen, and say.

3 Complete the pictures. Point and say.

1

2

3

4

1 48 Listen and sing.

2 Find and circle the four animals in the song.

Learning outcomes:
- to sing a song

New language: *Can you find ... ?*

Recycled language: animals, *zoo*, *see*

Materials: flashcards 36–41 (animals), animal shadows or animal outlines

Warm-up

Aim: to review new language
- Ask three students to go out of the classroom.
- Hand out an *animals* flashcard for a student to hide in the classroom.
- Ask the three students to come back into the classroom, and ask in chorus: *Can you find the (lion)?*
- Students search for the missing flashcard.
- Continue with other flashcards and participants.

1 48 ▶ 49 SB p42 Listen and sing.

Aim: to sing a song with the class
- Students look at the picture in their books.
- Play the audio (48).
- Students listen and look at the picture.

For song lyrics, see TB p106.
- Play the audio again and sing with the class.
- Play the song video, pausing after each verse for students to repeat.
- When students have learned the song, use the karaoke version of the video or audio (49) to practice the song with the whole class.

Practice

Aim: to practice the song
- Divide the class into five groups.
- Assign a part of the song to each group.
- Play the karaoke version (49) again for the groups to sing.
- Swap verses among groups so each group has a chance to sing the two main verses.

2 SB p42 Find and circle the four animals in the song.

Aim: to practice new language
- Students look at the picture in their books.
- They do the activity in pairs.

Key: lion, zebra, fish, parrot

1 WB p42 Look. Count and write numbers. Say.

Aim: to improve visual recognition

Key: 4 small lions, 2 zebras, 9 small fish, 2 big fish, 7 green and orange parrots, 3 green and red parrots

2 39 WB p42 Listen and point.

Aim: to identify vocabulary in the song

For song lyrics, see TB p106.

Ending the lesson

Aim: to identify animals
- Take out the animal shadows or outlines. (see Materials)
- Call on individual students and ask *Can you find the animal?*
- Students make guesses.
- Continue with the rest of the shadows/outlines.

Extension activity

Aim: to practice new language
- Point to the lion in the picture in Activity 1.
- Say *It's a small, yellow lion.*
- Volunteer students describe other animals in the picture.
- Encourage students to provide two adjectives per animal.

Extra support: Review all the colors students have learned so far before doing the Extension activity.

Learning outcomes:
- to improve listening and oral skills

New language: *What's your favorite (animal)?, A penguin!*

Recycled language: color, animals

Materials: toy animals (students bring one from home)

Warm-up

Aim: to introduce new language
- Tell students what your favorite color, animal, and number is, e.g., *My favorite color is green.*
- Draw a big heart on the board and write or draw your preferences inside.
- Students do the same in their notebooks.
- Ask individual students about their favorite things: *What's your favorite* (*color*)?
- Teach new animal names.

1 50 SB p43 Listen and check ☑.

Aim: to improve students' listening skills
- Give students time to look at the pictures in Activity 1.
- Explain the activity to students.
- Play the recording for students to complete the activity.
- Check results as a class.

For script, see TB p106.

Key: 2 the parrot, 3 the fish, 4 the zebra

2 ▶ SB p43 Watch and listen.

Aim: to focus students on grammatical form
- Play the *Penny the Penguin* video.
- Students watch and listen.
- Ask *What is Penny's favorite animal?*

For script, see TB p106.

- Play the recording again.
- Students repeat.

3 SB p43 Draw for you. Then ask and answer.

Aim: to practice new language
- Model the oral activity. Ask a volunteer: *What's your favorite animal?*
- The volunteer answers, and you draw the animal on the board.
- Continue with *What's your favorite color?*
- The volunteer answers, and you draw a squiggle of the color under the animal on the board.
- Then it is your turn to answer and the volunteer's turn to draw.
- Students work in pairs and complete the charts in their books.

Note: In modeling this activity, you help teach any unknown animals the children want to know.

1 40 WB p43 Listen and check ☑.

Aim: to practice new language

For script, see TB p106.

Key: 2 parrot, 3 fish, 4 zebra

2 41 WB p43 Listen and circle. Ask and answer.

Aim: to practice new language and review colors and numbers

For script, see TB p106.

Key: 1 green, 2 1

Ending the lesson

Aim: to practice new language
- Place the *animal* flashcards on the board.
- Ask volunteer students to draw more animals they have learned in previous units or lessons next to the flashcards, e.g., butterfly, shark, penguin, squirrel, chicken, dog, duck, cat.
- Students draw a 2x2 grid in their notebooks.
- They draw four different animals from the board in the grid.
- Play *Picture Bingo.*
- Say *My favorite animal is a (dog).*
- Students check the animals that you mention.
- Students who complete the grid first shout *Bingo!*

Extra support: Students draw the grids in groups of three or in pairs.

Extension activity

Aim: to review new language
- Students take out their toy animal.
- Model the activity by showing a toy animal and saying: *This is my favorite animal. It's a big, yellow and black giraffe.*
- Students go around the classroom introducing their toy animal to their classmates.
- Check performance.

1 Listen and check ☑.

2 Watch and listen.

3 Draw for you. Then ask and answer.

	You	Friend
Favorite animal? 		
Favorite color? 		

My Favorite Animal

1 51 Watch and listen to the story.

1

2

3

4

5

6

Learning outcomes:
- to listen to, read, watch, and act out a picture story
- to act out an interview
- to review language from the unit

New language: *stripes, happy*

Recycled language: animals, *big, small, How many … ?, Do you have … ?, What's your name?, What's your favorite animal?, What color is it?, Is it big or small?*

Value: friendship

Materials: microphone (a real one or one made from cardboard) (optional)

Warm-up

Aim: to introduce the story
- Students look at the story frames.
- Ask simple questions, e.g., *What animals can you see? Are Whisper and Misty in the story?*
- Teach *happy*. Ask *Is Misty happy?*
- Teach *stripes*. Ask *What color are the zebra's stripes?*

My Favorite Animal

1 51 SB pp44–45 **Watch and listen to the story.**

Aim: to present a picture story
- Play the audio as students follow the story in their books.
- Ask general comprehension questions, e.g., *Is the lion big or small? What's the fish's name? Who is the small fish? What is Misty's favorite animal?*

For script, see TB page 106.

- Play the *My Favorite Animal* video to the end.
- Talk about the story value: friendship.
- Ask students why friends are important and what they do for their friends.
- Discuss whether Whisper is a good friend or not.

Note: Some of the discussion will need to be in L1.
- Play the video again. Students watch, listen, and repeat.

1 42 WB p44 **Listen and number.**

Aim: to review the unit story

For script, see TB p107.

Key: a 2, (b 1), c 4, d 3

2 43 WB p44 **Listen and check ☑.**

Aim: to review the unit story

For script, see TB p107.

Key: 1 a, 2 b

Ending the lesson

Aim: to act out the story
- Model the story with five students. Play Whisper's part.
- Make groups of six students.
- Students practice the story and perform in front of the class.

Extension activity

Aim: to act out an interview
- Write these questions on the board: *What's your name? What's your favorite animal? What color is it? Is it big or small?* Read them and ask students to repeat.
- Hand out the microphone to a volunteer (see Materials) to act as an interviewer.
- He/She asks you the questions on the board, and you answer them.
- Ask a pair of students to act out the interview in front of the class.
- Make pairs of students.
- They interview each other.
- Go around the classroom to check performance.
- In their notebooks, students draw their favorite animal and color it.

Learning outcomes:
- to review language from the story and the unit

Value: friendship

Critical thinking: Solves simple puzzles

Critical thinking (WB): Identifies characters, setting, plots, and theme in a story

Critical thinking (WB): Sorts and arranges things by shapes, size, color, weight, texture, and positions

Warm-up

Aim: to improve visual recognition
- Students work with books closed.
- They draw any of the animals from the picture story in their notebook.
- Encourage students to draw the animals as similar to the original ones as possible.
- Compare students' versions with the original animals in the story.
- Hold a class vote for the drawings that look the most similar to the original ones.

2 SB p45 What's different? Look and circle.

Aim: to identify differences
- Students open their books to page 45 and look attentively at the pictures.
- They circle the differences.
- Elicit the differences orally, e.g., *The lion in the story is big. This lion is very big! The zebra in the story is big. This zebra is small.*

Key: 2 the lion (it's big), 3 the parrot (it's red and blue, not red, yellow, and blue), 4 the zebra (it's small, and it's orange and white)

1 WB p45 What's good? Draw ☺.

Aim: to revisit the unit value

Key: 1

2 WB p45 Look at the friends. Write 1, 2, and 3.

Aim: to revisit the unit value

Key: Students' own answers

Ending the lesson

Aim: to review patterns
- Remind students of what a pattern is.
- Ask them to draw a pattern in their notebooks, e.g., a big red bird, a small red bird, a small blue bird, a big red bird, etc.
- Encourage students to draw things that are big or small or a different color.
- Students exchange notebooks for their partner to complete the pattern.

Extension activity

Aim: to focus on the value of friendship
- Ask students what they do for their friends and what they expect their friends to do for them.
- Talk about how they feel when they are with their friends.

Note: Some of this discussion will need to take place in L1.

2 What's different? Look and circle.

Think and Learn

Animal Habitats

Watch and listen.

1 52 Listen and point.

1 
monkey

2 
frog

3 
tree

4 
pond

5 
grassland

2 Where do these animals live? Draw lines.

1 

2 

3 

a 

b 

c 

4 

5 

6 

Learning outcomes:
- to integrate other areas of the curriculum through English: science

BIG QUESTION to answer the Big Question *Where can we find animals?*

New language: *monkey, frog, tree, pond, grassland, live, habitat*

Recycled language: *chicken, duck, cat, dog, squirrel, butterfly, shark*

Critical thinking: Sorts and classifies objects and activities according to key features

Materials: flashcards 36–41 (animals), soft ball or fluffy toy the size of a tennis ball, flashcards/pictures of a squirrel, butterfly, shark, duck, chicken, cat, dog, frog, monkey (optional)

Warm-up

Aim: to introduce the lesson topic
- Ask students to think of where people live.
- Elicit different types of homes, e.g., house, apartment, igloo, tent, van, houseboat, tree house, etc.
- Ask where animals live, e.g., forest, savannah, jungle, sea, etc.

Note: Some of this discussion will need to take place in L1.

SB p46 Watch and listen. What is an animal habitat?

Aim: to identify habitats
- With the Student's Books closed, play the *Think and Learn* video.

For videoscript, see TB p107.

- Elicit from students what animals they have seen in the video.
- Ask what a habitat is and if they remember the name of any of them from the video.

1 52 SB p46 Listen and point.

Aim: to present words to describe where animals live
- Students open their books.
- Play the recording.
- Students listen and point to the corresponding picture.
- Ask *Where does the monkey live? Where does the frog live? Where do lions and zebras live?*

2 SB p46 Where do these animals live? Draw lines.

Aim: to identify habitats
- Point to the pictures and ask what each animal and habitat is.
- Students do the activity individually.
- Check results by asking *Where does the lion live? (On the grassland.)*

Key: 2 c, 3 a, 4 a, 5 c, 6 b

1 44 WB p46 Listen and color. Say.

Aim: to practice new language
- Check that students know what they are going to color. (the edge of the picture)

For script, see TB p107.

Key: 1 monkey: orange, (2 frog: blue), 3 tree: red, 4 pond: green, 5 grassland: yellow

2 WB p46 Where do the animals live? Match and say.

Aim: to identify habitats

Key: 1 b, 2 c, 3 a

Ending the lesson

Aim: to review animal names
- Place the *animals* flashcards on the board, and ask students to tell you their names.
- Take out the new flashcards/pictures (see Materials), and place them on the board, too.
- Ask students what each animal is called.
- Make two or three groups.
- Draw a line on the floor that could be around two meters away from the board.
- Groups stand behind the line.
- Give the ball or toy (see Materials) to a member of one group.
- Say an animal that is on the board.
- The student throws the ball, aiming at the corresponding animal.
- If he/she hits the correct animal, his/her group gets a point.
- Continue with the other groups, and let students say the animals.

Note: Keep all the flashcards for future lessons.

Extension activity

Aim: to practice categorizing
- Draw a table on the board made up of three columns.
- Draw a picture at the top of each column, e.g., tree, pond, grassland.
- Place the *animal* flashcards and new flashcards/pictures face down on your desk.
- Ask volunteers to come to the front, take a flashcard, and place it under the habitat it belongs to.

Learning outcomes:
- to extend the focus on science through English
- to complete a project

Recycled language: animals, numbers, habitats

Critical thinking: Demonstrate understanding of links between new ideas

Creative thinking: Creates content for peers to use in class activities

Critical thinking (WB): Sorts and classifies objects and activities according to key features

Creative thinking (WB): Uses own ideas for doing creative activities like coloring, drawing, and building

Materials: letter-size paper (1 piece per student), flashcards 36–41 (animals), and flashcards from previous lesson

Warm-up

Aim: to identify differences
- Draw a pattern on the board, e.g., red splotch, black splotch, 10, yellow splotch.
- A volunteer student crosses out the one that doesn't belong. (10)
- Repeat with other patterns.
- Students make patterns in their notebooks for a partner to identify the one that doesn't belong.

3 SB p47 Look and circle the wrong animal.

Aim: to identify where animals belong
- Students work in pairs.
- Pairs look at the pictures in their books and identify the animals that do not belong to the habitats.
- They circle the animal that does not belong in each case.
- Check results.

Key: a the chicken, b the duck, c the fish

4 Project SB p47 Make a puzzle for your friend.

Aim: to enable students to apply what they have learned about where animals live
- Hand out a piece of paper per student. (see Materials)
- Write *Pond Animals* and *Grassland Animals* on the board.
- Show students how to make the puzzle.
- First, students place the piece of paper horizontally on their tables.
- Second, they fold it in half. They will draw on each "page."
- Students choose one habitat and write a title on the front page, e.g., *Pond Animals*.
- They open the piece of paper and draw the chosen habitat, e.g., a pond.
- They also draw animals that belong to that habitat, between 1 and 10 of each animal.
- Finally, on the back they write a key, i.e., one drawing of each animal they drew and the number of each they have drawn, e.g., (drawing of a fish) 4.
- Students swap their puzzles with a partner.
- They open the puzzles and find and count the animals in their partner's picture.
- Then they say the result, e.g., *Four fish.*
- Their partner confirms whether they are correct and says *Yes. That's right!* or *No.* with a shake of the head.
- Take photos of the puzzles and save them to students' digital portfolios.

3 WB p47 Look and circle the wrong animal.

Aim: to identify where animals belong

Key: 1 parrot, 2 lion, 3 monkey

4 WB p47 Choose your favorite place. Draw ☺.

Aim: to communicate preferences

Key: Students' own answers

Lesson review

- With students, review what they have learned in the lesson and if they liked the project.
- Students tell you if they could solve their partner's puzzle easily or found it difficult.

Extension activity

Aim: to review animals
- Take out the *animals* flashcards.
- Make two or three groups.
- Place five flashcards on the board or on your desk.
- One member per group memorizes them.
- Ask the students to close their eyes.
- Take away one of the flashcards and scramble the rest.
- The first student to guess the missing animal wins a point for his/her group.
- Continue with a set amount of points in mind.

3 Look and circle the wrong animal.

4 Project Make a puzzle for your friend.

Do That!

1 53 Listen and act it out with your teacher. Then listen again and match.

1 2 3 4 5 6

Learning outcomes:
- to act out a story

New language: *jungle*

Recycled language: animals, animal sounds

Creative thinking: Listens and responds physically to songs, rhymes, chants

Creative thinking (WB): Creates texts that express personal interests, emotions, or identity

Materials: binoculars (real or made of cardboard rolls; students bring them from home)

Warm-up

Aim: to practice the unit language
- Say *Woof, woof* and elicit what animal students think this sound is produced by.
- Continue with *meow, cluck,* and *quack.*
- Encourage students to produce the sounds of some animals from the unit, e.g., monkey, frog, lion, parrot.
- Students sit in a circle.
- One student produces an animal sound.
- The student on his/her right, produces the same sound and another different sound.
- The next student has to produce the two previous sounds and a new one.
- The game continues until a student makes a mistake and is out.
- The game starts all over again.

1 53 SB p48 **Listen and act it out with your teacher. Then listen again and match.**

Aim: to activate students' creativity
- Work with books closed.
- Play the recording, and act it out as you listen to the story.

For script, see TB p107.

- Teach the word *jungle.*
- Play the recording again for students to act it out with you.
- Students open their books.
- Give them time to examine the pictures.
- Play the recording for a third time for students to do the activity.
- Check results as a class.

Key: 2 pink, 3 orange, 4 red, 5 green, 6 yellow

1 45 WB p48 **Listen and number. Say.**

Aim: to practice new language

For script, see TB p107.

Key: a 3, b 2, c 5, d 4, (e 1)

2 WB p48 **Draw a picture of your favorite animal.**

Aim: to communicate preferences

Ending the lesson

Aim: to review language
- Model a dialogue with a volunteer.
- Say *Let's go to the grassland.*
- Take your binoculars (see Materials), and pretend you are looking through them.
- Imagine you are looking at a lion and say *Can you see the lion?*
- Encourage your partner to say something about the lion, e.g., *Yes, it's big.*
- Continue with another example.
- Students work in pairs.
- They take out their binoculars.
- They invent a short dialogue following your model dialogue.
- Go around the classroom and check performance.
- Invite pairs to perform in front of the class.

Extension activity

Aim: to activate creativity
- Play *Charades* with the class.
- Make two groups.
- Whisper the name of an animal to one member of a group.
- He/She acts as that animal.
- His/Her group guesses what the animal is.
- Continue with a set amount of animals.

Learning outcomes:
- to review language from the unit by taking a quiz
- to reflect on learning

BIG QUESTION to think about how the unit has helped them answer the Big Question *Where can we find animals?*

Recycled language: vocabulary and grammar from the unit

Creative thinking (WB): Draws pictures to represent vocabulary and familiar concepts

Cognitive control functions (WB): Cognitive flexibility

Materials: pictures of the animals students have learned (they should be cut in half, as if they were a 2-piece puzzle), bag, two small boxes

Warm-up

Aim: to review vocabulary from the unit
- Put one half of the puzzles in a bag, and the other half face up on your desk. (see Materials)
- Students work in two groups.
- They stand in line, only one meter away from your desk.
- Give a box to each group.
- The second student in line holds the box.
- When you say *Go!* the first students in line run to the desk, take a piece from the bag, and find the missing half on your desk to complete a puzzle.
- Students run back to their group and leave the puzzle in the box.
- The student who is holding the box passes it to the next student in line and runs to get another puzzle.
- The winner is the group with the most puzzles.

1 54 SB p49 **Listen and point. Then say.**

Aim: to review key words from the unit
- Play the recording.
- Students listen, point to the corresponding picture, and say it.

For script, see TB p107.

Key: parrot, lion, fish, zebra, big fish, small fish

2 55 SB p49 **Listen and number.**

Aim: to review language from the unit
- Give students time to identify the animals in the pictures.
- Play the recording.
- Students number the pictures individually.
- Check results as a class.

For script, see TB p107.

Key: 2 c, 3 b, 4 a

3 SB p49 **Draw the missing animal. Then say.**

Aim: to review language from the unit
- Students look at the pictures and draw the animals that are missing.
- Check results orally.

Key: 1 Students draw a parrot.
2 Students draw a frog.

1 WB p49 **Look and say. Circle ☺, 😐, or ☹.**

Aim: to assess performance

2 WB p49 **Where do they live? Look and check ☑.**

Aim: to revisit the unit Big Question

Key: 1 c, 2 b, 3 a, 4 c

3 WB p49 **Look and think. Draw animals in the pictures.**

Aim: to review animal habitats

Key: Students' own answers

Ending the lesson

Aim: to enable students to express their preferences
- Ask students what their favorite activity is from the unit (e.g., the song, chant, or one of the games) and hold a class vote.
- Repeat the most popular activity with the class.

Extension activity

Aim: to enable students to share what they have learned
- Put students into groups of four.
- Each student opens their Workbook to page 49.
- Students take turns showing what they have drawn for Activity 3 and saying something about the animals.

1 54 Listen and point. Then say.

2 55 Listen and number.

a

b

c

d

1

3 Draw the missing animal. Then say.

1

2

5 My Food

1 56 Listen and point. Say the words.

BIG QUESTION What food do we eat?

2 57 Listen and chant.

Learning outcomes:
- to name and talk about food
- to say a chant

BIG QUESTION to start to think about the Big Question *What food do we eat?*

New language: *oranges, pears, tomatoes, milk, chocolate, cupcakes, picnic, water, share*

Recycled language: numbers, colors, *park*

Cognitive control functions: Working memory

Materials: flashcards 42–47 (food), paper

Warm-up

Aim: to introduce the unit topic
- Draw a plate on the board and draw your favorite food on it.
- Say *This is my favorite food. What is your favorite food?*
- Invite students to come to the board and draw their favorite food.
- See what the most popular food is. Count with students.

Presentation

Aim: to present new vocabulary
- Take out the *food* flashcards and say the words.
- Students repeat after you.
- Show each flashcard again and ask what color each food is.
- Place the flashcards on the board and ask students what their favorite food on the flashcards is.

1 56 SB p50 Listen and point. Say the words.

Aim: to practice food
- Students look at the picnic scene in their Student's Book.
- Ask *Where are Misty and Whisper? (At the park.) What food can you see? How many are there?*
- Teach the word *picnic*, and explain that a cupcake is a small cake.
- Play the recording. Students listen and point to the corresponding food.

For script, see TB p107.

- Play the recording again for students to repeat the words.

BIG QUESTION What food do we eat?

Aim: to make students aware of the food they eat
- Read the Big Question. Ask students what they usually eat.
- Ask if they consider the food they eat to be healthy or unhealthy.
- Take out the *food* flashcards and ask students if they consider the food on the flashcards healthy or unhealthy.

Note: Some of the discussion will need to be in L1.

2 57 SB p50 Listen and chant.

Aim: to give students practice with new language
- Elicit from students what they can see in the picture scene.
- Play the recording.
- Students listen and follow the chant in their Student's Books.
- Teach the word *share*.

For chant script, see TB p107.

- Play the recording again, pausing for students to repeat.
- Say the chant as a class and then in groups.

Practice

Aim: to personalize and practice the new language
- Ask volunteer students to come to the front and draw the food items from the chant in the order they appear, i.e., a drawing of an orange, a tomato, cupcake, chocolate, milk, pear.
- Point to each drawing as you chant with students.
- Change the pace at which you point to the drawings so that the chant is said more slowly or faster.

1 WB p50 Match and say.

Aim: to review new language

Key: 2 d, 3 e, 4 b, 5 a, 6 c

2 WB p50 Look and count. Say.

Aim: to review new language and numbers

Key: 2 four chocolates, 3 eight pears, 4 nine cupcakes

Ending the lesson

Aim: to review food
- Place the flashcards on the board.
- Elicit the names of the food items.
- Invite volunteers to write the beginning letter of each food item under the corresponding flashcard.
- Leave the flashcards and the text on the board for the Extension activity.

Extension activity

Aim: to review language from the unit
- Ask students to draw on paper two items of food they see on the flashcards (tennis ball sized drawings).
- Students cut the two drawings out separately.
- Invite four or five students to collect the drawings.
- These students will act as grocery store owners.
- They first arrange the food on your desk.
- Act as a customer using simple language students are already familiar with, e.g., *Hello. Pears, please. How many? Two. Thank you. Goodbye.*
- Keep the food drawings for another lesson.

Learning outcomes:
- to talk about likes and dislikes

New language: *I like (oranges)., I don't like (milk)., yum, yummy, yuck*

Recycled language: food, color, animals

Creative thinking (WB): Creates texts that express personal interests, emotions, or identity

Materials: Unit 5 stickers, flashcards 1–6 (colors), 36–39 (animals), and 42–47 (food)

Warm-up

Aim: to introduce the grammar point of the lesson
- Place the *food* flashcards on the board.
- Point to each of them and say whether you like them or not using *yum, yummy,* and *yuck* or *yucky*.
- For example, point to the chocolate and say *Yummy! I like chocolate* and make a gesture of satisfaction.
- Then point to the milk and say *Yuck! I don't like milk.*
- Elicit examples from volunteer students.

1 58 SB p51 Listen and stick ☺ or ☹.

Aim: to improve students' listening skills
- Students take out their stickers.
- Show each of the emoji, and make sure students understand what they stand for, i.e., *like, don't like.*
- Give students time to look at the pictures in their books.
- Play the recording.
- Students place the stickers where they belong.

For script, see TB p107.

- Play the recording again for students to check their work.
- Students stick the emoji in the corresponding place on the page.

Key: 1 ☺, 2 ☺, 3 ☹, 4 ☹, 5 ☺, 6 ☹

2 59 SB p51 Look, listen, and say.

Aim: to practice new language
- Students look at the pictures in Activity 1.
- Play the recording for students to listen and repeat.

For script, see TB p107.

3 SB p51 Talk about food.

Aim: to give students practice with *I like* and *I don't like*
- Students work in pairs.
- With a volunteer, give an example of how to do the activity, e.g., Say *I like cupcakes. I don't like pears.*
- Then it is the other student's turn to talk about likes and dislikes.
- Students take turns talking about their likes and dislikes.
- Change pairs twice or three times.

1 46 WB p51 Listen and check ☑ or X ☒.

Aim: to improve listening skills

For script, see TB p107.

Key: Tom ☑ ☑ ☒, Ruby ☑ ☒ ☑

2 WB p51 Circle ☺ or ☹ for you. Say.

Aim: to give students practice with *I like* and *I don't like*

Key: Students' own answers

Ending the lesson

Aim: to practice new language
- Take out the *color* and *animals* flashcards.
- Put them in a pile face down.
- Go around the classroom and ask students to take the first flashcard on the pile.
- They turn the chosen flashcard over and say if they like or don't like what they see, e.g., *I don't like blue.*
- You could also ask students about animals they already know but are not on the flashcards, e.g., *squirrel, chicken, dog, duck, cat, kitten, puppy, chick, duckling, shark, monkey, frog.*
- You could also ask about more colors students already know, e.g., *black, white.*

Extension activity

Aim: to expand on the new language from the lesson
- Draw two columns on the board.
- Draw a smiley face on top of the first column and a face showing dislike on top of the second.
- Students copy the table and emoji into their notebooks.
- They draw food, animals, and colors they like or dislike in the corresponding column.
- They work in pairs or small groups and tell each other what they like or don't like.
- Students will use the *like/don't like* table in their notebooks in the following lesson.

1 58 Listen and stick 😊 or 😔.

1

2

3

4

5

6

2 59 Look, listen, and say.

3 Talk about food.

cupcake

tomatoes

milk

oranges

chocolate

pears

1 60 Listen and sing.

2 Look, think, and draw 😊 or 😔.

Learning outcomes:
- to sing a song

Recycled language: *I like (oranges).*, *I don't like (milk).*, animals, colors, food

Creative thinking: Creates texts that express personal interests, emotions, or identity

Materials: *like/don't like* tables (see Extension activity in previous lesson), 3 smiley faces and 3 faces showing dislike on sticks (they should be a size that can be seen from the back of the classroom) (optional)

Warm-up

Aim: to review new language
- Students open their notebooks to use the *like/don't like* tables from the previous lesson.
- Students work in pairs.
- Ask students to take out a green and red pencil.
- Pairs compare their tables and circle the things they both like green.
- Then they circle the things they both don't like red.
- Students will reuse the table in their notebooks later.

1 60 ▶ 61 SB p52 **Listen and sing.**

Aim: to sing a song
- Students look at the picture in their books.
- Play the audio (60).
- Students listen and sing with you.

For song lyrics, see TB p107.

- Play the song video, pausing after each verse for students to repeat.
- When students have learned the song, use the karaoke version of the video or audio (61) to practice the song with the whole class.

Practice

Aim: to practice the song
- Divide the class into two groups, girls and boys.
- Assign the girl's part to the girls and the boy's part to the boys.
- Play the karaoke version (61) again for the class to sing.

2 SB p52 **Look, think, and draw ☺ or ☹.**

Aim: to practice new language
- Students look at the table in their books.
- Tell students that the girl and boy are the ones from the song.
- In pairs, they complete the table.
- Check results as a class.

Key: girl: ☺ chocolate, tomato, ☹ pear, milk; boy: ☺ orange, tomato, ☹ pear, cupcake

1 47 WB p52 **What do they like? Listen and circle.**

Aim: to practice the song

For song lyrics, see TB p107.

Key: 1 a and c, 2 a and c

2 WB p52 **Color, trace, and say.**

Aim: to practice a line from the song

Ending the lesson

Aim: to practice new language
- Students use their *like/don't like* tables in their notebooks. (see Materials)
- They work with the same pair they worked with when they compared their tables.
- Students practice a new version of the last verse of the song by choosing something they both like and something they both dislike, which has already been circled by them in green or red.
- Students sing in front of the class. Example: *I don't like blue. Yes, it's true. But I like yellow, and I like you.*

Extension activity

Aim: to practice new language
- Take out the emoji sticks. (see Materials)
- Show them to the class and say what they represent, i.e., *I like, I don't like.*
- Make two groups and hand out a pair of emoji per group, one of each kind.
- Keep two sticks for yourself.
- Mention a color, animal, or food, e.g., *apples.*
- Groups have to make a guess by showing you either the *I like* emoji or the *I don't like* one.
- You then show the emoji that communicates your preference and you say *I like (apples)* or *I don't like (apples).*
- Groups get a point per each correct guess.
- Set a total number of points the groups have to get to be the winners.

Learning outcomes:
- to improve listening and oral skills

New language: *Do you like (pink)?, Yes, I do. / No, I don't.*

Recycled language: color, food

Creative thinking: Participates in investigative, exploratory, open-ended tasks

Cognitive control functions: Cognitive flexibility

Materials: flashcards 1–6 (colors), a toy penguin, blindfold, soft ball (optional)

Warm-up

Aim: to review colors
- Place the *color* flashcards on the board.
- Elicit the name of each color.
- Ask students to take colored pencils for each of the colors on the flashcards.
- Students open their notebooks.
- Dictate colors. Students draw a circle for each color in a row.
- Students check their work in pairs.

1 62 SB p53 Listen and draw ☺ or ☹.

Aim: to improve students' listening skills
- Give students time to identify the colors in the picture.
- Explain how the activity works to students.
- Play the recording for students to complete the activity.
- Check results as a class.

For script, see TB p108.

Key: ☺: pink, orange; ☹: yellow, red, green

2 SB p53 Watch and listen.

Aim: to focus students on grammatical form
- Play the *Penny the Penguin* video.
- Students watch and listen.
- Take out the toy penguin (see Materials) and pretend you are asking it questions.
- Follow the dialogue in the video.
- Act out the penguin's part by making a fun voice.

For script, see TB p108.

- Play the recording again.
- Invite pairs of students to perform with the penguin in front of the class.

3 SB p53 Ask and answer. Draw ☺ or ☹.

Aim: to practice new language
- Model the oral activity with a volunteer by asking *Do you like … ?*
- Encourage the volunteer to provide complete answers, i.e., *Yes, I do. No, I don't.*
- Draw faces on the board as you interview the volunteer.
- Students complete the first column of the table about themselves.
- Make pairs.
- Students complete the second column.
- Make new pairs.
- Students complete the third column.

1 48 WB p53 Listen and write *yes* or *no*.

Aim: to practice new language

For script, see TB p108.

Key: 2 yes, 3 no, 4 no, 5 yes, 6 no

2 WB p53 Look and ask.

Aim: to practice speaking skills

Key: *Do you like cake/oranges/pears/milk/chocolate? Yes, I do. / No, I don't.*

Ending the lesson

Aim: to practice new language
- Students sit or stand in a circle.
- A volunteer (student A) goes to the middle of the circle and is blindfolded.
- Turn student A around so that he/she loses sense of direction.
- Student A points at someone in the circle (student B) he/she can't see.
- Student A asks a question using *Do you like … ?*
- Student B answers either by saying *Yes, I do.* or *No, I don't.*
- Student A guesses who is speaking.
- If he/she is right, it is another student's turn to act as student A.
- Continue with the game as many times as you consider appropriate.

Extension activity

Aim: to review new language
- Students sit in a circle.
- Take out the soft ball. (see Materials)
- Throw the ball to a student, and ask him/her a question with *Do you like … ?*
- The student answers your question.
- Then it is his/her turn to ask a question.
- Continue until everyone has participated.

1 62 Listen and draw 😊 or 😣.

2 Watch and listen.

3 Ask and answer. Draw 😊 or 😣.

	Me	My Friend ______	My Friend ______
pink			
blue			
green			
pears			
chocolate			
tomatoes			

The Cupcakes

1 63 Watch and listen to the story.

Learning outcomes:
- to listen to, read, watch, and act out a picture story
- to review language from the unit

Recycled language: numbers, food, *squirrel*, *have*

Critical thinking (WB): Solves simple puzzles

Cognitive control functions (WB): Cognitive flexibility

Value: sharing

Materials: 4 boxes or toy cupcakes

Warm-up

Aim: to introduce the story
- Students look at the story frames.
- Ask simple questions, e.g., *Where are Whisper and Misty? What food can you see? What animal can you see? Is Misty happy?*

The Cupcakes

1 63 SB pp54–55 Watch and listen to the story.

Aim: to present a picture story
- Play the audio as students follow the story in their books.
- Ask general comprehension questions, e.g., *How many cupcakes are there? Are the cupcakes big or small? Is the squirrel a friend?*

For script, see TB page 108.

- Play *The Cupcakes* video to the end.
- Talk about the story value: sharing.
- Ask students what they share with friends and family.
- Talk about what you get back when you share something with someone else.

Note: Some of the discussion will need to be in L1.
- Play the video again. Students watch, listen, and repeat.

1 WB p54 Follow the lines. check ☑ or X ☒.

Aim: to review the unit picture story

Key: squirrel ☑, Whisper ☒, Misty ☒

2 WB p54 What's different? Look and say.

Aim: to improve visual skills

Key: four oranges/no oranges, three tomatoes/two tomatoes, no cupcakes/four cupcakes, milk on the left/milk on the right

Ending the lesson

Aim: to act out the story
- Take out the four boxes or toy cupcakes. (see Materials)
- Use them as props to model the story with volunteer students.
- The student who plays the squirrel should take one box/cupcake at a time.
- Assign two scenes from the story to different groups of students.
- Students perform in front of the class.

Extension activity

Aim: to act out a new version of the story
- Make groups.
- Groups make up a new version of the story.
- They choose other food and another animal.
- Encourage groups to draw props for their performance.
- They perform in front of the class.

Stronger students: Students add a new dialogue to the original story, e.g., a dialogue with the squirrel asking his name.

Learning outcomes:
- to review language from the story and the unit

Value: sharing

Critical thinking: Solves simple puzzles

Critical thinking (WB): Identifies characters, setting, plots, and theme in a story

Cognitive control functions (WB): Cognitive flexibility

Flashcards: 42–47 (food)

Warm-up

Aim: to improve visual intelligence
- Place the *food* flashcards on the board in random order.
- Ask a volunteer to look at them attentively.
- Then ask the volunteer to turn around.
- Change the order of the flashcards.
- Ask the volunteer to face the board again.
- He/She has to put the flashcards in their original place.
- Repeat with other students and let them take your role as well.

Stronger students: Do the same activity, but using the flashcards showing the side with words and not the pictures.

2 SB p55 Look and draw the cupcakes.

Aim: to improve memory
- Students work in pairs.
- Without looking at the story scenes on the previous page, they complete the pictures with the missing cupcakes.

Key: 1 two cupcakes, 2 one cupcake, 3 four cupcakes, 4 three cupcakes

1 WB p55 What's good? Draw ☺.

Aim: to focus on the value of sharing

Key: 1

2 WB p55 Complete the picture. Draw what a good friend does.

Aim: to focus on the value of sharing

Ending the lesson

Aim: to practice spelling
- Students work in pairs.
- In their notebooks, they draw things from the story scenes they know the names of in English.
- Then they open their Student's Book, search for the words, and write them under each drawing.
- Go around the classroom, and check spelling.

Extra support: Instead of writing the words under the drawings, they say the words out loud in the class as they show their drawings.

Extension activity

Aim: to focus on the value of sharing
- Ask students why they think Misty and Whisper share the last cupcake with the squirrel.
- Explain to students the importance of teaching others to share.
- Ask students how they think Whisper, Misty, and the squirrel feel at the end of the story.

Note: Some of this discussion will need to take place in L1.

2 Look and draw the cupcakes.

Think and Learn

Fruit and Vegetables

Watch and listen.

1 64 Listen and point.

1 potatoes

2 carrots

3 bananas

4 ground

2 Where does our food come from? Draw lines.

1

2

Learning outcomes:
- to integrate other areas of the curriculum through English: science
- BIG QUESTION to answer the Big Question *What food do we eat?*

New language: *potatoes, carrots, bananas, ground, tree, fruit, vegetables, grow, come from*

Recycled language: food

Critical thinking (SB & WB): Sorts and classifies objects and activities according to key features

Materials: flashcards 42–47 (food), drawings or pictures of fruits and vegetables (pineapple, apple, peach, beetroot, onion, broccoli, pumpkin, peppers), a poster made of construction paper with a drawing of a big tree in the center and a line under it that represents the ground (optional)

Warm-up

Aim: to introduce the lesson topic
- Write the words *FRUITS* and *VEGETABLES* on the board.
- Take out the *oranges*, *pears*, and *tomatoes* flashcards.
- Show the *oranges* flashcard, and say *This is a fruit.*
- Place the flashcard under *FRUITS.*
- Continue with the pears and tomatoes. Explain to students that, even though many people think the tomato is a vegetable, it is actually a fruit.
- Leave the flashcards on the board.

SB p56 Watch and listen. Where does our food come from?

Aim: to learn where fruits and vegetables come from
- With the Student's Books closed, play the *Think and Learn* video.

For videoscript, see TB p108.

- Elicit from students what fruits and vegetables they have seen in the video.
- Ask volunteers to draw them on the board under the corresponding title, i.e., *FRUITS* or *VEGETABLES.*
- Leave the board as it is for the Ending the lesson activity.

1 64 SB p56 Listen and point.

Aim: to present words to describe where food comes from
- Students open their books.
- Play the recording.
- Students listen and point to the corresponding picture.
- Say incomplete sentences for students to complete by saying *the ground* or *a tree*, e.g., *Potatoes come from … Pears grow on …*
- Play the video again, if necessary.

2 SB p56 Where does our food come from? Draw lines.

Aim: to identify where food grows
- Elicit what students see in the pictures.
- Students do the activity in pairs.
- Pairs work with another pair to check results. They use (*Potatoes*) *come from the ground.* (*Oranges*) *grow on trees.*

Key: 1 ground: carrots, potatoes; 2 trees: pears, bananas

1 WB p56 Which one is different? Circle.

Aim: to categorize

Key: 1 c, 2 b, 3 c

2 WB p56 Where does it come from? Trace and check ☑.

Aim: to identify where food grows

Key: tree: 2 orange, 4 banana, 5 pear; ground: 3 potato, 6 carrot

Ending the lesson

Aim: to review vocabulary from the lesson
- Take out the drawings/pictures of fruits and vegetables. (see Materials)
- Volunteer students come to the front, take one drawing/picture and place it under the correct category on the board, i.e., *FRUITS* or *VEGETABLES.*
- Students copy what is on the board in to their notebooks.

Note: Keep the drawings/pictures for the Extension activity.

Extension activity

Aim: to categorize
- Take out the poster and place it on the board. (see Materials)
- Put the drawings/pictures from the previous activity and the *food* flashcards in a pile.
- Explain to students that the poster shows where fruits and vegetables can grow.
- Tell students that some fruits and vegetables can grow above the ground or below it.
- Provide an example by using the pictures of an apple, pumpkin, and carrots.
- Draw the apple on the tree, the pumpkin above the ground, and the carrots below the ground. (You can use the flashcards and pictures instead.)
- Continue with the rest of the fruits and vegetables.
- Encourage students to provide more examples.
- Display the poster in the classroom.

Learning outcomes:
- to extend the focus on science through English
- to complete a project

Recycled language: food, *come from*, *grow*

Critical thinking: Solves simple puzzles

Creative thinking: Uses different media to make and describe his/her own designs

Creative thinking (WB): Draws pictures to represent vocabulary and familiar concepts

Materials: letter-size paper (1 piece per student), blindfold, food students have already learned: chocolate, nut, orange, pear, tomato, cupcake, potato, carrot, banana, bottle of water, an empty milk carton. Put the food in a grocery bag that should be big enough for students not to see the food that is inside. (optional)

Warm-up

Aim: to review language
- Use the poster from the Extension activity in the previous lesson to review vocabulary.
- Point to the pictures and ask students what they are.
- Then say the words and ask students to point to the corresponding picture/ drawing.
- Speed up the pace every time you invite a new student to participate.

3 SB p57 Look and circle the wrong one.

Aim: to review language
- Students work in pairs.
- Pairs look at the pictures in their books and identify the fruits and vegetables that are in the wrong place.
- They circle them in their books.
- Check results as a class.

Key: 1 the orange, 2 the potato

4 Project SB p57 Make a food picture. Say.

Aim: to enable students to apply what they have learned about where food comes from
- Hand out a piece of paper per student. (see Materials)
- Ask students to draw a tree and the ground below it.
- Students choose a vegetable and a fruit.
- They draw several of them where they normally grow, either on the tree or in the ground.
- Students then color their drawings.
- Give an example of how to talk about their drawings by using the poster used in the previous lesson.
- Say *Oranges grow on trees. Carrots come from the ground.*
- Make groups of four.
- Students talk about their drawings.
- Go around the classroom to check performance.
- Display the drawings around the classroom. Take pictures of them and save them to students' portfolios.

3 WB p57 How many? Write.

Aim: to identify quantity

Key: b 6, c 7, d 10

4 WB p57 Draw the fruit. Trace.

Aim: to activate creativity

Lesson review

- With students, review what they have learned in the lesson and if they liked the project.
- Ask students to look around the classroom and say which food pictures are the most similar.

Extension activity

Aim: to review vocabulary
- Make two groups.
- Take out the grocery bag with food inside. Tell students you have gone shopping.
- Call on one member of a group (group A) and blindfold him/ her.
- Take out something from the grocery bag.
- The student touches the food and has to guess what it is.
- If he/she guesses correctly the first time, group A gets a point.
- Continue with group B.
- The winning team is the one that makes the most correct guesses.

3 Look and circle the wrong one.

1

2

4 Project Make a food picture. Say.

Create That!

1 65 Listen and imagine. Then draw your picture.

2 Show your plate to your friend. Say.

Learning outcomes:
- to activate creativity

New language: *party, lots of*

Recycled language: food

Creative thinking: Chooses options to create something new

Creative thinking (WB): Uses different media to make and describe his/her own designs

Cognitive control functions: Inhibitory control

Warm-up

Aim: to introduce the lesson topic
- Teach the word *party.*
- Ask students what parties they like going to.
- Ask questions using *Do you like … ?* For example, *Do you like birthdays? Do you like cupcakes? Do you like big or small parties?*
- Teach the word *lots of.* You could ask *Do you have lots of pencils/books?*

Note: Some of the discussion will need to be in L1.

1 65 SB p58 Listen and imagine. Then draw your picture.

Aim: to activate students' creativity
- Work with books closed.
- Students rest their heads down on their tables and close their eyes.
- Play the recording.

For script, see TB p108.

- When students open their eyes, ask them to open their books.
- They draw what they imagined on their plate.

2 SB p58 Show your plate to your friend. Say.

Aim: to practice speaking skills
- Show the class how to speak about their plates by calling a volunteer student and guiding him/her to talk about his/her plate.
- Students work in small groups.
- They show their plates to their partners and say what their favorite food is.
- Encourage them to ask questions to their partners using *Do you like … ?*

1 WB p58 Make a "Super Fruit."

Aim: to activate creativity

2 WB p58 Show a friend.

Aim: to practice speaking skills

Ending the lesson

Aim: to review language
- Students work in pairs.
- One of them (student A) stands behind the other (student B) and draws a fruit or vegetable with his/her finger on his/her partner's back.
- Student B has to guess the food by asking *Do you like … ?*
- Students swap roles.

Extension activity

Aim: to review language
- Play *I Spy with My Little Eye* with the class.
- Use the posters and drawings around the classroom to play the game.
- Say *I Spy with My Little Eye something …* and then say a color, the word *fruit, vegetable* or *on a tree, in the ground.*

Learning outcomes:
- to review language from the unit by taking a quiz
- to reflect on learning

BIG QUESTION to think about how the unit has helped them answer the Big Question *What food do we eat?*

Recycled language: vocabulary and grammar from the unit

Creative thinking (WB): Creates texts that express personal interests, emotions, or identity

Cognitive control functions (WB): Cognitive flexibility

Materials: letter-size paper

Warm-up

Aim: to review vocabulary from the unit
- Write the first letters of a fruit or vegetable on the board, e.g., *pe*.
- Encourage students to guess what food you are referring to.
- Ask a volunteer to complete the word on the board. (pear)

Stronger students: Students take your role.

1 SB p59 Read and match.

Aim: to review key words from the unit
- Students do the activity individually.
- Check answers as a class.

Key: 1 orange, 2 pear, 3 cupcake

2 SB p59 Read and draw ☺ or ☹.

Aim: to review language from the unit
- Students read in pairs and complete the faces.

Key: 1 ☹, 2 ☺

3 SB p59 Which food is different? Circle.

Aim: to review language from the unit
- Give students time to identify the one that doesn't belong.
- Ask them what they have circled and why.

Key: the orange

1 WB p59 Look and say. Circle ☺, 😐, or ☹.

Aim: to review language from the unit

2 WB p59 Tree or ground? Circle.

Aim: to review language from the unit

Key: 1 ground, 2 tree, 3 ground, 4 tree

3 WB p59 Choose and draw your picture.

BIG QUESTION Aim: to enable students to revisit the Big Question

Ending the lesson

Aim: to enable students to express their preferences
- Ask students what their favorite activity is from the unit (e.g., the song, chant, or one of the games) and hold a class vote.
- Repeat the most popular activity with the class.

Extension activity

Aim: to enable students to share what they have learned
- Put students into groups of four.
- Each student opens their Workbook to page 59.
- Students take turns showing their drawings from Activity 3 and talking about their pictures.

1 Read and match.

1

2

3

pear   cupcake   orange

2 Read and draw 😊 or 😣.

1

I don't like cake.

2

Do you like chocolate?

Yes, I do.

3 Which food is different? Circle.

6 My Town

1 66 Listen and point. Say the words.

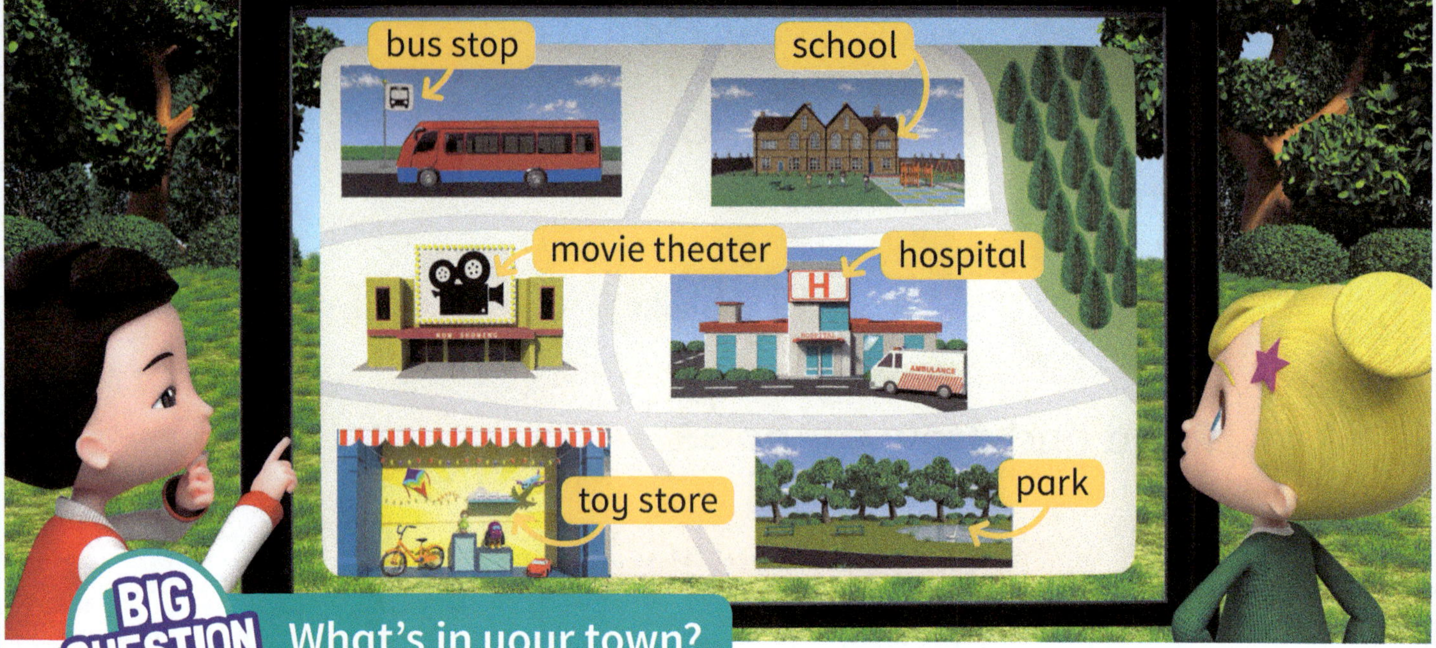

BIG QUESTION What's in your town?

2 67 Listen and chant.

Learning outcomes:
- to name and talk about places in a town
- to say a chant

BIG QUESTION to start to think about the Big Question *What's in your town?*

New language: *school, hospital, park, toy store, bus stop, movie theater, town, city, park*

Cognitive control functions: Working memory

Materials: flashcards 48–53 (places in a town), pictures of cities and towns

Warm-up

Aim: to introduce the unit topic
- Show a picture of a town (see Materials) and introduce the word *town.*
- Do the same with a picture of a city to introduce the word *city.*
- Show the other pictures of cities and towns, and ask students to identify them.
- Ask students if they live in cities or towns.
- Discuss the differences between a town and a city, e.g., size, population, transportation, etc.

Presentation

Aim: to present new vocabulary
- Take out the *places in a town* flashcards and say the words.
- Students repeat after you.
- Show each flashcard again, and ask students to mention the name of these places in their town/city, e.g., *Joy is a toy store in my town.*

1 66 SB p60 Listen and point. Say the words.

Aim: to practice places in a town
- Students look at the illustration of the town in their Student's Book.
- Ask *Where are Misty and Whisper?*
- Play the recording. Students listen and point to the corresponding place.

For script, see TB p108.

- Play the recording again for students to repeat the words.

BIG QUESTION What's in your town?

Aim: to enable students to describe where they live
- Read the Big Question.
- Ask questions about each of the places on the unit flashcards, e.g., *Is there a toy store in your town/city?*
- Encourage students to mention other places there are in their town/city.
- Students tell you where they usually go and what their favorite place is.

Note: Some of the discussion will need to be in L1.

2 67 SB p60 Listen and chant.

Aim: to give students practice with new language
- Ask students to tell you what places they can identify in the scene.
- Ask general questions, e.g., *How many places can you see? Is this a town or a city?*
- Point to the places from left to right for students to mention them in order.
- Play the recording.
- Students listen and follow the chant in their Student's Books.

For chant script, see WB 108.

- Play the recording again, pausing for students to repeat.
- Say the chant as a class and then in groups.

Practice

Aim: to practice the new language
- On the board, place the *places in a town* flashcards in the order they are in the chant. Leave enough space between them.
- Take a book or a backpack to pretend you are a student.
- Say the chant and move toward the *school* flashcard, stopping next to each place in town on the flashcards you mention.
- Invite volunteers to do the same.
- Leave the flashcards on the board for the Ending the lesson activity.

1 49 WB p60 Listen and number.

Aim: to practice new language

For script, see TB p108.

Key: a 3, b 4, c 5, (d 1), e 2, f 6

2 WB p60 Point and say.

Aim: to practice new language

Key: 2 hospital, 3 school, 4 toy store, 5 movie theater, 6 park

Ending the lesson

Aim: to review places in a town
- Invite a volunteer to the front.
- Say a place for the student to touch the corresponding flashcard.
- Continue with the rest of the places in random order.
- Invite pairs of students to do the same.

Extension activity

Aim: to review vocabulary from the unit
- Write scrambled versions of the words students have already learned on the board. Ask students in small groups to unscramble the words. Names of places vocabulary: school, movie theater, hospital, park, toy store, bus stop.

Extra support: Arrange groups in mixed abilty to allow peers to support each other.

Learning outcomes:
- to talk about places in a town

New language: *There's/There ...*

Recycled language: *How many ... ?*, things in the classroom

Creative thinking: Creates texts that express personal interests, emotions, or identity

Materials: paper (optional)

Warm-up

Aim: to identify singular and plural forms
- On the board, make a mind map of the things and people there are in your classroom.
- Write *Our Classroom* in the center and these words around it: *window, door, desk/ table, chair, teacher, student.*
- Students tell you how many things/people there are.
- Write the quantity under each word, e.g., *2 windows, 1 teacher*, etc.
- Focus students' attention on the difference between singular and plural nouns.
- Introduce *there is* and *there are* orally by giving an example, e.g., *There are two windows in our classroom.*
- Ask questions to students using *How many ... are there in our classroom?*
- Encourage students to use *there is* and *there are* in their answers.

1 68 SB p61 Listen and match.

Aim: to improve students' listening skills
- Allow students time to look at the maps and read the names of the children.
- Play the recording.
- Students match the maps to the children.

For script, see TB p108.

- Check answers as a class.

Key: 2 Tom, 3 Lola, 4 Flo

2 69 SB p61 Look, listen, and say.

Aim: to practice new language
- Students look at the pictures in Activity 1.
- Play the recording and pause after each child speaks for students to repeat.

For script, see TB p108.

- Ask questions using *How many ... are there in (Lola's) town?* to practice the new grammar point.

3 SB p61 Draw your town. Say.

Aim: to give students practice with *there is* and *there are*
- Students look at the child's map.
- Ask a volunteer to describe the town using *there is* and *there are*.
- Students draw a simple map of their town/city using the sample from the book in their notebooks.
- Students work in pairs to talk about their maps.
- Go around the classroom to check performance.
- Invite students to the front to describe their maps.

1 50 WB p61 Listen and color.

Aim: to improve students' listening skills
- Check that students know what they are going to color. (the edge of the picture)

For script, see TB p108.

Key: 1 red, 2 blue, (3 yellow), 4 green

2 WB p61 Look at the maps. Point and say.

Aim: to practice new language

Ending the lesson

Aim: to practice new language
- Go back to some of the introductory scenes of previous units in the book and ask questions about what there is in the scenes. For example, go to page 50 and ask about the food students can see.
- Ask students to choose other pictures in the book to describe what they see by using *there is* and *there are*.
- Students describe the pictures to the class or they work in small groups.

Extension activity

Aim: to expand on the new language from the lesson
- Students work in small groups.
- Hand out pieces of paper.
- Students draw a park and things they can name in English in it. For example, they could draw trees, a parrot in a tree, frogs in a pond, food, etc. If necessary, use previous unit flashcards to give students more guidance.
- Groups show their parks to the class and describe what there is in it, e.g., *There are three trees in the park. There is a boy and a girl.*

1 68 Listen and match.

1

2

Will Lola Tom Flo

3

4

2 69 Look, listen, and say.

3 Draw your town. Say.

1 70 Listen and sing.

2 Where do these people work? Point and say.

1 

2 

3 

4 

Learning outcomes:
- to sing a song

Recycled language: *There's/There ...* vocabulary from previous units

Cognitive control functions (WB): Working memory

Materials: flashcards 48–53 (places in a town), paper, worksheet with 5 sentences to complete (1 per student): *There are ________ at the toy store/school/hospital/park/movie theater* (optional)

Warm-up

Aim: to review vocabulary
- Students work in groups of three.
- Hand out paper.
- Write a category on the board and say it. Students draw three things that belong to that category, e.g., *school: a drawing of a pencil, a teacher, a ruler.*
- Continue with other categories, e.g., food, animals, colors.
- When the activity is over, invite groups to show their drawings to the class and mention what they have drawn for each category.

1 70 ▶ 71 SB p62 Listen and sing.

Aim: to sing a song
- Students work with books closed.
- Play the recording.
- Students listen to the song.

For song lyrics, see TB p109.

- Ask questions to see how much students remember from the song, e.g., *How many stores are there in the town? Is there a hospital?*
- Students open the books and look at the map.
- Play the audio again, and sing with the class.
- Play the song video, pausing after each verse for students to repeat.
- When students have learned the song, use the karaoke version of the video or audio (71) to practice the song with the whole class.

Practice

Aim: to practice the song
- Divide the class into three groups and assign different parts of the song to each one.
- Use the karaoke version (71) to sing the song again.

2 SB p62 Where do these people work? Point and say.

Aim: to practice new language
- Students look at the pictures in their books.
- Teach what each person's job is, i.e., *nurse, ticket collector, salesclerk, teacher.*
- Ask where each person works.

Key: 1 hospital, 2 movie theater, 3 store, 4 school

1 51 WB p62 Listen. What can you remember? Draw.

Aim: to practice the song

For song lyrics, see TB p109.

2 WB p62 Look and write.

Aim: to review new language

Key: 1 park, 2 hospital, 3 store

Ending the lesson

Aim: to practice new language
- Place the *places in a town* flashcards on the board.
- Invite volunteer students to draw things that they could find in each place, e.g., a tree in a park, a bed at a hospital, a doll at a toy store, etc.
- Students work in their notebooks.
- They choose a place, write its name, and draw things they can find in the place they have chosen to make a mind map.
- Record the words on the board for students to refer to in the Extension activity.

Stronger students: Students write the things they can find in the place of their choice instead of drawing.

Extension activity

Aim: to practice new language
- Students work in small groups.
- They use their drawings from the Ending the lesson activity to complete the four sentences on the worksheet (see Materials), e.g., *There are __dolls__ at the toy store. There are __books__ at school.*
- Check the use of plurals.

Stronger students: Students write a whole sentence to describe what they could find at the bus stop: *There are __________ at the bus stop.*
Extra support: Provide students with consonants for a missing word for them to fill in the vowels, e.g., b_ _ ks.

Learning outcomes:
- to improve listening and oral skills

New language: *Where's the (park)?, It's (over) there., market*

Recycled language: *pear, cake, lion, milk*, things in the classroom

Critical thinking (WB): Solves simple puzzles

Materials: flashcards 17–22 (classroom objects), 36–41 (animals), 42–47 (food) and 48–53 (places in a town), big labels with these words: *zoo, market, school*, tape, soft ball (optional)

Warm-up

Aim: to introduce new language
- Put your bag, pen, book, etc. in different parts of the classroom that are far away from students.
- Pretend you are an absent-minded person and ask students where your things are, e.g., *Where's my bag?*
- Encourage students to say *It's there* or *It's over there.*
- Invite a volunteer to give you four of his/her things, and ask them to leave the classroom while another student puts the items around the room.
- Invite the volunteer to come back to the classroom, and ask *Where's my … ?*
- Students answer by pointing and saying *It's (over) there.*
- The volunteer picks up his/her things.
- Repeat with other students.

1 72 SB p63 Listen and draw Max's route.

Aim: to improve students' listening skills
- Give students time to identify the places on the map.
- Students tell you the places they can see on the map, e.g., *There's a park.*
- Explain how the activity works, i.e., students draw a line from the park past all the places mentioned.
- Play the recording for students to complete the activity.
- Check results as a class.

For script, see TB p109.

Key: the park – the toy store – the bus stop – the movie theater

2 SB p63 Watch and listen.

Aim: to focus students on grammatical form
- Play the *Penny the Penguin* video.
- Students watch.

For script, see TB p109.

- Play the audio.
- Invite pairs of students to repeat after the audio.

3 SB p63 Ask a partner. Find and answer.

Aim: to practice new language
- Model the oral activity with a volunteer by asking *Where's the pear?*
- Encourage the volunteer to provide the answer, i.e., *It's there.*
- Students work in pairs.
- They take turns asking about the rest of the hidden things.

1 WB p63 Look and number.

Aim: to practice new language

Key: 2 hospital, 3 toy store, 4 bus stop, 5 school, 6 movie theater

2 WB p63 Look at the map. Ask and answer.

Aim: to practice new language

Ending the lesson

Aim: to practice new language and review vocabulary
- Take out the labels. (see Materials)
- Stick them in three different places around the classroom.
- Teach the word *market.*
- Students stand in two lines, line A and line B.
- Hand out the *food, animals,* and *classroom objects* flashcards to the students in line A so that each one has a flashcard.
- Students in line B will answer questions.
- The first student in line A asks the first student in line B where the thing on his/her flashcard is, e.g., *Where's the lion?*
- The student in line B answers and points to the right label, e.g., *It's over there.* (Points to the *zoo* label.)
- The student holding the *lion* flashcard goes to the "zoo" and stands there.
- Continue with the rest of the students and then swap roles.

Extension activity

Aim: to review new language
- Place the labels on the board. Leave a big distance among them.
- Put the *food, classroom objects,* and *animals* flashcards face down in a pile.
- Make two teams, A and B.
- Give a soft ball (see Materials) to a student on team A.
- A student from team B takes a flashcard from the pile and asks the student from team A who holds the ball where the thing on the flashcard is, e.g., *Where's the pear?*
- The student holding the ball aims at the corresponding label on the board. If he/she hits the correct label, the team gets a point.
- Continue until all the flashcards have been used.

1 72 Listen and draw Max's route.

2 Watch and listen.

3 Ask a partner. Find and answer.

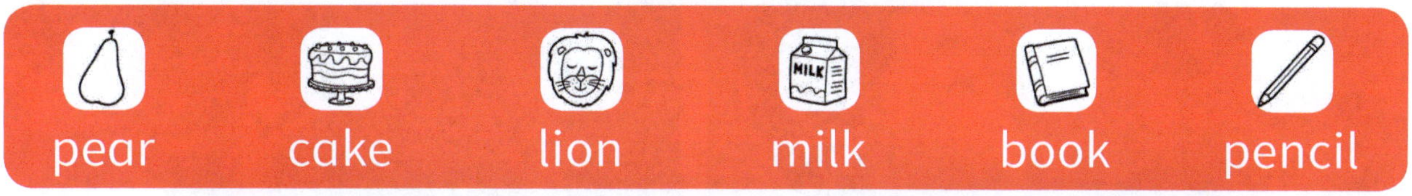

The Toy Store

1 73 Watch and listen to the story.

Learning outcomes:
- to listen to, read, watch, and act out a picture story
- to review language from the unit

New language: *pigeon, helmet*

Value: being kind

Warm-up

Aim: to introduce the story
- Students look at the story frames.
- Ask simple questions, e.g., *What's the name of the story? Where are Whisper and Misty?*
- Teach the words *pigeon* and *helmet.*

The Toy Store

1 73 SB pp64–65 Watch and listen to the story.

Aim: to present a picture story
- Play the audio as students follow the story in their books.
- Ask general comprehension questions, e.g., *Who helps Whisper and Misty? Is there a toy store in town?*

For script, see TB page 109.

- Play *The Toy Store* video to the end.
- Talk about the story value: being kind.
- Ask students who is kind in the story.
- Ask why Whisper gives a present to the pigeon.
- Elicit examples of kindness, e.g., let someone go ahead of you in line, help your parents without being asked, donate toys, help an elderly person, greet people, thank people, etc.

Note: Some of the discussion will need to be in L1.
- Play the video again. Students watch, listen, and repeat.

1 52 WB p64 Listen and number.

Aim: to identify the story scenes

For script, see TB p109.

Key: b 4, c 3, d 2

2 53 WB p64 Who says it? Listen and match.

Aim: to identify characters in the unit story

For script, see TB p109.

Key: 1 Misty, 2 Whisper, 3 Pigeon

Ending the lesson

Aim: to practice language from the story
- Write *Whisper, Misty,* and *Pigeon* on the board.
- Tell students you will say something from the story and they have to tell you who said it.
- For example, say *Here you go.* Students say *Whisper.*

Extension activity

Aim: to act out the story
- Act out the story with two volunteers.
- Make groups of three.
- Assign a character to each student.
- Students practice the story in groups.
- Go around the classroom to help students.
- Volunteer groups perform in front of the class.

Learning outcomes:
- to identify sequences of events

Recycled language: vocabulary from previous units

Value: being kind

Critical thinking: Solves simple puzzles

Critical thinking (WB): Identifies characters, setting, plots, and theme in a story

Cognitive control functions (WB): Cognitive flexibility

Materials: 1 piece of construction paper with a title on it: Kindness; 4 big color labels with text on them: *sorry*, *thank you*, *excuse me*, *please*. The labels should fit on the construction paper. (optional)

Warm-up

Aim: to improve memory
- Play a memory game.
- Sit in a circle.
- Say a category, e.g., food.
- One student says a word that belongs to the category, and the student on his/her right repeats that word and adds another one of the same category.
- Continue until a student makes a mistake or runs out of options.
- Start all over again with other categories, e.g., places, colors, animals.

2 SB p65 **Look, find, and write the picture number.**

Aim: to identify sequences and improve visual memory
- Students work in pairs.
- Students look at the pictures of the pigeon in Activity 2.
- They then look back at the story scenes to identify which scene each picture belongs to.
- Students number the pictures in Activity 2 based on the picture numbers in the story.
- Check results as a class.

Key: b 3, c 8, d 4, e 5, (a 6), f 7

1 WB p65 **What's good? Draw ☺.**

Aim: to understand the meaning of being kind

Key: 2

2 WB p65 **Finish the picture. Draw what a good friend does.**

Aim: to understand the meaning of being kind

Ending the lesson

Aim: to identify literary elements in a story
- Write CHARACTER and SETTING on the board.
- Explain the meaning of each word to the class.
- Students give you examples of characters and settings from well-known children's stories.

Stronger students: Students write the characters and setting of *The Toy Store* under the words on the board.

Extension activity

Aim: to focus on the value of being kind
- Take out the labels. (see Materials)
- Teach students the words and expressions on the labels.
- Create situations in which students can use them, e.g., borrow a ruler, bump into someone's backpack, etc.
- Take out the piece of construction paper. (see Materials)
- Invite volunteers to glue the labels on the paper to make a kindness poster for the class.
- Encourage students to use the words during lessons.

2 Look, find, and write the picture number.

a

6

b

☐

c

☐

d

☐

e

☐

f

☐

Think and Learn

Maps and Towns

Watch and listen.

1 74 Listen and point.

1 market

2 café

3 playground

4 sports center

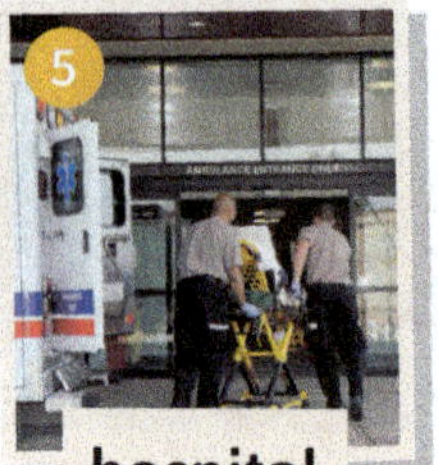

5 hospital

6 movie theater

2 Look and match. Write the numbers.

a 4

b

c

d

e

f

3 Look and stick.

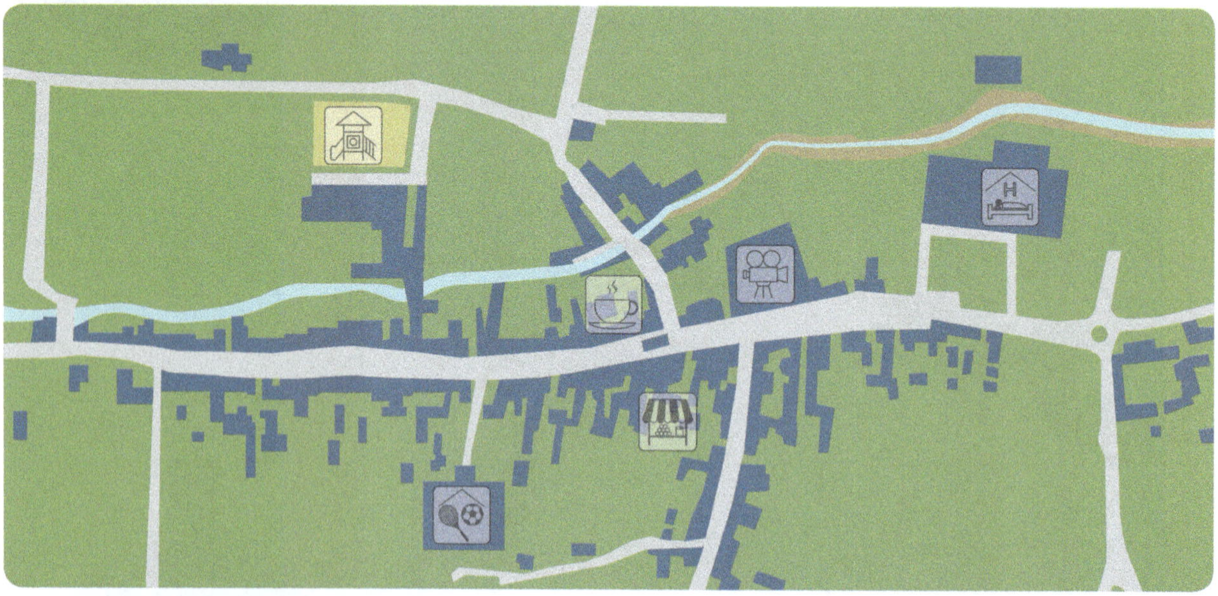

Learning outcomes:
- to integrate other areas of the curriculum through English: geography

BIG QUESTION to answer the Big Question *What's in your town?*

New language: *café, playground, sports center, map*

Recycled language: *market, hospital, movie theater*

Critical thinking: Compares different types of information

Materials: flashcards 48–53 (places in a town), Unit 6 stickers, worksheets with four identical sentences for students to complete: *There is a ________ in the town.* (1 per student), pictures of objects related to each place in town (3 different objects per place) (optional)

Warm-up

Aim: to introduce the lesson topic
- Take out the *places in a town* flashcards and place them on the board.
- Draw a ruler on the board and ask students where they would usually find rulers. (*At school.*)
- Do the same with a park bench, a toy, a bus, and a movie ticket.
- Draw some fruit, and ask students where they would buy them. (*At the market.*)

SB p66 Watch and listen. What is a map of a town?

Aim: to understand maps
- With Student's Books closed, play the *Think and Learn* video.

For videoscript, see TB p109.

- Ask students what places they saw on the map in the video.
- Elicit new words: *café, playground, sports center.*
- Students answer general questions, e.g., *How many cafés are there? What is there in the market? Is there a hospital?*

1 74 SB p66 Listen and point.

Aim: to identify places in a town
- Students open their books.
- Play the recording.
- Students listen and point to the corresponding pictures.
- Say the places in random order. Students point to the corresponding pictures.

2 SB p66 Look and match. Write the numbers.

Aim: to practice association
- Elicit what students see in the icons.
- Students number the icons according to which place they represent. Provide an example.
- Students check results in pairs.

Key: b 3, c 6, d 1, e 2, f 5

3 SB p66 Look and stick.

Aim: to practice association
- Students work in small groups.
- Give students time to look at the map.
- They take out their stickers.
- They place them where they consider they belong and check results as a group.
- Students glue their stickers on the map.

1 WB p66 Where are they? Look and say.

Aim: to identify places in a town

Key: 2 café, 3 park, 4 sports center

2 WB p66 Look. Write and match.

Aim: to identify places in a town

Key: 2 c: café, 3 a: movie theater, 4 d: hospital

Ending the lesson

Aim: to review language
- Hand out the worksheets. (see Materials)
- In small groups, students complete the sentences with places they see on the map in Activity 3.
- Go around the classroom to check performance.
- Students stick the worksheets in their notebooks.

Extension activity

Aim: to review language from the unit
- Take out the pictures related to places in a town. (see Materials)
- Make two teams.
- Explain to students that you will show a picture to one team and they have to say the place the picture is related to.
- If they guess correctly, they get a point. If they don't, it's the other team's turn to guess.
- Continue until there is a winning team.
- Write the word TOWN in the center of the board.
- Place the *places in a town* flashcards around it to make a picture mind map.
- Invite students to place the pictures they used in the game next to the corresponding flashcard on the board.
- Students copy the picture mind map into their notebooks.

Learning outcomes:
- to extend the focus on geography through English
- to complete a project

Creative thinking: Based on a model, develops new ideas

Creative thinking: Participates in investigative, exploratory, open-ended tasks

Creative thinking (WB): Uses different media to make and describe his/her own designs

Cognitive control functions: Cognitive flexibility

Materials: map of the students' town, construction paper (1 per group of 3 students), letter-size paper (1 or 2 pieces per group)

Warm-up

Aim: to review language
- Discuss with students what a symbol is and why they are important. Mention that they are important for easy communication and that some are universal so that people from different countries can understand them.
- Draw or show pictures of symbols, and elicit what they are associated with. For example, a fork and knife (café), a plane (airport), the silhouette of a woman/ man (restrooms), wi-fi symbol, a shopping cart (supermarket), etc.
- Encourage students to provide more examples.

4 SB p67 Draw symbols. Then say.

Aim: to activate creativity
- Students work individually.
- They draw one well-known map symbol and then invent a new one that represents one of the places they have learned.
- They show their creations to the class and say what they represent or let the class guess.

5 Project SB p67 Make a map of your dream town.

Aim: to enable students to apply what they have learned about what a town is
- Show students the map of the town, and elicit the meaning of the words *map*, *road*, *street*, and *dream*.
- Students work in groups of three.
- Hand out pieces of paper.
- Students draw six or eight big map symbols that represent places they would like to include in their dream town, e.g., a cup of coffee to represent a café, a swing to represent a playground, etc. Students can refer to the map symbols on page 66.

Note: Make sure students draw the symbols the correct size to fit the map on the construction paper you will be using. You could show a sample.
- Students cut out their symbols.
- Hand out construction paper.
- Help groups draw a main road in the middle of the construction paper and some streets to make a simple map.
- Students decide where on the map they would like to place the symbols they have drawn. If students want to draw more symbols, give them the freedom to do so.
- Groups stick their symbols on the map and decorate their dream town by drawing trees, people, cars, bus stops, etc. Encourage students to use a variety of materials to make their map more attractive.
- Students show their creations to their classmates and describe them.
- Display students' dream towns around the classroom. Take photos of them and save them to students' digital portfolios.

3 54 WB p67 Listen and draw a line. Start at X.

Aim: to review new language

For script, see TB p109.

Key: 1 the school, 2 the movie theater, 3 the hospital, 4 the park, 5 the bus stop, 6 the toy store

4 WB p67 Draw a place you know.

Aim: to activate creativity

Lesson review

- With students, review what they have learned in the lesson and if they liked the project.
- As a class, compare the maps to find similarities and differences.

Extension activity

Aim: to share work results with other students
- Organize a school art exhibition.
- Display the maps somewhere in the school for other students to see.

4 Draw symbols. Then say.

5 Project Make a map of your dream town.

Do That!

1 75 Listen and act it out with your teacher. Listen again and match.

1 2 3 4 5 6

Learning outcomes:
- to activate creativity

New language: *at home, in bed*

Recycled language: places in town

Creative thinking: Listens and responds physically to songs, rhymes, chants

Materials: blindfold (optional)

Warm-up

Aim: to activate students' imagination
- Act out situations in different places for students to guess where you are.
- Ask *Where am I?* and pretend you are drinking a cup of tea.
- Students make guesses.
- Continue with other situations, e.g., looking at the time while waiting for a bus, eating popcorn while you are watching a movie, holding your arm as if it hurt, etc.
- Invite volunteer students to perform for the class to guess.

1 75 SB p68 **Listen and act it out with your teacher. Listen again and match.**

Aim: to activate students' creativity
- Work with books closed.
- Play the recording, and act it out at the same time for students to follow you.

For script, see TB p109.

- Play the recording for a second time, and let students perform freely without your guidance.
- Students open their books.
- Play the recording.
- Students match the numbers to the pictures.

Key: 2 green, 3 yellow, 4 pink, 5 red, 6 orange

1 55 WB p68 **Listen and color.**

Aim: to practice listening skills
- Check that students know what they are going to color. (the edge of the picture)

For script, see TB p109.

Key: 1 blue, 2 orange, 3 green, 4 yellow, 5 pink, (6 red)

2 WB p68 **Look at the pictures again. Circle a face for you.**

Aim: to show preferences

Key: Students' own answers

Ending the lesson

Aim: to review language from the unit
- Students work in pairs or small groups.
- Say a place, e.g., *market*.
- Students write as many sentences as they can describing what they imagine there is in that place, e.g., *There are bananas.*
- Go around the classroom to check the correct use of *there is/are* and singulars/plurals.

Extra support: Provide worksheets with incomplete sentences with *There is …* and *There are …* for students to complete to describe the place you mention.

Extension activity

Aim: to review language
- Make two teams, A and B.
- A student from team A is blindfolded.
- Put a set quantity of school objects on your desk.
- The blindfolded student touches the objects and then has to say what there is on the table, e.g., *There is a ruler. There are two pencils.*
- A point is awarded for each correct sentence. The correct use of grammar and plurals should be taken into consideration in the score.
- Continue with team B.
- Other objects, apart from school ones, can be used as long as students know how to say them in English. For example, food or toy animals.

Learning outcomes:
- to review language from the unit by taking a quiz
- to reflect on learning

BIG QUESTION to think about how the unit has helped them answer the Big Question *What's in your town?*

Recycled language: vocabulary and grammar from the unit

Creative thinking (WB): Creates texts that express personal interests, emotions, or identity

Cognitive control functions (WB): Cognitive flexibility

Warm-up

Aim: to review vocabulary from the unit
- Students draw a 3x2 grid in their notebooks that will act as a map.
- Draw your own grid, and draw a place inside each square. This will be your map. Don't show it to the class.
- Tell students you will say places, and they have to draw them in any of the squares in the grid.
- When students have completed their maps, show your map to them.
- Students check their maps against yours to see if they match.
- The winners are the students who distributed the places on their map as you did.

1 SB p69 Read and match.

Aim: to review key words from the unit
- Students do the activity individually.
- They check results in pairs.

Key: 1 school, 2 toy store, 3 movie theater, 4 bus stop

2 SB p69 Write.

Aim: to review language from the unit
- Students look at the pictures and complete the blanks.

Key: 1 hospital, 2 park

3 SB p69 Read and check ☑ or put an X ☒.

Aim: to review language from the unit
- Students look at the pictures, read the sentences, and check the correct ones.
- Guide students to identify the mistakes and correct them.

Key: 1 There's a pen. 2 There are four pens.

1 WB p69 Look and say. Circle ☺, 😐, or ☹.

Aim: to assess performance

2 WB p69 What's in your town? Write *yes* or *no*.

BIG QUESTION **Aim:** to revisit the unit Big Question

Key: Students' own answers

3 WB p69 Draw a picture.

Aim: to personalize language

Ending the lesson

Aim: to enable students to express their preferences
- Ask students what their favorite activity is from the unit (e.g., the song, chant, or one of the games) and hold a class vote.
- Repeat the most popular activity with the class.

Extension activity

Aim: to enable students to share what they have learned
- Put students into groups of three.
- Each student opens their Workbook to page 69.
- Students take turns showing what they have drawn for Activity 3 and saying something about their pictures.

1 Read and match.

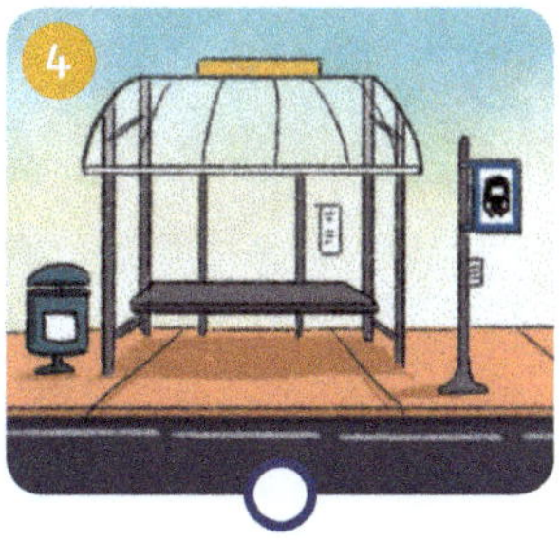

toy store | movie theater | bus stop | school

2 Write.

This is a ___ospital.

This is a ___ark.

3 Read and check ☑ or put an X ☒.

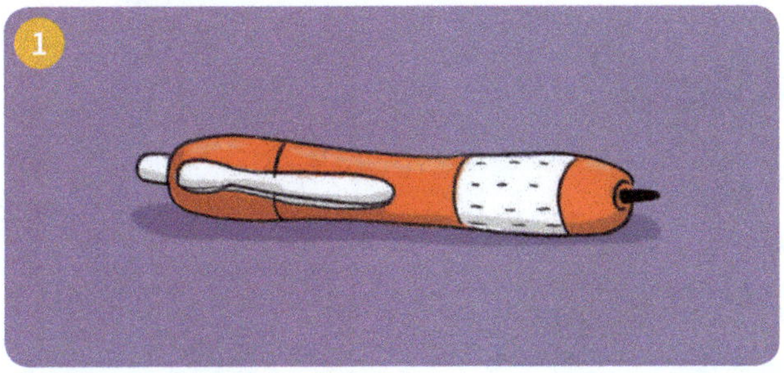

There's a pen. ☐

There are pen. ☐

There's four pens. ☐

There are four pens. ☐

7 Jobs

1 76 Listen and point. Say the words.

BIG QUESTION What's a job?

2 77 Listen and chant.

Learning outcomes:
- to name and talk about jobs
- to say a chant

BIG QUESTION to start to think about the Big Question *What's a job?*

New language: *teacher, doctor, gardener, vet, police officer, firefighter*

Recycled language: *Is this a … ?, Yes, it is./No, it isn't., Is there a … ?, Where's … ?*

Critical thinking (WB): Solves simple puzzles

Cognitive control functions: Working memory

Materials: flashcards 54–59 (jobs), pictures of objects students could associate with each job (2 or 3 pictures per job), e.g., shovel, gloves, and plant pot (gardener)

Warm-up

Aim: to introduce the unit topic
- Ask students what their parents, grandparents, aunts, and uncles do.
- Students tell you what their favorite job would be.

Note: Some of the discussion will need to be in L1.

Presentation

Aim: to present new vocabulary
- Take out the *jobs* flashcards.
- Students repeat after you.
- Take one flashcard and ask *Is this a (doctor)?*
- Students answer using *Yes, it is.* or *No, it isn't.*
- Continue with the rest of the flashcards.

1 76 SB p70 Listen and point. Say the words.

Aim: to practice jobs
- Students look at the pictures in their Student's Book.
- Point to the two characters, and ask where they are and what jobs are in the poster.
- Play the recording. Students listen and point to the corresponding picture.

For script, see TB p110.

- Play the recording again for students to repeat the words.

BIG QUESTION What's a job?

Aim: to make students aware of what a job is
- Read the Big Question.
- Ask students why they think having a job is important.
- Students choose a job and tell you what a person who has that job does.

Note: Some of the discussion will need to be in L1.

2 77 SB p70 Listen and chant.

Aim: to give students practice with new language
- Elicit from students what they can see in the pictures.
- Ask questions about the scene using *Is there … ? Where is … ?* to review grammar from previous units.
- Play the recording.
- Students listen and follow the chant in their Student's Books.

For chant script, see TB p110.

- Play the recording again, pausing for students to repeat.
- Say the chant as a class and then in groups.

Practice

Aim: to practice new language
- Take out the *jobs* flashcards, and place them on the board in random order.
- Students work in small groups.
- Groups practice saying the original chant following the new order of jobs on the board.
- Volunteer groups chant the new version of the chant.
- Change the order and repeat.

1 WB p70 Match and say.

Aim: to practice new language

Key: 1 f teacher, 2 e doctor, 3 d gardener, 4 c vet, 5 a police officer, (6 b firefighter)

2 WB p70 Look and write.

Aim: to practice new language

Key: 1 teacher, 2 doctor, 3 gardener, 4 vet, 5 police officer, 6 firefighter

Ending the lesson

Aim: to review vocabulary
- Place the *jobs* flashcards on the board.
- Take out the pictures and put them in a pile. (see Materials)
- A volunteer student takes a picture, shows it to the class, and sticks it next to the correct job.
- Continue with the rest of the pictures.

Stronger students: Volunteer students write the job titles next to the flashcards.

Extension activity

Aim: to review language from the unit
- Play *Charades*, i.e., students mime a job and the rest of the class guesses the job.
- Play the chant.
- Students chant as they mime the jobs.

Learning outcomes:
- to talk about jobs

New language: *woman, man, He's/She's a (gardener).*

Recycled language: members of the family, *boy, girl*

Materials: flashcards 30–35 (family), students bring a family photo from home, students choose one of the jobs they have learned, and bring a costume to dress up (optional)

Warm-up

Aim: to teach new language
- Place the *family* flashcards on the board and elicit the names.
- Teach *she/he* by pointing to each flashcard and saying *She is a girl. He is a boy. She is a woman. He is a man.*
- Write *Misty is a girl. She is a girl.*
- A volunteer writes about Whisper, i.e., *Whisper is a boy. He is a boy.*

Stronger students: In their notebooks, students write more examples about their classmates using *she* or *he.*

1 78 SB p71 Listen and check ☑.

Aim: to improve students' listening skills
- Point to the pictures of the male and female teachers, and elicit *he* and *she.*
- Play the recording and pause for students to do the first point.
- Play the rest of the recording.

For script, see TB p110.

- Check results as a class.

Key: 2 male police officer, 3 female doctor, 4 male vet, 5 female firefighter, 6 female gardener

2 79 SB p71 Look, listen, and say.

Aim: to practice new language
- Students look at the pictures in Activity 1.
- Play the recording again for students to repeat.

For script, see TB p110.

3 SB p71 Look and draw lines. Say.

Aim: to give students practice with new grammar
- Students choose a job for each person by drawing a line from the person to the object representing the job.
- Students work in pairs and take turns saying their sentences for their chosen people and jobs, *She's a gardener. He's a teacher.*

1 56 WB p71 Listen. Write *yes* or *no*.

Aim: to practice new language

For script, see TB p110.

Key: 2 no, 3 yes, 4 no, 5 yes, 6 yes

2 WB p71 Look at the pictures again. Say.

Aim: to practice new language

Key: 1 *He's a gardener. (2 She's a police officer.) 3 She's a firefighter. 4 He's a doctor. 5 He's a teacher. 6 She's a vet.*

Ending the lesson

Aim: to review language
- Students take out their family photos. (see Materials)
- Show a photo of your family.
- Point to one member of the family and say *This is (Juliet). (She's) my (sister).*
- Continue with the rest of the family members.
- Ask a volunteer to present his/her family using names and *he/she.*
- Students work in pairs and present their family to their partners.

Extension activity

Aim: to expand on the new language from the lesson
- Students dress up. (see Materials)
- Assign a place in the classroom that will be a runway.
- Ask a volunteer to walk as a model as if walking on a runway.
- Say *This is* (*Jane*). *She's a* (*vet*).
- Volunteers act as announcers.
- They say who the model is and what he/she is.
- Keep the costumes for future lessons.

1 78 Listen and check ☑.

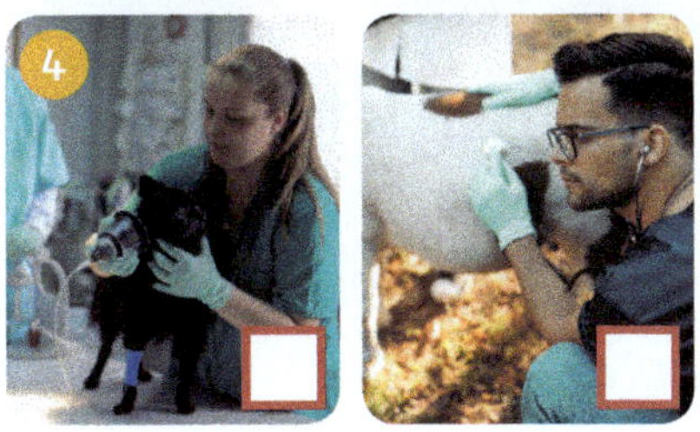

2 79 Look, listen, and say.

3 Look and draw lines. Say.

He's a police officer.

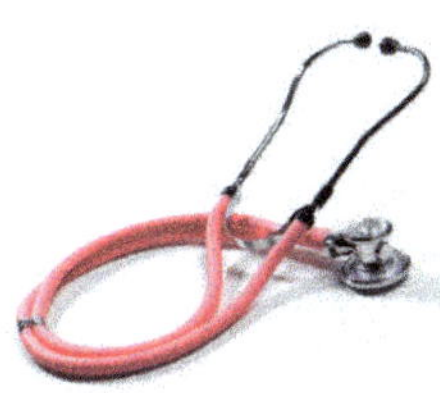
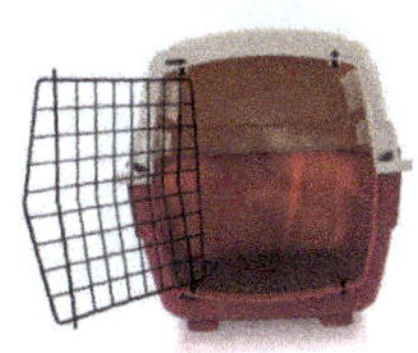

1 80 Listen and sing.

2 Mime a job for your partner to guess. Wave and say *Hello* if they're correct!

Learning outcomes:
- to sing a song

Recycled language: *hello, hi, goodbye, bye*, jobs, *he's, she's, walk, run, wave, bend, shake, stretch, jump*

Creative thinking: Participates in activities that involve taking the role of familiar people (e.g., being a teacher, parent, doctor, police)

Materials: costumes from previous lesson, flashcards 54–59 (jobs), fun music (optional)

Warm-up

Aim: to get students ready for singing
- Perform these actions from Unit 2 and name them: *walk, run, wave, bend, shake, stretch, jump.*
- Play *Simon Says* with the class.

1 80 81 SB p72 Listen and sing.

Aim: to sing a song with the class
- Students look at the picture in their books.
- They work in pairs to describe the people they see by using *she* and *he*, e.g., *She's a vet.*
- Go around the classroom to check performance.
- Play the audio (80).
- Students listen and sing with you.

For song lyrics, see TB p110.

- Play the song video, pausing after each verse for students to repeat.
- When students have learned the song, use the karaoke version of the video or audio (81) to practice the song with the whole class.

Practice

Aim: to practice the song
- Students dress up. (see Materials)
- Call a male teacher, a male police officer, a female vet, a female doctor, a male firefighter, a female gardener to stand at the front with you.
- Use the karaoke version (81) to sing the song while students perform, e.g., *He's a teacher.* (Point to the teacher.) *Say hello.* (The class says hello while the teacher waves.)
- Continue with the rest of the song.
- Repeat for all students so that everyone has a chance to act at the front with you.

2 SB p72 Mime a job for your partner to guess. Wave and say *Hello* if they're correct!

Aim: to practice new language
- Students work in pairs.
- They mime a job for their partner to guess.
- If they guess correctly the first time, they wave and say *hello*.
- If they don't guess, they wave and say *goodbye*.

1 57 WB p72 Listen and trace.

Aim: to practice new language

For song lyrics, see TB p110.

Key: 1 hello, 2 hello, 3 hi, 4 hello, 5 hi, 6 hi

2 WB p72 Say "goodbye." Write.

Aim: to practice new language

Key: goodbye

Ending the lesson

Aim: to review new language
- Take out the *jobs* flashcards and place them on the board.
- Write a sentence about one of the flashcards on the board, e.g., *She's a vet.*
- Following your model sentence, volunteer students write sentences about the rest of the flashcards.
- Check the correct use of *she's* and *he's*.

Extension activity

Aim: to practice new vocabulary
- Play *Musical Statues*.
- Play music. (see Materials)
- Students dance around the classroom.
- Pause the music.
- Point to one student and ask him/her to mime a job.
- The class guesses what job the student is miming.
- Play the music again and repeat the game.

Learning outcomes:
- to improve listening, reading, and oral skills

New language: *Is he/she a (firefighter)?, Yes, he/she is., No, he/she isn't.*

Recycled language: jobs

Flashcards: 54–59 (jobs)

Warm-up

Aim: to introduce new language
- Place the *jobs* flashcards on the board.
- Point to one flashcard, and ask *Is she a doctor?*
- Encourage students to provide the complete answer *Yes, she is.*
- Continue with the rest of the flashcards.
- Volunteer students come to the front and ask questions.

1 82 SB p73 Listen, read, and check ☑.

Aim: to improve students' listening and reading skills
- Give students time to look at the pictures in Activity 1.
- Volunteer students read the words aloud.
- Play the recording for students to check the correct option.
- Check results as a class by using *Is (she) … ?*

For script, see TB p110.

Key: 2 teacher, 3 police officer, 4 firefighter

2 ▶ SB p73 Watch and listen.

Aim: to focus students on grammatical form
- Play the *Penny the Penguin* video.
- Students watch and listen.
- Ask general comprehension questions, e.g., *Is Penny's mother a gardener?*

For script, see TB p110.

- Play the audio.
- Students repeat.
- Volunteer students perform the dialogue between Penny and her friend in front of the class.

3 SB p73 Point. Ask and answer.

Aim: to practice new language
- Give students time to look at the pictures.
- Model the oral activity.
- Ask questions using *Is she/he … ?*
- Students work in pairs.
- They ask and answer each other's questions using *Is she/he … ?*

1 58 WB p73 Look. Listen and check ☑.

Aim: to practice listening skills

For script, see TB p110.

Key: 1 a, 2 b, 3 a

2 WB p73 Point and say.

Aim: to practice speaking skills

Key: Example *He's a police officer.*

Ending the lesson

Aim: to practice new language
- Make two teams, A and B.
- Ask two volunteers from team A to come to the front.
- Whisper a job to them and assign roles, i.e., one of them answers questions and the other is the one who has the job.
- Team B has to ask questions to guess what the job is, e.g., *Is he/she a doctor?*
- If team B guesses correctly the first time, they get three points. If they guess the second time, they get two points. If they guess the third time, they get one.
- Continue until there is a winning team.

Extension activity

Aim: to review vocabulary
- Draw a 10x10 grid on the board and teach students how to make a word search.
- Write the six jobs students know in random order, horizontally and vertically.
- Complete the empty squares with letters.
- Students work in pairs to make word searches.
- Pairs swap the word searches and solve them.

1 Listen, read, and check ☑.

82

1

- doctor ☐
- gardener ☑

2

- teacher ☐
- doctor ☐

3

- firefighter ☐
- police officer ☐

4

- firefighter ☐
- vet ☐

2 Watch and listen.

3 Point. Ask and answer.

Is she a vet?

Yes, she is.

The Teacher

1 83 Watch and listen to the story.

Learning outcomes:
- to listen to, read, watch, and act out a picture story
- to review language from the unit

New language: *What's his/her job?, his/her, Ouch!, Oh, no., That's great!*

Recycled language: *potatoes*, jobs

Value: appreciating others

Materials: paper, flashcards 54–59 (jobs)

Warm-up

Aim: to introduce the story topic
- Ask students to draw a portrait of you or any other teacher they have at school.
- Students draw and then write the teacher's name under the drawing.
- Students show the portraits to the class.
- Vote for the portraits that look the most similar to the teachers chosen.
- Display the portraits around the classroom.

The Teacher

1 83 SB pp74–75 Watch and listen to the story.

Aim: to present a picture story
- Students look at the scenes in the picture story.
- Play the audio as students follow the story in their books.
- Ask general comprehension questions, e.g., *Where are Misty and Whisper? Who else is in the story?*

For script, see TB page 110.

- Play *The Teacher* video to the end.
- Talk about the story value: appreciating others.
- Ask if the teacher is really a police officer, a doctor, and a gardener.
- Ask why Misty and Whisper say that the teacher does so many jobs.
- Students talk about how important it is to recognize what people do for us.

Note: Some of the discussion will need to be in L1.
- Play the video again. Students watch, listen, and repeat.

1 WB p74 Who is it? Look and match.

Aim: to practice new language

Key: 1 doctor, 2 gardener, 3 police officer

2 WB p74 Who wears it? Write *Whisper, Misty,* or *teacher.*

Aim: to identify characters

Key: 2 Misty, 3 Whisper, 4 teacher, 5 Misty, 6 Whisper

Ending the lesson

Aim: to review language from the story
- Review expressions from the story, i.e., *ouch, that's great, oh, no* by creating situations in which you would use them. For example, pretend you hit your elbow against a table and say *Ouch.*
- Take out the *jobs* flashcards, point to one of them and ask *What's his/her job?*
- Volunteer students ask questions about the rest of the flashcards.
- Number the flashcards and write two sample sentences on the board: *She's a* __________. *He's a* __________.
- Students work in pairs.
- They use the sample sentences to write about each of the flashcards, e.g., *1 She's a doctor.*
- Go around the classroom to monitor performance.

Extension activity

Aim: to act out the story
- Act out the story with the class.
- Assign roles to students so that the scenes in the characters' thought bubbles are played by different students.
- Hand out the *police officer, doctor,* and *gardener* flashcards as props.
- Groups of students perform in front of the class.

Learning outcomes:
- to review language from the story and the unit

Recycled language: school objects, numbers, colors, *there is*, *there are*

Value: appreciating others

Critical thinking: Solves simple puzzles

Critical thinking (WB): Identifies characters, setting, plots, and theme in a story

Creative thinking (WB): Creates texts that reflect personal interests, emotions, or identity

Cognitive control functions (WB): Cognitive flexibility

Materials: a drawing of a classroom (include six tables, two windows, one door, one board, six chairs, books, etc.), paper

Warm-up

Aim: to improve visual intelligence
- Take out the drawing of a classroom (see Materials), but do not show it to the students.
- Hand out paper to small groups of students.
- Tell students you will describe a classroom and they have to draw it. Describe the drawing of the classroom you have brought from home. (see Materials)
- Use *there is/are*, e.g., *There are two windows in the classroom.*
- Mention colors, e.g., *The windows are blue.*
- Students draw the classroom as they imagine it.
- Once you have finished describing the classroom, students show you their classrooms.
- They compare their drawings against your version.
- The winning group is the one whose drawing is the most similar to your drawing.

2 SB p75 **Look at picture 6. Circle four differences.**

Aim: to identify differences
- Students open their books to page 75 and look attentively at the scene.
- They compare the scene against scene 6 in the picture story.
- They then circle the four differences between them.
- Elicit the differences orally.

Key: the teacher's hair, the flowers, (the boy), the carrot

1 WB p75 **What's good? Draw ☺.**

Aim: to understand the meaning of appreciating others

Key: 1

2 WB p75 **Complete the picture.**

Aim: to understand the meaning of appreciating others

Ending the lesson

Aim: to focus on the value of appreciating others
- Ask students to think of one of their parents or someone they admire.
- Discuss what these people do every day and what they do for others.
- Talk about how important it is to respect what others do.

Note: Some of this discussion will need to take place in L1.

Extension activity

Aim: to focus on the unit value
- Students draw the person they thought of in the Ending the lesson activity, e.g., they draw their mom.
- They then think of the things the person does and draw him/her in different costumes. For example, if their mom does the gardening, they draw their mom as a gardener. If their mom also does the cooking, they draw her as a chef, etc.
- Students show their drawings in groups and talk about them, e.g., *This is my mom. She is a gardener, a chef, …*
- Students give their drawing to the person they have chosen to show appreciation. They could even write a thank-you note to them.

2 Look at picture 6. Circle four differences.

Think and Learn

INSIDE AND OUTSIDE JOBS

Watch and listen.

1 84 Listen and point.

1 farmer

2 salesclerk

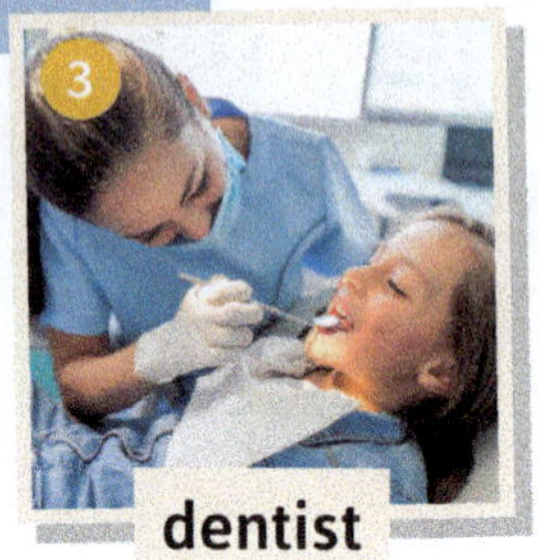
3 dentist

4 inside

5 outside

2 Look and stick.

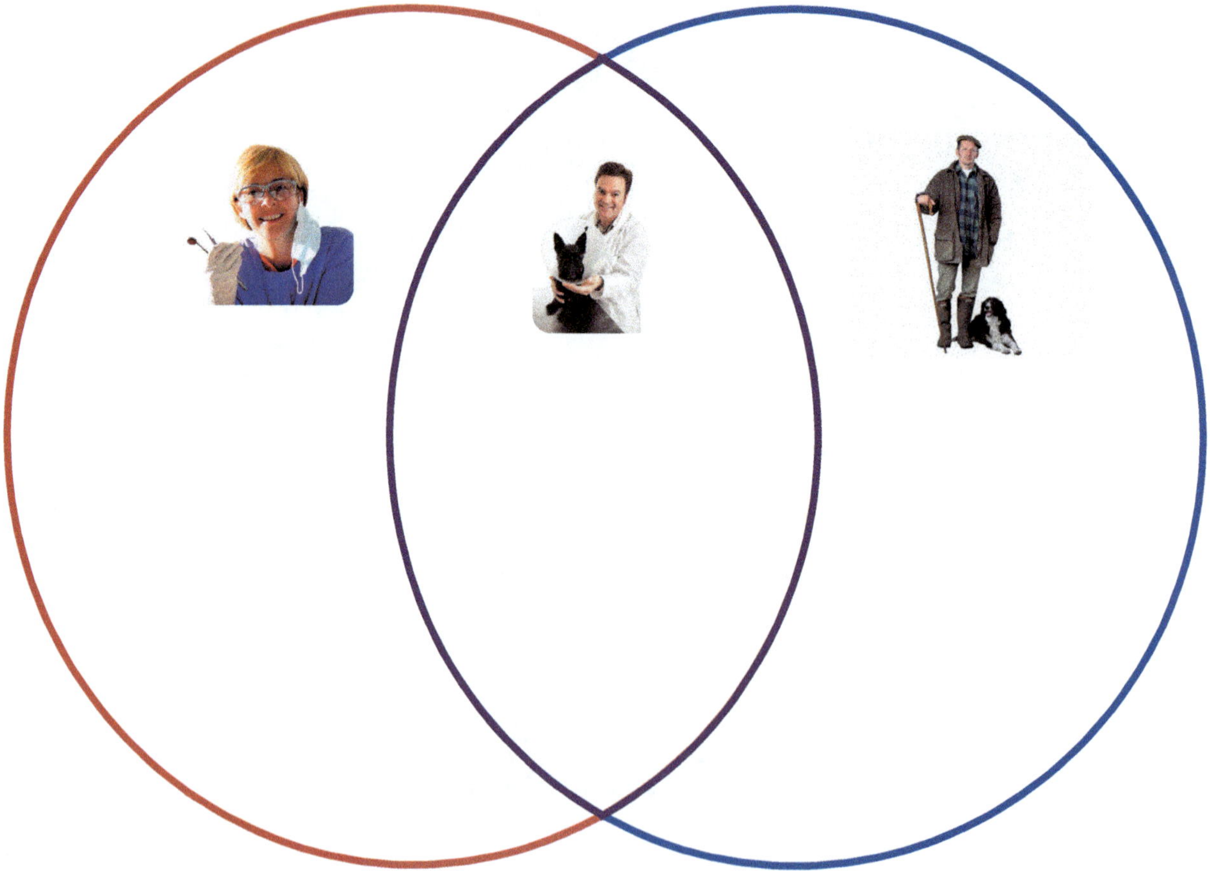

Learning outcomes:
- to integrate other areas of the curriculum through English: social science

BIG QUESTION to answer the Big Question *What's a job?*

New language: *farmer, salesclerk, dentist, inside, outside*

Recycled language: jobs, places

Critical thinking (SB & WB): Sorts and classifies objects and activities according to key features

Cognitive control functions: Cognitive flexibility

Materials: flashcards 50–52 (places in a town) and 54, 56, and 58 (jobs), Unit 7 stickers

Warm-up

Aim: to introduce the lesson topic

- Place the *school, hospital,* and *park* flashcards on the board and elicit their names.
- Take out the *teacher, doctor,* and *gardener* flashcards and ask where each person works.
- Volunteers students place the *jobs* flashcards next to the corresponding *places* flashcards on the board.
- Teach *inside* and *outside* by comparing the teacher and doctor to the gardener. Use arrows to communicate the concept and write the words *inside* and *outside*.
- Leave the flashcards on the board.

SB p76 Watch and listen. Which jobs are inside, and which are outside?

Aim: to categorize jobs

- With the Student's Books closed, play the *Think and Learn* video.

For videoscript, see TB p111.

- Elicit from students the jobs mentioned in the video. Then ask if the jobs are done inside or outside.
- Write the jobs on the board, the ones that are done inside below the flashcards of the *teacher* and *doctor* and the ones that are done outside below the flashcard of the *gardener.*

1 84 SB p76 Listen and point.

Aim: to present words relating to jobs

- Students open their books.
- Play the recording.
- Students listen and point to the corresponding picture.

2 SB p76 Look and stick.

Aim: to categorize jobs

- Students look at the examples in the Venn diagram.
- Explain what a Venn diagram is and how it works.
- Help students identify that the red circle is for jobs done inside, the blue one for jobs done inside, and the purple section for jobs that are done both inside and outside.
- Students take out their stickers.
- They place them where they consider they belong.
- Before sticking them, students check their answers in pairs.
- Students glue their stickers in place.

Key: inside: teacher, salesclerk, doctor; outside: gardener; both: police officer, firefighter

1 WB p76 Write the first letters.

Aim: to practice new language

Key: 1 farmer, 2 dentist, 3 salesclerk

2 WB p76 Circle the correct words.

Aim: to practice new language

Key: 1 He is outside. 2 She is inside.

Ending the lesson

Aim: to review language

- Students use the Venn diagram in the Student's Book to talk about jobs.
- Students work in pairs.
- They point to the people and say, e.g., *She's a dentist. He's inside. He's a vet. He's inside and outside.*
- Go around the classroom to check performance.

Extension activity

Aim: to review language

- Elicit from students the jobs they have learned, i.e., *teacher, doctor, gardener, vet, police officer, firefighter, farmer, salesclerk, dentist.*
- Students work in small groups.
- With your guidance, they draw a Venn diagram in their notebooks and draw three jobs, one for each section in the Venn diagram.
- Check results as a class.

Learning outcomes:
- to extend the focus on social science through English
- to complete a project

New language: *fisherman, chef, receptionist, painter/decorator, scientist, postal worker*

Recycled language: jobs, *inside, outside, he/she*

Creative thinking: Uses different media to make and describe his/her own designs

Creative thinking (WB): Draws pictures to represent vocabulary and familiar concepts

Materials: letter-size paper (2 per group, see Project), strips of paper with incomplete sentences to complete: *He's a* ___________. *She's a* ___________. (1 per student)

Warm-up

Aim: to identify jobs
- Students work in groups.
- Hand out paper. (see Materials)
- Groups draw ten objects related to jobs they have learned in this unit, e.g., a rake (gardener), a board (teacher), a tooth (dentist), etc.
- Students cut out the drawings and give them to you.
- Put the drawings face down in a pile.
- Make two teams, A and B.
- A student from team A takes a drawing, looks at it, and says the job.
- If he/she is right, team A gets a point.
- Continue with the game.
- The winner is the team that gets the most points.

3 SB p77 Where do they work? Look and write *I* for *inside*, *O* for *outside*, or *B* for *both*.

Aim: to categorize jobs
- Teach the new jobs, i.e., *fisherman, chef, receptionist, painter/decorator, scientist, postal worker.*
- Students work in pairs.
- They label the pictures *I, O,* or *B*.
- Check results as a class.

Key: b I, c I, d B, e B, f B

4 Project SB p77 Make a class poster. Say.

Aim: to enable students to apply what they have learned about jobs
- This activity works well as a class activity with a small number of students. If you have a larger class, put students into groups of four or five before handing out paper.
- Each student in the group says the job he/she would like to draw for the poster and decides whether he/she wants to draw a woman or man.
- Students say the jobs for their poster out loud. Ask *Are they inside or outside jobs?*
- Each student in the group draws a person doing the job, colors it, and cuts it out.
- Once students have finished their drawings, they place and stick them on their paper.
- Read the two sentences about the farmer on page 77.
- Write model sentences on the board:
  He's a ________. *He's inside/ outside.*
  She's a ________. *She's inside/ outside.*
- Students write the two sentences below their drawing on the poster.
- Each group holds up their poster and speaks about their drawings.
- Take photos of the posters and save them to students' digital portfolios.

Extra support: Hand out the strips of paper with incomplete sentences. (see Materials) Students complete the sentences and stick them below their drawings on the poster.

3 WB p77 Where are they? Look and say.

Aim: to practice new language

Key: 1 She is inside. 2 She is inside. (3 He is outside.) 4 He is inside. 5 She is outside. 6 He is outside.

4 WB p77 Trace and color.

Aim: to practice fine motor skills

Lesson review

- With students, review what they have learned in the lesson and if they liked the project.
- Students count how many posters show jobs outside and inside.

Extension activity

Aim: to review jobs
- Show students on the board how to create two- or three-word "pictures" using the job titles.
- For example, write the word *teacher* vertically and then write the word *vet* horizontally, sharing the letter *e* with *teacher.*
- Guide the class to add at least two more jobs to the "picture."

Stronger students: Make small groups and let students invent new "pictures."
- Go around the classroom to check results.

3 Where do they work? Look and write *I* for *inside*, *O* for *outside*, or *B* for *both*.

a 
O

b 

c 

d 

e 

f 

4 Project Make a class poster. Say.

Create That!

1 85 Listen and imagine. Then draw your picture.

2 Show your picture to your friend. Say.

Learning outcomes:
- to follow instructions
- to trigger imagination

New language: *window cleaner*

Recycled language: jobs, *What's his/her job?, He/She is ....*

Creative thinking: Chooses options to create something new

Creative thinking (WB): Uses different media to make and describe his/her own designs

Cognitive control functions: Inhibitory control

Materials: soft music

Warm-up

Aim: to get ready for Activity 1
- Play soft music.
- Guide students to do some stretching activities to set the mood for Activity 1.

1 85 SB p78 **Listen and imagine. Then draw your picture.**

Aim: to activate students' creativity
- Play the recording.

For script, see TB p111.

- Students draw what they have imagined in their books.
- Some students may prefer to draw in their notebooks.

2 SB p78 **Show your picture to your friend. Say.**

Aim: to practice oral skills
- Students work in pairs.
- They show their drawings from Activity 1 to their partner and say what job they have.

1 WB p78 **Make a job picture.**

Aim: to activate students' creativity

2 WB p78 **Trace the title.**

Aim: to activate students' creativity

Key: My Job Picture

Ending the lesson

Aim: to practice oral skills
- Students work in small groups.
- They work with their drawings from Activity 1.
- Model a short dialogue for students to follow. Use *What's your job? What's his/her job? Are you a (doctor)? Is he/she a (vet)?*
- Go around the classroom and check oral performance. Make sure everyone participates.

Extension activity

Aim: to activate creativity
- Play *Telephone* with the class.
- Students sit in a circle.
- A student whispers a job to the student on his/her right.
- He/She then whispers the word to the next student until it reaches the last player in line.
- The last player says the word out loud to see how accurate the word is in comparison to the first whisper.

Stronger students: Encourage students to say phrases or complete sentences to make the game more fun and challenging.

Learning outcomes:
- to review language from the unit by taking a quiz
- to reflect on learning

BIG QUESTION to think about how the unit has helped them answer the Big Question *What's a job?*

Recycled language: vocabulary and grammar from the unit

Creative thinking (WB): Creates texts that express personal interests, emotions, or identity

Cognitive control functions (WB): Cognitive flexibility

Materials: ABC box: squares of around 2x2 cm with letters of the alphabet written on them (around 15 per each letter of the alphabet). Take into consideration that these are the highest frequency letters in the English alphabet: E, T, A, O, I, N, S, R, H, D, L, U.

Warm-up

Aim: to review vocabulary and practice spelling
- Take out the ABC box. (see Materials)
- Make three groups.
- Spread the letters on one big table or several smaller desks.
- Say a job and when you say *Go!* students work in groups to spell the word.
- The group that finishes first says *Stop!*
- Assign a point if the word is spelled correctly. If not, give the other groups the opportunity to get the point.
- Continue until you have mentioned all the jobs students have learned.
- Keep the ABC box for future vocabulary review.

1 SB p79 Read and match.

Aim: to review key words from the unit
- Volunteer students read the key words out loud.
- Students match the words to the pictures individually.
- Check results as a class.

Key: 1 firefighter, 2 teacher, 3 doctor, 4 police officer

2 SB p79 Complete the words.

Aim: to review language from the unit
- Students do the activity individually.
- They complete the missing blanks.
- Check results as a class by writing the complete sentences on the board.

Key: 1 She's a gardener. 2 He's a vet. 3 She's a firefighter.

3 SB p79 Read and check ☑.

Aim: to review language from the unit
- Students look at the pictures, read, and check the correct options.
- Check results orally.

Key: 1 No, she isn't. 2 Yes, he is. 3 teacher

1 WB p79 Look and say. Circle ☺, 😐, or ☹.

Aim: to assess performance

2 WB p79 Inside or outside? Circle.

Aim: to review language from the unit

Key: 1 outside, 2 inside, 3 inside, 4 inside

3 WB p79 Draw your favorite job.

BIG QUESTION Aim: to revisit the unit Big Question

Ending the lesson

Aim: to enable students to express their preferences
- Ask students what their favorite activity is from the unit (e.g., the song, chant, or one of the games) and hold a class vote.
- Repeat the most popular activity with the class.

Extension activity

Aim: to enable students to share what they have learned
- Put students into groups of four.
- Each student opens their Workbook to page 79.
- Students take turns showing what they have drawn for Activity 3 and saying something about it.

1 Read and match.

1 

2 

3 

4 

teacher | firefighter | police officer | doctor

2 Complete the words.

1 

She' s a ___ardener.

2 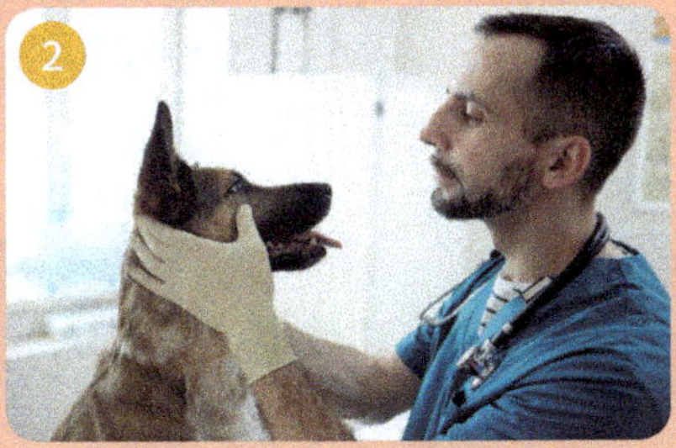

___ ___'s a vet.

3 

___ ___ ___'s a ___irefighter.

3 Read and check ☑.

1 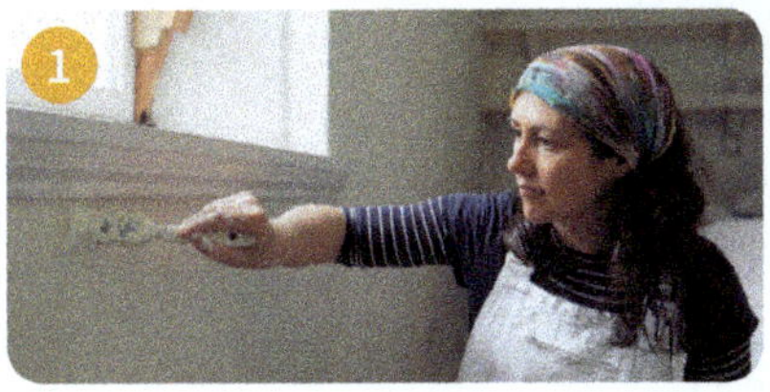

Is she a doctor?

Yes, she is. ☐

No, she isn't. ☐

2 

Is he a police officer?

Yes, he is. ☐

No, he isn't. ☐

3 

She's a …

police officer. ☐

teacher. ☐

8 My Clothes

1 🎧86 Listen and point. Say the words.

BIG QUESTION What clothes do we need?

2 🎧87 Listen and chant.

Learning outcomes:
- to name and talk about clothes
- to say a chant

BIG QUESTION to start to think about the Big Question *What clothes do we need?*

New language: *hat, scarf, gloves, coat, boots, sweater, jeans, T-shirt*

Recycled language: colors, *big/small*

Critical thinking (WB): Solves simple puzzles

Cognitive control functions: Working memory

Flashcards: 60–67 (clothes)

Warm-up

Aim: to introduce the unit topic
- Draw a sun and a snowflake on the board.
- Draw a scarf under the snowflake and a T-shirt under the sun.
- Students work in pairs to draw clothes for each category in their notebooks.
- Go around the classroom to check performance.

Presentation

Aim: to present new vocabulary
- Take out the *clothes* flashcards and say the words.
- Students repeat after you.
- Show each flashcard again and ask what color the pieces of clothing are.
- Volunteer students place the flashcards in alphabetical order on the board.

1 86 SB p80 Listen and point. Say the words.

Aim: to practice clothes
- Students look at the scene in their Student's Book.
- Ask general questions, e.g., *Where is Misty? Is Misty with Whisper? What pieces of clothing can you see? Is there a scarf in the room?*
- Play the recording. Students listen and point to the corresponding clothes.

For script, see TB p111.

- Play the recording again for students to repeat the words.

BIG QUESTION What clothes do we need?

Aim: to make students aware of what clothes they need
- Read the Big Question. Ask students what they usually wear in different seasons.
- Students tell you what their favorite clothes are.

Note: Some of the discussion will need to be in L1.

2 87 SB p80 Listen and chant.

Aim: to give students practice with new language
- Elicit from students what they can see in the picture scene.
- Ask what pieces of clothing they can see.
- Students tell you the colors they are and if they are big or small.
- Play the recording.
- Students listen and follow the chant in their Student's Books.

For chant script, see TB p111.

- Play the recording again, pausing for students to repeat.
- Say the chant as a class and then in groups.

Practice

Aim: to practice the new language
- Place the *clothes* flashcards on the board showing the spelling of them.
- Ask pairs to challenge each other to spell the words without looking at the board. One student spells a word out loud while the other student writes down the letters they say. Then they check spelling on the board before swapping roles.

1 WB p80 Find the words.

Aim: to practice new language

Key: Word search items: jeans, scarf, sweater, gloves, T-shirt, boots, hat

2 WB p80 Look at pictures 1–8. Say.

Aim: to practice new language

Key: 1 coat, 2 jeans, 3 scarf, (4 sweater), 5 gloves, 6 T-shirt, 7 boots, 8 hat

Ending the lesson

Aim: to review clothes
- Dictate the new lexical items in random order, e.g., *A red hat, blue boots, a green T-shirt …*
- Students draw them in a row in their notebooks.
- Check results as a class.

Extension activity

Aim: to review language from the unit
- Volunteers place the *clothes* flashcards on the board following the order in the chant.
- Students say the chant.
- A volunteer student changes the order of the flashcards on the board.
- The class sings the new version of the chant.
- Repeat the activity as many times as you consider appropriate.

Learning outcomes:
- to talk about the clothes you are wearing

New language: *I'm wearing (a hat).*

Recycled language: clothes, colors

Creative thinking (WB): Draws pictures to represent vocabulary and familiar concepts

Materials: a hat, scarf, gloves, *colors* flashcards from U0 and *clothes* flashcards; if students wear a school uniform, ask them to bring to school one of the pieces of clothing that are key words in the unit – make sure they bring something that is easy to put on and take off, i.e., a hat, scarf, gloves, coat, sweater (optional)

Warm-up

Aim: to introduce the grammar point of the lesson
- Take out a hat (see Materials) and put it on.
- Say *I'm wearing a (blue) hat.*
- Continue with the scarf and gloves.
- Write the new structure on the board.

1 88 SB p81 Listen and check ☑.

Aim: to improve students' listening skills
- Students look at the pictures in their books.
- Play the recording.
- Students work individually.
- Check answers as a class.

For script, see TB p111.

Key: 2 child with sweater and hat, 3 child with coat and hat, 4 child with jeans and T-shirt

2 89 SB p81 Look, listen, and say.

Aim: to practice new language
- Students look at the pictures in Activity 1.
- Play the recording for students to listen and repeat.

For script, see TB p111.

Stronger students:
- Write four incomplete sentences on the board about the kids that have been checked for students to complete, e.g., *I'm wearing* ________ *and* ________.
- Make sure students use *a* when referring to singular pieces of clothing.

3 SB p81 Choose and color your outfit. Say.

Aim: to give students practice with *I'm wearing*
- Students choose pieces of clothing from the pictures to make an outfit.
- They color the outfit.
- Students work in pairs to describe their outfits, e.g., *I'm wearing blue jeans, a yellow coat, and brown boots.*
- Go around the classroom to check performance.
- Some students tell the class about their outfits.

1 59 WB p81 Listen and draw.

Aim: to practice listening skills

For script, see TB p111.

Key: 2 a scarf, 3 boots, 4 a sweater

2 WB p81 Circle your clothes. Draw and say.

Aim: to practice oral skills

Ending the lesson

Aim: to practice new language
- Put the *color* and *clothes* flashcards in two piles. (see Materials)
- A volunteer takes one flashcard from each pile and says what he/she is wearing, e.g., *I'm wearing a red T-shirt.*
- Continue and shuffle the flashcards from time to time.

Extension activity

Aim: to expand on new language from the lesson
- Students use the pieces of clothing they have brought from home. (see Materials)
- Students show what they are wearing as if they were models in a fashion show in front of the class.
- Students exchange pieces of clothing and describe what they are wearing.

Note: Keep the pieces of clothing for the following lesson.

1 88 Listen and check ☑.

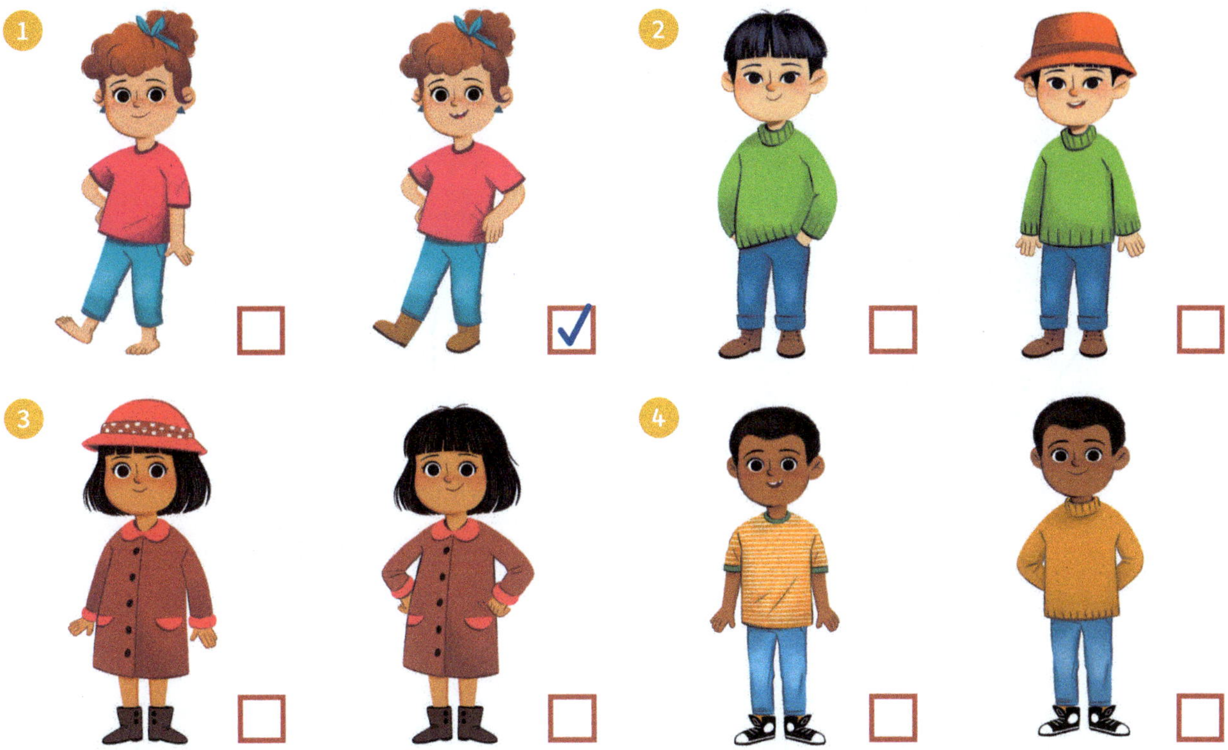

2 89 Look, listen, and say.

3 Choose and color your outfit. Say.

1 90 Listen and sing.

2 Read and number the clothes in order.

☐ scarf ☐1 jeans ☐ coat ☐ hat

Learning outcomes:
- to sing a song

Recycled language: colors, *I'm wearing (a hat).*, *cold*, *put on*, *That's good for you! That's so cute!*

Critical thinking (WB): Sorts and classifies objects and activities according to key features

Cognitive control functions (WB): Cognitive flexibility

Materials: pieces of clothing from previous lesson, blindfold, paper, lollipop sticks (1 per student), tape, scissors (optional)

Warm-up

Aim: to review new language
- Students put on the pieces of clothing they brought from home. (see Materials)
- Students memorize what each classmate is wearing.
- Make two teams, A and B.
- A volunteer from team A is blindfolded.
- A volunteer says what another student is wearing using *I'm wearing …* e.g., *I'm wearing a green scarf.*
- The blindfolded student has to say the name of the person who is wearing a green scarf.
- If he/she is right, team A gets a point. If not, it is team B's turn.
- Students take turns so that everyone participates.

1 90 ▶ 91 SB p82 **Listen and sing.**

Aim: to sing a song
- Students look at the pictures in their books.
- Elicit from students the pieces of clothing the boy is wearing and their color.
- Say *It's cold! (Pedro), put on your (coat).* When the student is ready, say *That's good for you!*
- Repeat with other students so that students get familiar with new vocabulary before listening to the song.
- Play the audio (90).
- Students listen as they look at the pictures in their books.

For song lyrics, see TB p111.

- Play the boy's part of the song and encourage students to sing the rest.
- Play the song video, pausing after each verse for students to repeat.
- When students have learned the song, use the karaoke version of the video or audio (91) to practice the song with the whole class.

Practice

Aim: to practice the song
- Use the karaoke version (91) to sing the song again.
- Students use the pieces of clothing from the Warm-up activity and put them on as they sing the song, e.g., those students who have brought a hat from home put it on as they sing *I'm wearing my hat.*

2 SB p82 **Read and number the clothes in order.**

Aim: to practice new language
- Based on the song, students put the words in order.
- Check results as a class.

Key: 2 hat, 3 coat, 4 scarf

1 60 WB p82 **What clothes do you need? Listen and circle.**

Aim: to practice listening skills

For song lyrics, see TB p111.

Key: sweater, hat, coat, boots, scarf

2 WB p82 **Look at the picture. Check ☑ the clothes you need.**

Aim: to practice new language

Key: 2, 7

Ending the lesson

Aim: to practice new language
- Students put the pieces of clothing they brought from home on your desk.
- Make two teams, A and B.
- A student from each team stands at the same distance from the desk.
- Give an instruction, e.g., *Put on a scarf.*
- The two students run to get a scarf and put it on.
- The first student who puts on a scarf wins a point for his/her team.
- Continue with a set number of points in mind.

Extension activity

Aim: to practice new language
- Hand out paper.
- Students draw a person, animal, or character wearing clothes they have learned in the unit.
- They cut them out.
- Hand out the lollipop sticks. (see Materials)
- Help students tape the sticks behind the drawings to make a puppet.
- Students act as if they were their puppets and describe what they are wearing.

Learning outcomes:
- to improve listening and oral skills

New language: *Is he/she wearing (a coat)?, Yes, he/she is., No, he/she isn't.*

Recycled language: clothes

Materials: Students bring one or two pictures of people from magazines wearing different outfits. They cut them in two vertical pieces so that the pictures become two-piece puzzles. Note: Students will use these in this lesson and in the lesson on page 85.

Warm-up

Aim: to improve visual skills
- Make two teams, A and B.
- Students take out their puzzles. (see Materials)
- Put the pictures of team A on one table, table 1, and the pictures of team B on another, table 2.
- Mix the pieces on each table.
- Teams A and B stand in different lines.
- The first two students in line run to the tables, team A to table 2 and team B to table 1.
- Each student makes a puzzle and gives it to you.
- Keep the puzzles from each team separately.
- Teams continue playing.
- When you say *Stop!*, the game is over and it is time to count how many puzzles each team has solved.

Note: Students keep their puzzles for the lesson on page 85.

1 92 SB p83 Listen and stick.

Aim: to improve students' listening skills
- Give students time to look at the pictures of the two children.
- Students take out their stickers.
- Play the recording.
- Students place the stickers where they belong.

For script, see TB p111.

- Students check results in pairs and glue the stickers in place.

Key: Will: blue coat, orange hat, red boots; Fran: green sweater, orange scarf, blue boots

2 SB p83 Watch and listen.

Aim: to focus students on grammatical form
- Play the *Penny the Penguin* video.
- Students watch and listen.
- Ask questions using *Is he/she wearing … ?* about Paul and Penny to check comprehension.

For script, see TB p111.

- Play the audio.
- Write two questions on the board, one about Penny and the other about Paul, e.g., *Is Penny wearing a _____?*

Stronger students: Choose students to write questions on the board.
- Volunteer students come to the board and provide the correct answer in writing, e.g., *Yes, she is.*

3 SB p83 Work with a partner. Play *Guess Who?*

Aim: to practice new language
- Model the oral activity with a volunteer.
- The volunteer chooses a child from the book and does not tell you his/her name.
- Ask questions to guess which child from the book the volunteer has chosen, e.g., *Is this person a girl or a boy? Is (he) wearing (boots)?*
- Make a guess, e.g., *Is she (Eva)?*
- After showing how the activity works, ask students to work in pairs.
- Go around the classroom to check performance.

1 61 WB p83 Listen. Write *yes* or *no*.

Aim: to practice new language

For script, see TB p112.

Key: 2 no, 3 no, 4 yes, 5 yes, 6 no

2 WB p83 Look at the pictures. Point and ask.

Aim: to practice new language

Key: e.g., *Is he wearing a scarf? No, he isn't.*

Ending the lesson

Aim: to practice new language
- Play *Guess Who?* but instead of using the pictures from the book, students guess about their classmates.
- A volunteer chooses a classmate and the class asks questions.

Extension activity

Aim: to review new language
- In their notebooks, students draw a child wearing an outfit.
- Make pairs of students by choosing students that sit far away from each other.
- Students must not show their drawings to each other, but only say if their character is a girl or boy.
- Each student has four questions available to make about his/her partner's drawing, e.g., *Is she wearing a scarf?*
- The student who guesses the most pieces of clothing after asking the four questions wins.

1 Listen and stick.

2 Watch and listen.

3 Work with a partner. Play *Guess Who?*

Hot or Cold?

1 93 Watch and listen to the story.

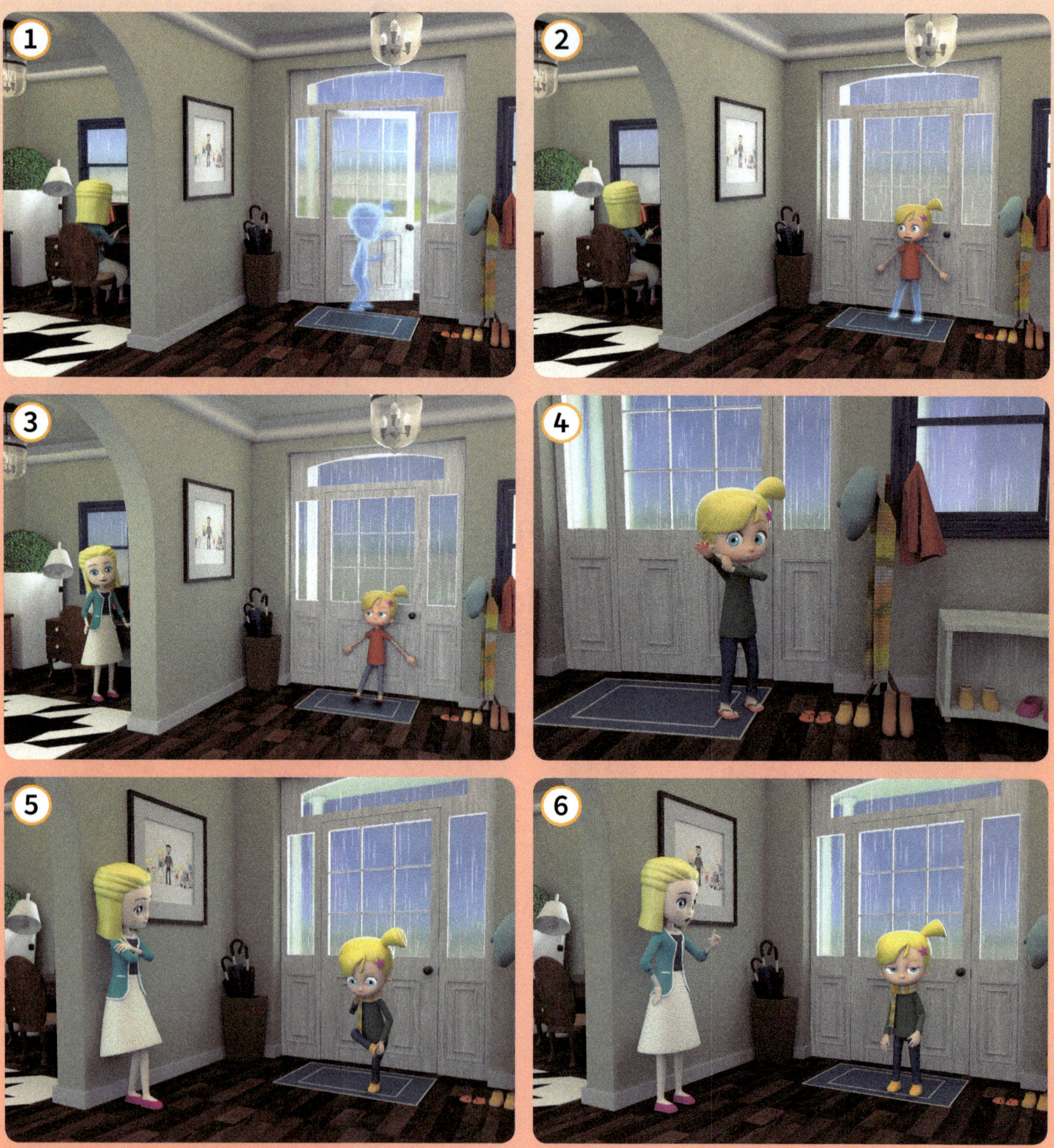

Learning outcomes:
- to listen to, read, watch, and act out a picture story
- to review language from the unit

New language: *hot*, *take off*

Recycled language: *I'm wearing (a coat)?*, *cold*, *put on*, clothes

Value: being prepared

Materials: tape, pictures (the size of a flashcard) that show examples of *hot* and *cold*, e.g., fire, the sun, ice, boiling water, glacier, iron, oven, desert, ice cream, snowman, igloo, etc.; props: sweater, boots, scarf, coat, two hats

Warm-up

Aim: to practice vocabulary
- Teach the word *hot*, and review the word *cold*.
- Write HOT and COLD on the board.
- Show the pictures (see Materials), and ask students what they associate them with, *hot or cold?*
- Students come to the front and place the pictures under the correct category.

Note: Keep the pictures for the lesson on page 87.

Hot or Cold?

1 93 SB pp84–85 Watch and listen to the story.

Aim: to present a picture story
- Play the audio as students follow the story in their books.
- Ask general comprehension questions, e.g., *Who is in the story? What clothes are mentioned? Is Misty cold at the end?*

For script, see TB page 112.

- Play the *Hot or Cold?* video to the end.
- Talk about the story value: being prepared.
- Students give you examples of clothes or objects they should remember to take before leaving home.
- Help them think why it is important to remember about them in each case.

Note: Some of the discussion will need to be in L1.
- Play the video again. Students watch, listen, and repeat.

1 WB p84 What's she wearing? Color and say.

Aim: to practice new language

Key: For example: 1 *She's wearing jeans.* 2 *She's wearing a scarf.* 3 *She's wearing a hat.*

2 62 WB p84 Who says it? Listen and check ☑.

Aim: to identify characters from the picture story

For script, see TB p112.

Key: 2 a, 3 b, 4 a

Ending the lesson

Aim: to act out the story
- Take out the props to act out the story. (see Materials)
- Act out the story with a volunteer student.
- Invite pair of students to act it out in front of the class.

Extension activity

Aim: to practice new language
- Put on a hat, and take it off to teach *take off*.
- Play a simple version of *Simon Says*, just by using *put on* and *take off*.
- Make two teams. Ask a student from each to come to the front and take a hat. (see Materials)
- Give instructions: *Put on the hat, take off the hat, put on …*
- The student who wins gets a point for his/her team.
- Continue with other students from each team.

Learning outcomes:
- to review language from the story and the unit

Value: being prepared

Critical thinking (WB): Identifies characters, setting, plots, and theme in a story

Materials: flashcards 60–67 (clothes), two-piece puzzles from the lesson on page 83

Warm-up

Aim: to improve visual skills
- Place the *clothes* flashcards on the board in random order.
- Ask a volunteer to look at them attentively.
- Then ask the volunteer to turn around.
- Change the order of the flashcards.
- Ask the volunteer to face the board again.
- He/She has to put the flashcards in their original place.
- Repeat with other students, and let them take your role as well.

2 SB p85 Look and read. Check ☑ Misty's clothes.

Aim: to improve visual skills
- Students work in pairs.
- They look at the pictures and check the pieces of clothing Misty is wearing in each scene.
- Pairs ask questions to each other to check their work, e.g., *In this picture, is Misty wearing a scarf? Yes, she is.*

Key: Column 1: T-shirt, jeans; Column 2: scarf, jeans, coat, hat, sweater, T-shirt; Column 3: jeans, sweater, T-shirt; Column 4: scarf, jeans, sweater, T-shirt

1 WB p85 What's good? Draw ☺.

Aim: to understand the meaning of the value of being prepared

Key: 2

2 WB p85 Trace the answer.

Aim: to understand the meaning of the value of being prepared

Key: OK, Mom.

Ending the lesson

Aim: to practice vocabulary
- Students take out their two-piece puzzles and stick them in their notebooks. (see Materials)
- They copy the list of pieces of clothing in Activity 2 and check those that are in their puzzles.

Extension activity

Aim: to focus on the value of being prepared
- Ask students what problems they can avoid if they are prepared for different situations.
- For example, talk about the moment they get ready for school and prepare their backpacks, or when they get ready to go to the park.
- Elicit what they should take to different places to be prepared, e.g., mosquito repellent if they go camping.

Note: Some of this discussion will need to take place in L1.

2 Look and read. Check ☑ Misty's clothes.

scarf				
jeans	✓			
coat				
hat				
sweater				
T-shirt				

Different Clothes

Watch and listen.

1 94 Listen and point.

1 
soft

2 
hard

3 
cold

4 
hot

5 
belt

6 
sunglasses

2 Is it soft or hard? Draw lines.

1 

2 

3 

soft

hard

4 

5 

6 

Learning outcomes:

- to integrate other areas of the curriculum through English: science

BIG QUESTION to answer the Big Question *What clothes do we need?*

New language: *soft*, *hard*, *belt*, *sunglasses*

Recycled language: *cold*, *hot*, clothes

Critical thinking: Demonstrate understanding of links between new ideas

Warm-up

Aim: to introduce the lesson topic

- Write the question *How are clothes different?* on the board.
- Discuss the topic with students.
- Refer to differences among clothes based on weather, texture, situations in which students would wear a specific piece of clothing, etc.

Note: Some of the discussion will need to be in L1.

SB p86 Watch and listen. How are clothes different?

Aim: to identify differences

- With the Student's Books closed, play the *Think and Learn* video.
- Elicit from students the names of the pieces of clothing mentioned in the video.
- On the board, write the names of the pieces of clothing from the video with the vowels missing.
- Volunteer students complete the words on the board.
- Play the video again and elicit the meaning of *soft* and *hard* from students.
- Students touch things in the classroom that are soft or hard to give you examples.

For videoscript, see TB p112.

1 94 SB p86 Listen and point.

Aim: to present words relating to clothes

- Students open their books.
- Play the recording.
- Students listen and point to the corresponding picture.

2 SB p86 Is it soft or hard? Draw lines.

Aim: to identify soft and hard objects

- Ask students what they see in the pictures.
- Students do the activity in pairs.
- Check results as a class by asking questions, e.g., *Is the scarf soft or hard?*

Key: 2 hard, 3 soft, 4 hard, 5 hard, 6 soft

1 WB p86 Complete the words. Match.

Aim: to practice new vocabulary

Key: 2 hot: b, 3 soft: d, 4 hard: a

2 WB p86 Write *soft* or *hard*.

Aim: to identify soft and hard objects

Key: 2 soft, 3 hard, 4 soft, 5 soft, 6 hard

Ending the lesson

Aim: to review vocabulary from the lesson

- Students draw four things in their notebooks: some should be soft, and others hard.
- Students work in small groups and ask each other questions about their drawings, e.g., *Is the chair soft or hard?*
- Students write *soft* or *hard* under their drawings.

Extension activity

Aim: to practice writing skills

- Students work in pairs.
- In their notebooks, students write three questions using this structure: *Is … soft or hard?* and a picture to complete it, e.g., *Is (picture of a pencil) soft or hard?*
- Pairs exchange notebooks with another pair.
- Students answer the other pair's questions by writing *H* for *hard* and *S* for *soft* next to the questions, e.g., *Is (picture of a pencil) soft or hard? H*

Stronger students: Students write complete answers, i.e., *It's hard/soft.*

Learning outcomes:
- to extend the focus on science through English
- to complete a project

Recycled language: *soft*, *hard*, *hot*, *cold*, clothes

Creative thinking: Participates in investigative, exploratory, open-ended tasks

Critical thinking (SB & WB): Sorts and classifies objects and activities according to key features

Creative thinking (WB): Uses different media to make and describe his/her own designs

Cognitive control functions (WB): Cognitive flexibility

Materials: pictures from the lesson on page 84, a piece of paper with a table like the one on page 87 drawn on it (1 per small group of students), students bring pictures of pieces of clothing from magazines or from the internet

Warm-up

Aim: to review language
- Take out the pictures from the lesson on page 84. (see Materials)
- Review *hot* and *cold* by showing the pictures to the class.

3 SB p87 Circle the items red for hot weather and blue for cold weather.

Aim: to review language
- Students work in pairs.
- Pairs look at the pictures in their books and circle them.
- Students work with another pair to check results.

Key: 2 red, 3 red, 4 blue, 5 blue, 6 blue, 7 red, 8 blue, 9, blue

4 Project SB p87 Draw clothes in a table.

Aim: to enable students to apply what they have learned about differences in clothes
- Ask students to look at the clothes they are wearing.
- They stand up when you say the clothes, e.g., soft sweater, soft jeans, hard boots, soft T-shirt, hard belt.
- Students look at the table on page 87.
- Say *A T-shirt is soft. It's for hot weather.*
- Students look at the items in Activity 3.
- In pairs, they draw the items to complete the table in their Student's Book.
- Check results as a class.
- Make small groups.
- Hand out the tables. (see Materials)
- Students take out their pictures and figure out where each one should go in the table.
- Go around the classroom to discuss choices with groups.
- Students stick the pictures where they belong.
- If they don't agree on where a picture goes, they can draw the same picture in another place in the table.
- Groups show their work to the class and say sentences about it.
- Take photos of the completed tables and save them to students' digital portfolios.

3 WB p87 Complete the words. Draw lines and match.

Aim: to review language

Key: hot: 1 T-shirt, 2 sunglasses, 3 sandals, (6 sunhat) cold: 4 sweater, 5 scarf, 7 gloves, 8 coat

4 WB p87 Complete the picture. Trace.

Aim: to personalize the unit topic

Key: Me on a cold day

Lesson review

- With students, review what they have learned in the lesson and if they liked the project.
- Display the tables around the classroom.

Extension activity

Aim: to trigger creativity
- As homework, ask students to make a pair of sunglasses with cardboard.
- Students decorate them and bring them to class.
- Students put on their sunglasses and describe them to the class, e.g., *I'm wearing blue and red sunglasses.*

3 Circle the items red for hot weather and blue for cold weather.

4 Project Draw clothes in a table.

	soft	hard
hot		
cold		

Do That!

1 95 Listen and act it out with your teacher. Listen again and match.

1 2 3 4 5 6

Learning outcomes:
- to activate creativity

New language: *mirror*

Recycled language: *put on*, *take off*, clothes

Creative thinking: Listens and responds physically to songs, rhymes, chants

Warm-up

Aim: to review language
- Teach students how to make a two- or three-word "picture" with new vocabulary.
- For example, write *gloves* vertically and *coat* horizontally so that the words share the letter *o*.
- Students work in pairs to make new word "pictures" in their notebooks.
- Go around the classroom to check results.

Extra support: Provide two or three set words for pairs to make the new acrostics. Tell them which word should go vertically and write it on the board. Another alternative is to hand out incomplete acrostics for pairs to complete.

1 95 SB p88 **Listen and act it out with your teacher. Listen again and match.**

Aim: to activate students' creativity
- Students stand up.
- Play the recording and encourage students to follow you while you act out the instructions in the audio.

For script, see TB p112.

- Students stand in a circle.
- Play the recording again for the class to act it out while they look at each other.
- Students go back to their tables, open their books, and match the numbers to the pictures.

Key: 2 red, 3 pink, 4 orange, 5 green, 6 blue

1 63 WB p88 **Listen and color.**

Aim: to improve listening skills
- Check that students know what they are going to color. (the edge of the picture)

For script, see TB p112.

Key: 2 yellow, 3 blue, 4 orange, 5 red

2 WB p88 **Look at the pictures again. Circle a face for you.**

Aim: to show preferences

Key: Students' own answers

Ending the lesson

Aim: to review language
- Pretend you are putting on a hat and then take if off.
- Give students instructions using *put on* and *take off*.
- Volunteer students give instructions to the class.

Extension activity

Aim: to review language
- Play *I Spy with My Little Eye …* with the class.
- Use new vocabulary, e.g., *I spy with my little eye something that is yellow and hard. I spy with my little eye something that is blue and soft.*
- Play in two teams.

Learning outcomes:
- to review language from the unit by taking a quiz
- to reflect on learning

BIG QUESTION to think about how the unit has helped them answer the Big Question *What clothes do we need?*

Creative thinking (WB): Creates texts that express personal interests, emotions, or identity

Cognitive control functions (WB): Cognitive flexibility

Recycled language: vocabulary and grammar from the unit

Warm-up

Aim: to review vocabulary from the unit
- Teach students how to scramble a word, e.g, *e u b l* for *blue.*
- Students work in pairs and write scrambled words from the unit in their notebooks.
- Pairs exchange their notebooks and unscramble the words.

Extra support: Write scrambled words on the board instead of asking students to write them, and solve them as a class.

1 SB p89 Read and match.

Aim: to review key words from the unit
- Students do the activity individually.
- Check answers as a class.

Key: 1 gloves, 2 coat, 3 sweater, 4 boots

2 SB p89 96 Listen and write *S* for *Sally*, *T* for *Tim*, and *K* for *Kate*.

Aim: to improve listening skills
- Students look at the pictures.
- Play the recording.

For script, see TB p112.

- Students write the initials in the boxes.
- Check answers as a class.

Key: 1 S, 2 T, 3 K

3 SB p89 Look and circle *soft* or *hard*.

Aim: to review language from the unit
- Students look at the pictures and circle the correct options.
- Check results as a class.

Key: 1 soft, 2 soft, 3 hard, 4 soft

1 WB p89 Look and say. Circle ☺, 😐, or ☹.

Aim: to assess performance

2 WB p89 Hard or soft? Circle.

Aim: to review language

Key: 1 hard, 2 hard, 3 soft, 4 hard

3 WB p89 Finish the picture.

BIG QUESTION Aim: to revisit the unit Big Question

Ending the lesson

Aim: to enable students to express their preferences
- Ask students what their favorite activity is from the unit (e.g., the song, chant, or one of the games) and hold a class vote.
- Repeat the most popular activity with the class.

Extension activity

Aim: to enable students to share what they have learned
- Put students into groups of four.
- Each student opens their Workbook to page 89.
- Students take turns showing what they have drawn for Activity 3 and saying something about their picture, e.g., *This is my favorite T-shirt. It's green and blue. It's for hot weather.*
- The class votes for the most original T-shirt.

1 Read and match.

1 
2 
3 
4 

coat gloves boots sweater

2 Listen and write *S* for *Sally*, *T* for *Tim*, and *K* for *Kate*.

96

1  ☐
2  ☐
3  ☐

3 Look and circle *soft* or *hard*.

1 
soft
hard

2 
soft
hard

3 
soft
hard

4 
soft
hard

9 My Hobbies

1 97 Listen and point. Say the words.

BIG QUESTION What are hobbies?

2 98 Listen and chant.

Learning outcomes:
- to name and talk about hobbies
- to say a chant

BIG QUESTION to start to think about the Big Question *What are hobbies?*

New language: *read, swim, dance, paint a picture, play soccer, run*

Recycled language: *Do you like … ?, Do you have … ?, What's your favorite … ?*

Cognitive control functions: Working memory

Materials: flashcards 68–73 (hobbies), pictures of various hobbies (e.g., making origami, playing the guitar, cooking, etc.), pictures of sports (e.g., tennis, basketball, rugby, baseball, etc.), music representing different dancing styles (e.g., hip-hop, rock, R&B, classical, samba, etc.) (optional)

Warm-up

Aim: to introduce the unit topic
- Place the pictures of hobbies (see Materials) on the board.
- Tell students that the pictures represent hobbies.
- Use grammar structures students already know (i.e., *Do you have any hobbies? Do you like music? What's your favorite hobby?*) to ask students about their hobbies.
- Leave the pictures on the board.

Presentation

Aim: to present new vocabulary
- Take out the *hobbies* flashcards and say the words.
- Students repeat after you.
- Place the flashcards on the board next to the pictures of hobbies.
- Individual students tell you which hobby from the board is their favorite.

1 97 SB p90 Listen and point. Say the words.

Aim: to practice vocabulary about hobbies
- Students look at the illustration of the school scene in their Student's Book.
- Ask *Where are Misty and Whisper?*
- Write *After School Clubs* on the board. Students tell you what after school clubs they are familiar with.
- Ask *What is Misty's favorite hobby? And Whisper's?*
- Play the recording. Students listen and point to the corresponding activity.

For script, see TB p112.

- Play the recording again for students to repeat the words.

BIG QUESTION What are hobbies?

Aim: to make students explain what a hobby represents
- Read the Big Question.
- Students tell you what a hobby is. They also tell you why a hobby is important, e.g., to have fun, to learn something new, to do something you love, to do something with your friends, etc.

Note: Some of the discussion will need to be in L1.

2 98 SB p90 Listen and chant.

Aim: to give students practice with new language
- Students tell you which hobbies they can identify in the scene.
- Play the recording.
- Students listen and follow the chant in their Student's Books.

For chant script, see TB p112.

- Play the recording again, pausing for students to repeat.
- Say the chant as a class and then in groups.

Practice

Aim: to practice new language
- On the board, place the *hobbies* flashcards in the order they are in the chant.
- Write the first two letters of a hobby, e.g., *sw*, on the board.
- Students identify the hobby you are referring to. (swim)
- A volunteer student comes to the front and completes the word.
- Continue with the rest of the hobbies.

1 WB p90 Circle the hobby.

Aim: to practice new vocabulary

Key: 1 read, 2 dance, 3 play soccer

2 WB p90 Look at the pictures. Write the words.

Aim: to practice spelling

Key: 1 swim, 2 paint a picture, 3 run

Ending the lesson

Aim: to review vocabulary from the lesson
- Play *Charades.*
- Students perform the hobbies in front of the class, and the rest of the students guess the hobby.

Extension activity

Aim: to review vocabulary from the lesson
- Write the word PLAY on the board.
- Students tell you what other sports you can play as a hobby.
- Take out the pictures of sports (see Materials).
- Students come to the front, take one of the pictures and say what sport it is.
- Write the word DANCE on the board.
- Students tell you what dancing styles they are familiar with.
- Play the music (see Materials).
- Students identify the different dancing styles.

Learning outcomes:
- to talk about hobbies

New language: *I'm (dancing).*, *slowly*, *quickly*

Recycled language: hobbies

Critical thinking: Solves simple puzzles

Cognitive control functions: Cognitive flexibility

Warm-up

Aim: to review vocabulary
- Draw a paintbrush on the board.
- Elicit from students what hobby students associate the object with.
- Continue with other objects, e.g., dancing shoes, story book, ball, running shoes.
- Students draw other objects that can be associated with the hobbies.

1 99 SB p91 Listen and number.

Aim: to improve students' listening skills
- Give students time to look at the pictures.
- Play the recording.
- Students add the numbers.

For script, see TB p112.

- Check answers as a class.

Key: a 6, b 2, c 4, d 3, (e 1), f 5

2 100 SB p91 Look, listen, and say.

Aim: to practice new language
- Students look at the pictures in Activity 1.
- Play the recording, and pause for students to repeat.

For script, see TB p112.

3 SB p91 What's next? Look, draw, and say.

Aim: to give students practice with grammar
- Use the first pattern of illustrations as a sample for students to understand how the activity works.
- Remind students of what a pattern is.
- Students draw themselves in the empty boxes.
- In pairs, students check results by saying *I'm (running)*.
- Go around the classroom to check understanding.

Key: 1 dancing, 2 painting, 3 playing soccer

1 WB p91 Draw lines.

Aim: to practice new language

Key: 2 I'm dancing. 3 I'm playing soccer. 4 I'm swimming. 5 I'm painting a picture. 6 I'm running.

2 WB p91 Draw yourself and write.

Aim: to practice new language

Key: Look! I'm swimming.

Ending the lesson

Aim: to practice new language
- Use the audio from Activity 1 and ask students to perform as a class.
- Demonstrate the actions when you repeat the lines in the audio. Ask students to copy the actions while repeating the words together. For example, *Look. I'm running.*, *Look at me. I'm swimming.*

Extension activity

Aim: to review new language
- Show how you run slowly and say *I'm running slowly.*
- Show how you run quickly and say *I'm running quickly.*
- Volunteer students perform the different hobbies slowly and quickly.
- A volunteer student gives directions to the class, e.g., *I'm playing soccer slowly.*
- Turn this activity into a game. Students who do not follow the instructions correctly are out of the game.

1 (audio 99) Listen and number.

2 (audio 100) Look, listen, and say.

3 What's next? Look, draw, and say.

I'm dancing!

1

2

3

1 101 Listen and sing.

2 Read, count the children, and write the number.

How many children are …

reading?	2	running?	☐
painting?	☐	swimming?	☐
dancing?	☐	playing soccer?	☐

Learning outcomes:
- to sing a song

Recycled language: hobbies, *how many*

Materials: flashcards 68–73 (hobbies), cards/strips of paper with one hobby written on each of them. There should be one card/strip of paper per student. Make sure the amount of hobbies is not even.

Warm-up

Aim: to review *how many*
- Hand out the cards/strips of paper to the class. (see Materials)
- Say one hobby, e.g., *I'm running.*
- Students who have the corresponding card start running.
- Ask a volunteer student *How many students are running?*
- Continue with the rest of the hobbies.
- Students exchange cards to perform other hobbies.

1 101 ▶ 102 SB p92 Listen and sing.

Aim: to sing a song
- Play the audio (101).
- Students listen to the song.

For song lyrics, see TB p112.

- Play the audio again and sing with the class.
- Play the song video, pausing after each verse for students to repeat.
- When students have learned the song, use the karaoke version of the video or audio (102) to practice the song with the whole class.

Practice

Aim: to practice the song
- Make six groups.
- Assign a hobby per group.
- Play the song for each group to sing its part. The chorus should be sung by everyone in the class.
- Use the karaoke version (102) to sing the song again.

2 SB p92 Read, count the children, and write the number.

Aim: to practice new language
- Students work in pairs.
- Pairs check results with another pair of students.

Key: painting: 4, dancing: 3, running: 5, swimming: 2, playing soccer: 6

1 64 WB p92 Listen and number 1–6.

Aim: to practice new language

For song lyrics, see TB p112.

Key: b 3, c 4, d 2, e 5, f 6

2 WB p92 Trace.

Aim: to practice new language

Key: Play today. I'm having fun.

Ending the lesson

Aim: to practice new language
- Place the *hobbies* flashcards on the board.
- Make two groups, A and B.
- Write a number next to a flashcard, e.g., 3 next to the *paint* flashcard.
- Ask *How many students are painting?* (*Three.*)
- Play a guessing game.
- Six students from team A sit with their backs to the board.
- Six students from team B write numbers from 1 to 10 next to each flashcard.
- Students from team B ask the students that are sitting questions, e.g., *How many children are* (*reading*)*?*
- Give students two chances to guess. They get one point when they guess correctly the first time or half a point when they guess the second time.
- The group that gets the most points is the winner.

Extension activity

Aim: to practice spelling of new words
- Students work in pairs.
- Write the word HOBBIES vertically on the board.
- Students use the word hobbies to write simple "pictures" using the hobbies they have learned in the unit, e.g., they use the letter O in the word hobbies for the word *soccer.* They write *soccer* horizontally sharing the letter *o* in *hobbies.*
- Go around the classroom to check performance.

Extra support: Write the word "hobbies" vertically on the board. Write words that share letters with the word on the board, e.g., soccer, swim, read, and complete a word "picture" with the class.

Learning outcomes:
- to improve listening and oral skills

New language: *Are you swimming?, Yes, I am. / No, I'm not.*

Recycled language: actions from Unit 2

Materials: Unit 9 stickers, flashcards 68–73 (hobbies), blindfold

Warm-up

Aim: to review actions
- Remind students of the verbs *walk, wave, shake, jump, stretch,* and *bend* (see Warm-up on page 27).
- Students perform the actions with you as if they were in a gym class.
- Whisper one of the verbs to one student.
- The volunteer student performs it, e.g., He/She stretches.
- Ask *Are you bending?*
- Elicit the answer.
- Other students participate by performing the actions you whisper to them.

1 103 SB p93 **Listen and stick.**

Aim: to improve students' listening skills
- Give students time to look at the illustrations in their books.
- Students take out their stickers.
- Play the recording.

For script, see TB p113.

- Students place the stickers where they consider they should go.
- Play the recording again to check results.
- Students glue the stickers in the right place.

Key: 1 swimming, 2 painting, 3 playing soccer, 4 reading, 5 dancing, 6 running

2 SB p93 **Watch and listen.**

Aim: to focus students on grammatical form
- Play the *Penny the Penguin* video.
- Students watch.

For script, see TB p113.

- Play the audio.
- Invite pairs of students to repeat after the audio.

3 SB p93 **Play the game.**

Aim: to practice new language
- Play *Charades*.
- Model the game with a volunteer.

1 65 WB p93 **Listen. Write *yes* or *no*.**

Aim: to practice new language

For script, see TB p113.

Key: 2 no, 3 no, 4 yes, 5 no, 6 yes

2 WB p93 **Look at the photos. Write.**

Aim: to practice new language

Key: 1 Are you playing soccer? Yes, I am. 2 Are you dancing? No, I'm not.

Ending the lesson

Aim: to practice new language
- Put the *hobbies* flashcards face down on your desk.
- A volunteer student takes one without showing it to the class.
- Another volunteer student guesses by asking *Are you (swimming)?*
- Turn this activity into a game by making two groups.
- Six students from group A come to the front, take a flashcard each, and do not show them to the class.
- Group B makes ten guesses by asking questions to any of the students in the front: *Are you (running)?*
- Students from Group A answer by saying *Yes, I am* or *No, I'm not*.
- Groups swap roles.
- The group that makes the most correct guesses is the winner.

Extension activity

Aim: to review new language
- Write the hobbies and verbs reviewed from Unit 9 on the board and say them out loud.
- Blindfold one student.
- Another student performs any of the actions on the board behind him/her.
- The blindfolded student has to guess what his/her classmate is doing, e.g., *Are you (stretching)?*
- Allow different students to participate.

1 103 Listen and stick.

1

2

3

4

5

6

2 Watch and listen.

3 Play the game.

Are you dancing?

Yes, I am!

Guess What I'm Doing?

1 104 Watch and listen to the story.

Learning outcomes:
- to listen to, read, watch, and act out a picture story
- to review language from the unit

New language: *my turn, sorry, guess, Not at all. / You're welcome.*

Value: saying sorry

Materials: 4 big cards to display around the classroom

Warm-up

Aim: to introduce the story
- Students look at the story frames.
- Ask simple questions, e.g., *What's the name of the story? Where are Whisper and Misty? Is Whisper dancing?*

Guess What I'm Doing?

1 104 SB pp94–95 Watch and listen to the story.

Aim: to present a picture story
- Play the audio as students follow the story in their books.
- Ask general comprehension questions.

For script, see TB page 113.

- Play the *Guess What I'm Doing?* video to the end.
- Talk about the story value: saying sorry.
- Ask students who says sorry in the story.
- Students give you examples of situations in which they have said sorry or should say sorry.
- Teach *Not at all / You're welcome.*

Note: Some of the discussion will need to be in L1.
- Play the video again. Students watch, listen, and repeat.

1 66 WB p94 Listen and number.

Aim: to review the picture story

For script, see TB p113.

Key: a 3, b 2, c 4, (d 1)

2 67 WB p94 Who says it? Listen and check ☑.

Aim: to identify characters

For script, see TB p113.

Key: 2 a, 3 a, 4 b

Ending the lesson

Aim: to practice values
- Elicit from students what Misty says when she wants to swap roles with Whisper. (*My turn.*)
- Discuss with students how important it is to take turns in games.
- Teach *Your turn.*
- Elicit from students the expression they learned to apologize (*sorry*) and to respond to an apology (*you're welcome / not at all*).
- Take out the cards (see Materials), and write the four expressions on them.
- Display the cards in the classroom for future use.

Extension activity

Aim: to act out the story
- Act out the story with a volunteer.
- Students practice the story in pairs.
- Volunteer pairs perform in front of the class.

Learning outcomes:
- to improve visual memory

Value: saying sorry

Recycled language: vocabulary from previous units

Critical thinking (WB): Identifies characters, setting, plots, and theme in a story

Flashcards: 68–73 (hobbies)

Warm-up

Aim: to improve visual memory
- Place the *hobbies* flashcards on the board in random order.
- Write numbers 1 to 6 under them.
- Take the flashcards from the board and put them in a pile.
- Groups of three students come to the front and put the flashcards in their original order.
- Repeat with other groups of students.

2 SB p95 Look and write the words. Check ☑ the activity from the story.

Aim: to improve visual memory
- Students work in pairs.
- They write the words and check the correct picture.
- Check results as a class.

Key: 2 read, 3 play soccer, 4 swim; *play soccer* is checked

1 WB p95 What's good? Draw ☺.

Aim: to understand the value of saying sorry

Key: 1

2 WB p95 Write.

Aim: to understand the value of saying sorry

Key: sorry

Ending the lesson

Aim: to act out the story
- Encourage students to come up with new versions of the story that would be easy to perform.
- For example, Whisper and Misty perform other hobbies, they are at a different club and, instead of hitting Whisper with a ball, Misty could step on his foot.
- Groups of students perform the new version of the story in front of the class.

Extension activity

Aim: to focus on the value of saying sorry
- Discuss how students feel before and after saying sorry and how they feel when someone apologizes.

2 **Look and write the words.**
Check ☑ the activity from the story.

swim ~~dance~~ play soccer read

1

☐

dance

2

☐

3

☐

4

☐

Think and Learn

BAR CHARTS

Watch and listen.

1 105 Listen and point.

bar chart

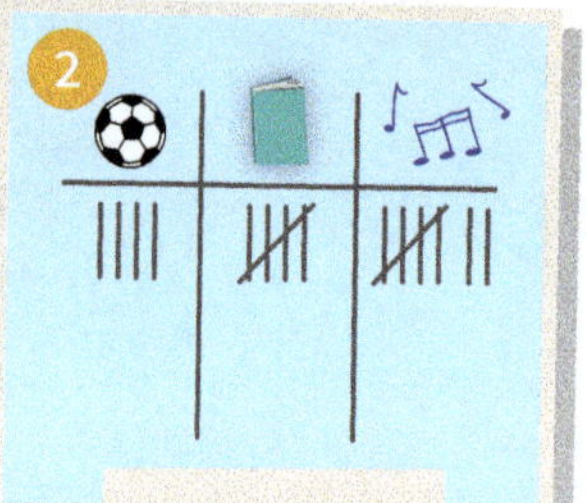

tally chart

computer games

movies

2 Look at the key and color the bar chart.

How many children like ... ?

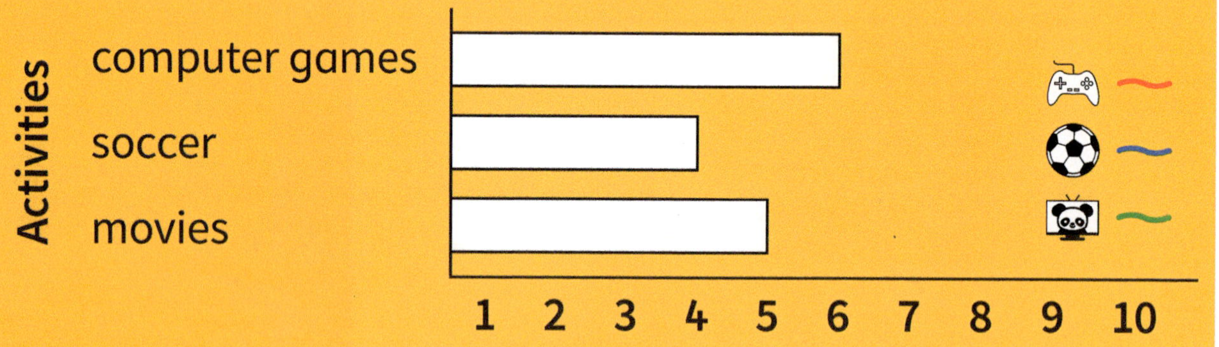

3 Look at the bar chart. Complete the tally chart.

Do you like ...?	
playing soccer	IIII
watching movies	
playing computer games	

Learning outcomes:
- to integrate other areas of the curriculum through English: math

BIG QUESTION to answer the Big Question *What are hobbies?*

New language: *bar chart, tally chart, computer games, movies*

Recycled language: colors, *Do you like ... ?*

Critical thinking: Demonstrate understanding of links between new ideas

Critical thinking (WB): Compares different types of information

Cognitive control functions (WB): Cognitive flexibility

Materials: pictures of simple tally charts and bar charts, paper

Warm-up

Aim: to identify charts
- Take out the pictures of tally charts and bar charts.
- Students pass them around, and tell you if they know what they are.
- Explain simply what tally charts and bar charts are and what they are used for.

SB p96 Watch and listen. How do we make a bar chart?

Aim: to learn how to collect data
- With Student's Books closed, play the *Think and Learn* video.

For videoscript, see TB p113.

- Ask students if the video is about tally charts or bar charts. (both)
- Ask *What is the chart in the video about?*

1 105 SB p96 Listen and point.

Aim: to present words relating to charts
- Students open their books.
- Play the recording.

For script, see TB p113.

- Students listen and point to the corresponding pictures.
- Play the recording again for students to repeat.

2 SB p96 Look at the key and color the bar chart.

Aim: to learn how to collect data
- Write the title *Favorite Pets* on the board.
- Draw axes. On the left, write only three categories, e.g., dog, cat, rabbit.
- At the lower end of the chart, write the numbers 1 to 10.
- Ten students come to the front.
- Start completing the chart while asking each student which pet from the chart is his/her favorite. If possible, use different colors for each pet.
- Student look at the bar chart in Activity 2.
- Ask general questions to help students identify the elements in the chart, e.g., *What is the chart about? How many categories are there?*
- Students complete the activity in pairs.

Key: computer games: red, soccer: blue, movies: green

3 SB p96 Look at the bar chart. Complete the tally chart.

Aim: To learn how to collect data
- Draw a table made up of two columns by eight rows on the board.
- Write a color for each row, e.g., blue, green, yellow, orange, pink, red, black, white.
- Say which color is your favorite, and draw a vertical dash (|), i.e., a tally line, in the correct category.
- Students tell you which color they like.
- Explain to students that five is represented by a horizontal line across the first four lines, i.e., ||||.
- Students complete the table with you.
- Keep for Ending the lesson.
- In pairs, students complete Activity 3.
- Check performance.

Key: movies: 5, computer games: 6

1 WB p96 Color the bars.

Aim: to learn how to collect data

Key: blue 5, red 7, yellow 2

2 WB p96 Count. Complete the sentences.

Aim: to learn how to collect data

Key: 1 5 children like blue. 2 7 children like red. 3 2 children like yellow.

Ending the lesson

Aim: to learn how to interpret data
- In pairs, students make a bar chart with the information from the tally chart on the board.
- They use the corresponding colors to paint the bars in the bar chart.

Extension activity

Aim: to review vocabulary
- Play *Scattergories*.
- Students work in pairs.
- Hand out one piece of paper per pair.
- Students draw five columns. They write a category at the top of each column. It can be any of the categories of vocabulary they have learned in previous units.
- The game consists of thinking of a word for each category that begins with a certain letter.
- Set a time limit and say a letter. Repeat with other letters.

Learning outcomes:
- to extend the focus on math through English
- to complete a project

Recycled language: *Do you like … ?*

Creative thinking: Participates in investigative, exploratory, open-ended tasks

Cognitive control functions (WB): Cognitive flexibility

Materials: construction paper (1 per group of around 10 students), letter-size paper

Warm-up

Aim: to review language
- Review the use of *Do you like … ?* with hobbies.
- Students ask you questions about your preferences.
- Make sure students use *-ing* when mentioning the hobbies, e.g., *Do you like swimming?*

4 Project SB p97 Make a bar chart about your friends.

Aim: to enable students to apply what they have learned about what a hobby is
- Draw three different tallies on the board to represent numbers 3, 5, and 8.
- Students tell you what numbers they represent.
- Volunteers write the numbers under the tallies on the board.
- Invite other students to draw tallies representing numbers 2, 4, 6, 9, and 10.
- Ask *Which numbers are missing?* (1 and 7)
- Students look at page 97. Ask one student the questions in the tally chart: *Do you like (reading)?*
- Encourage the student to answer using *Yes, I do* and *No, I don't.*
- A volunteer asks you the three questions in the tally chart.
- Students work in groups of a maximum of ten members.
- They ask the three questions to all the members in the group and complete the tally chart on page 97.
- In groups, students complete the bar chart on page 97.
- Hand out construction paper and letter-size paper.
- Students decide on three hobbies they would like to make a bar chart about.
- They draw an icon for each of the three hobbies, e.g., a drawing of running shoes to represent *running*, and cut them out.
- Groups also draw big numbers 1 to 10 and cut them out.
- Groups use the construction paper to make a bar chart about the three hobbies they have chosen.
- They stick the icons vertically on the left-hand side of the construction paper and the numbers horizontally in the lower part of the paper.
- Groups count how many in the group like each hobby and complete the bar chart by drawing bars.
- Groups compare their bar charts by asking *How many friends like ____? How many friends don't like ____?*
- Display the bar charts around the classroom. Take photos of them and save them to students' digital portfolios.

3 WB p97 Count and complete the tally chart.

Aim: to practice how to collect data

Key: apples 3, bananas 5, oranges 6

4 WB p97 Draw the bar chart.

Aim: to practice how to collect data

Key: bananas 5, apples 3, oranges 6

Lesson review

- With students, review what they have learned in the lesson and if they liked the project.
- Students tell you which one they like the most, the bar charts or the tally charts.

Extension activity

Aim: to review topics learned throughout the year
- Remind students of all the topics they have learned about throughout the year, i.e., school, body, family, animals, food, places, jobs, clothes, and hobbies.
- Hold a class vote for the three topics students liked the best.
- As a class, make a tally chart based on the three favorite topics.

4 Project Make a bar chart about your friends.

a Ask questions and complete the tally chart:

Do you like reading?

Yes, I do.

Do you like ...?	
reading 	
swimming 	
dancing 	

b Now draw a bar chart using the numbers on the tally chart.

c Color the bars.

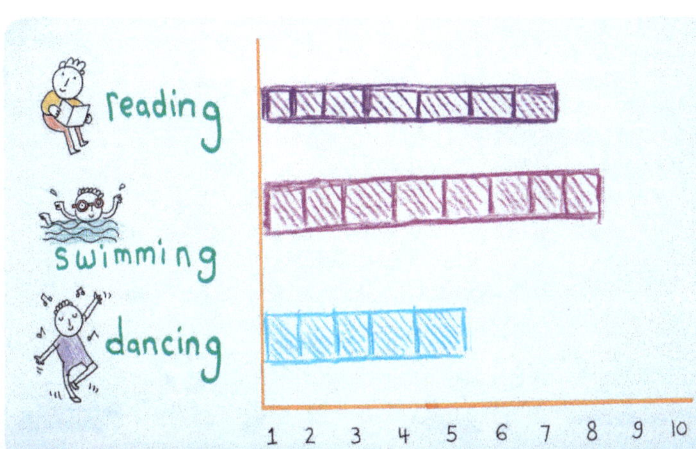

Create That!

1 106 Listen and imagine. Then draw your picture.

2 Show your picture to your friend. Say.

Learning outcomes:
- to activate creativity

Recycled language: hobbies, *How many … ?, big/small, Are you (running)?, Are you wearing … ?, I'm wearing (a T-shirt).*

Creative thinking: Chooses options to create something new

Creative thinking (WB): Uses different media to make and describe his/her own designs

Cognitive control functions: Inhibitory control

Materials: flashcards 60–67 (clothes) and 68–73 (hobbies), Students bring a photo of themselves that shows they are doing something e.g., a sport or a hobby (optional)

Warm-up

Aim: to activate students' imagination
- Place the Unit 8 and Unit 9 flashcards on the board.
- Write these places on the board: school, park, café, playground, sports center, home.
- Students choose a place, a hobby, and a piece of clothing from the board and they imagine a scene, e.g., a boy wearing a coat running at school.
- Students draw the scenes.

Stronger students: Instead of drawing, students work in pairs. They ask each other questions to guess their partner's choices, e.g., *Are you at the park? Are you wearing a coat? Are you running?*

1 106 SB p98 **Listen and imagine. Then draw your picture.**

Aim: to activate students' creativity
- Work with books closed.
- Students close their eyes.
- Play the recording.

For script, see TB p113.

- Students open their books and draw.

2 SB p98 **Show your picture to your friend. Say.**

Aim: to practice language
- Students work in pairs.
- They show their drawing to their partner and say what they are doing.

1 WB p98 **Make a guessing game.**

Aim: to activate students' creativity

Key: Students' own answer

Ending the lesson

Aim: to review language from the unit
- Students say more things about their drawings from Activity 1, e.g., *I'm with (friend's name).*

Stronger students: Students write sentences about their drawings from Activity 1, following a sample you write on the board, e.g., *I'm with* (*friends' names*). *We are in/at* (*place*). (*Tom*) *is* (*running*)., etc.
- Students swap notebooks with a partner. Partners check if the sentences are correct.

Extension activity

Aim: to review language
- Students take out a photo. (see Materials)
- They describe their photos to a classmate, e.g., *I'm at the park. I'm with my friends. I'm playing soccer. I'm wearing a blue T-shirt.*

Learning outcomes:
- to review language from the unit by taking a quiz
- to reflect on learning

BIG QUESTION to think about how the unit has helped them answer the Big Question *What are hobbies?*

Recycled language: vocabulary and grammar from the unit

Creative thinking (WB): Creates texts that express personal interests, emotions, or identity

Cognitive control functions (WB): Cognitive flexibility

Warm-up

Aim: to review how charts work
- Elicit from students the number of girls and boys there are in the class.
- Draw a tally chart and a bar chart with students' help to review how charts work.

1 SB p99 **Read and match.**

Aim: to review key words from the unit
- Students do the activity individually.
- They check answers in pairs.

Key: 1 read, 2 swim, 3 paint, 4 play soccer

2 SB p99 **Complete.**

Aim: to review language from the unit
- Students look at the pictures and complete the blanks.

Key: 1 Are, 2 I'm not, 3 playing; I am

3 SB p99 **Read and count. Write the numbers.**

Aim: to review how charts work
- Students look at the incomplete charts and write the numbers.

Key: 1 4, 2 8, 3 7

1 WB p99 **Look and say. Circle ☺, 😐, or ☹.**

Aim: to assess performance

2 WB p99 **Match the numbers and pictures.**

Aim: to review language

Key: a Reading: 3, b Dancing: 7, c Playing soccer: 5, d Swimming: 1

3 WB p99 **Draw your favorite hobby.**

BIG QUESTION Aim: to revisit the unit Big Question

Ending the lesson

Aim: to enable students to express their preferences
- Ask students what their favorite activity is from the unit (e.g., the song, chant, or one of the games) and hold a class vote.
- Repeat the most popular activity with the class.

Extension activity

Aim: to enable students to share what they have learned
- Put students into groups of four.
- Each student opens their Workbook to page 99.
- Students take turns showing what they have drawn for Activity 3 and saying something about it.

Stronger students: Provide a sample with incomplete sentences for students to complete about their drawing, e.g., *My hobby. I'm (action). I'm wearing ________. I'm (place).*

1 Read and match.

1 

2 

3 

4 

swim play soccer read paint

2 Complete.

1 

________ you running?
Yes, I am.

2 

Are you running?
No, ________
________.

3 

Are you ________ soccer?
Yes, ______ ______.

3 Read and count. Write the numbers.

1 

☐

2 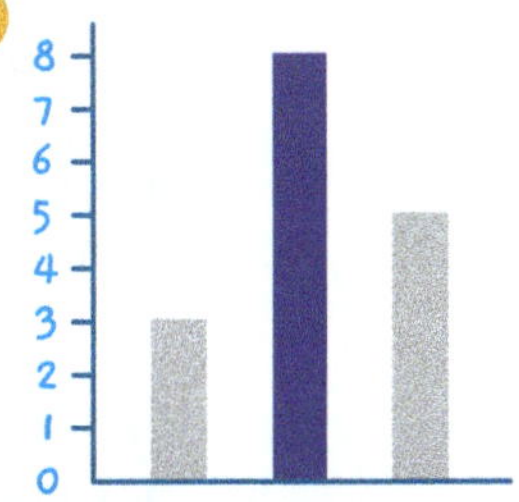

☐

3 

☐

Say *Hello*!

01 Student's Book p4, Act. 1

Misty: Hello, hello. What's your name?
Hello, hello. What's your name?
Whisper: I'm Whisper!
I'm Whisper!
I'm Whisper!
Misty: Hello, Whisper.
Hello, Whisper. Hello, Whisper.
Hey, Whisper. Let's be friends.
Whisper: Hello, hello. What's your name?
Hello, hello. What's your name?
Misty: I'm Misty!
I'm Misty!
I'm Misty!
Whisper: Hello, Misty.
Hello, Misty. Hello, Misty.
Hey, Misty. Let's be friends.

01 Workbook p4, Act. 1

Misty: Hello, what's your name?
Hello, what's your name?
Whisper: I'm Whisper!
Misty: Hello, Whisper.
Whisper, let's be friends.
Whisper: Hello, what's your name?
Hello, what's your name?
Misty: I'm Misty.
Whisper: Hello, Misty.
Misty, let's be friends.

03 Student's Book p5, Act. 1

Hello, what's your name?
Misty: I'm Misty.
Hello, what's your name?
Whisper: I'm Whisper.

02 Workbook p5, Act. 2

Misty: Hello, what's your name?
Whisper: I'm Whisper!
Whisper: Hello, what's your name?
Misty: I'm Misty.

04 Student's Book p6, Act. 1

blue
green
yellow
orange
red
pink

03 Workbook p6, Act. 1

One – red
Two – yellow
Three – green
Four – blue
Five – orange
Six – pink

05 Student's Book p7, Act. 1

one
two
three
four
five
six
seven
eight
nine
ten

04 Workbook p7, Act. 1

See above for script.

06 Student's Book p8, Act. 1

1 **Misty:** Oh, no!
Whisper: Poor rabbit.
2 **Whisper:** What's your name?
Rabbit: I'm Hop.
3 **Whisper:** Goodbye, Hop.
Misty: That's cool, Whisper! Watch this!
4 **Misty:** Close your eyes. Count to six.
Whisper: One, two, three, four, five, six.
5 **Whisper:** Where are you, Misty?
6 **Misty:** Here!
Whisper: Wow!
7 **Whisper:** Lets' be friends!
Misty: Yes, OK!
8 **Both:** Super friends!

05 Workbook p8, Act. 1

1 **Misty:** Oh, no!
Whisper: Poor rabbit.
2 **Whisper:** What's your name?
Rabbit: I'm Hop.
3 **Whisper:** Goodbye, Hop.
Misty: That's cool, Whisper! Watch this!
4 **Misty:** Close your eyes. Count to six.
Whisper: One, two, three, four, five, six.

06 Workbook p8, Act. 2

5 **Whisper:** Where are you, Misty?
6 **Misty:** Here!
Whisper: Wow!

1 My Classroom

07 Student's Book p10, Act. 1

Misty: Hello, Whisper.
Whisper: Hello, Misty.
Now say the words:
window
door
pencil
chair
book
table

08 Student's Book p10, Act. 2

One, two, three, four.
Table, chair, and a door.
Window, pencil, and a book.
Here's the classroom. Take a look.

07 Workbook p10, Act. 1

1 pencil
2 table
3 window
4 book
5 door
6 chair

08 Workbook p10, Act. 2

The table is blue and pink.
The window is orange and blue.
The chair is green and yellow.
The book is red and blue.
The pencil is yellow and blue.

09 10 Student's Book p11, Acts. 1 and 2

1 Open your book.
2 Close your book.
3 Stand up.
4 Sit down.

09 Workbook p11, Act. 1

Close your book. Color blue.
Sit down. Color yellow.
Open your book. Color red.
Stand up. Color green.

10 Workbook p11, Act. 2

Sit down.
Open your book.
Stand up.
Close your book.

11 Student's Book p12, Act. 1

Look! Look! It's my classroom.
Look! Look! It's my classroom.
Look! Look! It's my classroom.
Come along and see!

Tables, tables. Come and see.
Chairs, chairs. Come and see.
Doors, doors. Come and see.
Windows, windows. One, two, three.

(Repeat chorus)

Pencils, pencils. Come and see.
Books, books. Come and see.
Teacher, teacher. Come and see.
Children, children. One, two, three.

(Repeat chorus)

11 Workbook p12, Act. 1

See above for script.

13 Student's Book p13, Act. 1

1 What is it?
It's a pencil.
Yes, that's right.
2 What is it?
It's a table.
Yes!
3 What is it?
It's a book.
Yes, it is.
4 What is it?
It's a table.
No. What is it?
Ah, it's a chair.
Yes, that's right.

Student's Book p13, Act. 2

Penny: Sit down, Paul. Let's play.
Paul: OK.
Penny: What is it?
Paul: Hmmm. It's a book.
Penny: No, no, no.
Paul: Hmmm. It's a pencil.
Penny: No, no, no.
Paul: Hmmm. It's a table.
Penny: No, no, no.
Paul: What is it?
Penny: It's ice!
Paul: Ah, that's nice.

12 Workbook p13, Act. 1

1 What is it?
It's a book.
Yes, that's right.
2 What is it?
It's a chair.
Yes, that's right.
3 What is it?
It's a window.
Yes, that's right.
4 What is it?
It's a chair.
Yes, that's right.

13 Workbook p13, Act. 2

What is it?
It's a pencil.
Yes.

14 Student's Book pp14–15, Act. 1

1 **Misty:** Look! A butterfly.
2 **Misty:** Wow!
3 **Whisper:** Sit down, Misty. Close your eyes.
4 **Whisper:** Sit here, please, butterfly.
Butterfly: OK.
5 **Whisper:** Stand up, Misty.
Misty: OK.
6 **Whisper:** Sit here, butterfly. Open your eyes, Misty.
7 **Whisper:** Look!
Misty: It's beautiful.
8 **Whisper:** Shh … Be quiet, please.

14 Workbook p14, Act. 1

1 **Misty:** Look! A butterfly.
2 **Misty:** Wow!
3 **Whisper:** Sit down, Misty. Close your eyes.
4 **Whisper:** Sit here, please, butterfly.
Butterfly: OK.

15 Student's Book p16, Act. 1

1 crayon 2 pen 3 eraser

Student's Book p16

What is a pattern?
Look at the patterns!
What is it?
It's a crayon!
What color is it?
It's red!
It's a red crayon.
What is it?
It's a blue pen!
What is it?
It's a pink eraser!
Look at the pattern.
What's next?
It's a red crayon!
What is a pattern?
Let's find out more!

16 Student's Book p16, Act. 3

1 a red pen, a blue pencil, a red pen, a blue pencil, a red pen, a blue pencil
2 a green book, a yellow crayon, a green book, a yellow crayon, a green book, a yellow crayon
3 a pink eraser, an orange chair, a red pen, a pink eraser, an orange chair, a red pen

15 Workbook p16, Act. 1

a green book
a yellow pencil
a red and blue eraser

17 Student's Book p18, Act. 1

Close your eyes. Imagine a beautiful classroom ... a desk: what color is it?
Is it orange? Is it blue? Is it green?
And your chair: what color is it?
Is it pink? Yellow? Red?
Imagine a book and a pencil.
Imagine the door and the windows in your classroom.
Now open your eyes. Draw a picture of your beautiful classroom.

16 Workbook p18, Act. 1

Look at this beautiful butterfly. It's pink, yellow, and blue. It's so beautiful.
Look. Now it sits down on the red and blue desk.
Look. Now it sits down on the green book.
Look. Now it sits down on the pink and green pen.
Look. Now it sits down on the orange and yellow window.
Look. Now it sits down on the yellow and green door.

18 Student's Book p19, Act. 1

Open the window.
Close your book.
Sit down.
Stand up.

19 Student's Book p19, Act. 2

1 a green chair
2 an orange door
3 a red window
4 a yellow book

2 My Body

20 Student's Book p20, Act. 1

Whisper: Hi, Oscar.
Oscar: Hello, Whisper. Great costume!
Whisper: Thanks.

Now say the words:

ears
head
eyes
mouth
nose
arms
legs

21 Student's Book p20, Act. 2

A nose, a mouth.
Three legs, a head.
Four ears, three eyes.
And look! Five arms.
It's a monster!
Let's run, run, run!

17 Workbook p20, Act. 1

1 nose
2 arms
3 mouth
4 legs
5 ears
6 head
7 eyes

18 Workbook p20, Act. 2

Ears – pink. Color the ears pink.
Arms – blue. Color the arms blue.
Nose – green. Color the nose green.
Eyes – blue. Color the eyes blue.
Mouth – pink. Color the mouth pink.
Head – yellow. Color the head yellow.
Legs – orange. Color the legs orange.

22 Student's Book p21, Act. 1

1 I have one eye. Color me green.
2 I have three noses. Color me orange.
3 I have four eyes. Color me blue.
4 I have two noses. Color me red.

23 Student's Book p21, Act. 2

1 I have two noses.
2 I have four eyes.
3 I have three noses.
4 I have one eye.

19 Workbook p21, Act. 1

Monster 1: I have one eye. I'm monster one.
Monster 2: I have two noses. I'm monster two.
Monster 3: I have three legs. I'm monster three.
Monster 4: I have four ears. I'm monster four.

24 Student's Book p22, Act. 1

Run, run, run.
Here I come.
I'm a horrible monster.
I'm a horrible monster.

I have three arms, three legs,
Three noses, and one head.
I'm the chocolate monster.
My eyes are fiery red!

(Repeat chorus)

I have four arms, four legs,
Four noses, and I'm bold.
I'm the ice-cream monster.
My body is so cold!

(Repeat chorus)

I'm a horrible monster!

20 Workbook p22, Act. 1

See above for script.

26 Student's Book p23, Act. 1

Child: Hello, Monster.
Monster: Hello.
Child: How many eyes do you have?
Monster: I have one eye.
Child: How many noses do you have?
Monster: I have two noses.
Child: OK. You have two noses. How many ears do you have?
Monster: I have four ears.
Child: You have four ears. I see. How many arms do you have?
Monster: I have three arms.
Child: You have three arms. Uh-huh. And how many legs?
Monster: I have four legs.
Child: Four legs. OK. Thank you. Look at my picture of you.
Monster: That's nice!

Student's Book p23, Act. 2

Paul: How many eyes do you have?
Penny: Three. Three. I have three eyes.
Paul: How many heads do you have?
Penny: Two. Two. I have two heads.
Paul: How many noses do you have?
Penny: Five. Five. I have five noses.
Paul: How many legs do you have?
Penny: Six. Six. I have six legs.
Paul: Three eyes, two heads, five noses, six legs! Oh, no! A monster! Help!

21 Workbook p23, Act. 1

1 I have two heads.
2 I have three eyes.
3 I have four noses.
4 I have three arms.
5 I have three ears.
6 I have two mouths.

27 Student's Book pp24–25, Act. 1

1 **Misty:** Hello, Whisper.
Whisper: Oh!
2 **Whisper:** Where are you, Misty?
Misty: Here! I'm a monster.
3 **Whisper:** How many eyes do you have?
Misty: Four.
4 **Whisper:** How many noses do you have?
Misty: Two!
5 **Whisper:** And how many ears?
Misty: I have three.
6 **Whisper:** And how many arms?
Misty: Four arms.
7 **Misty:** Here I am. Look!
Whisper: Oh!
8 **Whisper and Misty:** Great costume!

22 Workbook p24, Act. 1

1 **Misty:** Hello, Whisper.
Whisper: Wooaahh!!!
2 **Whisper:** Where are you, Misty?
Misty: Here! I'm a monster.
3 **Whisper:** How many eyes do you have?
Misty: Four.

23 Workbook p24, Act. 2

4 **Whisper:** And how many ears?
Misty: I have three.
5 **Whisper:** And how many arms?
Misty: Four arms!

Student's Book p26

How does our skeleton move?
Look at the skeleton move!
Our skeleton has one head.
Shake your head!
Our skeleton has two legs.
Walk! Run! Sit!
Bend down and jump!
Our skeleton has two arms.
Stretch your arms!
Wave to your friends!
How does our skeleton move?
Let's find out more!

28 Student's Book p26, Act. 1

1 walk 2 run 3 wave

24 Workbook p26, Act. 1

1 Look. Number one. Wave.
2 Look. Number two. Stand.
3 Look. Number three. Run.
4 Look. Number four. Sit.
5 Look. Number five. Walk.

25 Workbook p26, Act. 2

1 run
2 wave
3 sit
4 run
5 walk

26 Workbook p27, Act. 3

1 leg – green
2 arms – blue
3 head – red
4 mouth – yellow

27 Workbook p27, Act. 4

1 Walk to the door.
2 Sit on the chair.
3 Stand near the table.
4 Say hello to butterfly. Wave.

29 Student's Book p28, Act. 1

1 Stand up.
2 Circle your head gently.
3 Stretch your arms.
4 Bend down.
5 Jump up high.
6 Wave to your friends.

28 Workbook p28, Act. 1

Crouch down. Down – down – down. Color it yellow.
Stand up. Up – up – up. Color it blue.
Circle your head gently. Gently – gently – gently. Color it orange.
Stretch your arms. Ahhhhhhhh. Stretch your arms. Color it green.
Jump up high. Wow! Jump up high! Color it pink.
Wave to your friends. Hello! Wave to your friends. Color it red.

30 Student's Book p29, Act. 1

eyes
ears
legs
mouth
arms

31 Student's Book p29, Act. 2

1 I have two ears and two legs. I have two mouths and two noses. I have four arms and four eyes. Red.
2 I have two ears and three legs. I have two arms and two noses. I have two eyes. Green.
3 I have four ears, four legs, and three eyes. I have two arms and one nose. Blue.
4 I have two ears and two legs. I have two mouths and three eyes. Pink.

3 My Family

32 Student's Book p30, Act. 1

Misty: Hey, Whisper. Look! This is my family.
Whisper: Wow! You have a big family.
Misty: Yes. This is my mom, and my dad, my sister, my brother, my grandma, and my grandpa.
Now say the words:
grandpa
grandma
mom
dad
sister
brother

33 Student's Book p30, Act. 2

Do you want to see
My crazy family?
There's my mom.
There's my dad.
There's my grandpa.
There's my grandma.
There's my sister.
There's my brother.
And there's me!
This is my crazy family!

29 Workbook p30, Act. 1

1 brother – pink
2 sister – green
3 grandpa – red
4 mom – yellow
5 dad – orange
6 grandma – blue

34 Student's Book p31, Act. 1

1 Hey, look. This is my family. Look. This is my brother, Tim.
Oh, yes, I see.
2 This is a photo of my family. Look. This is my dad. His name's Mike.
3 Look at my family. This is my grandpa.
4 This is my family. Look. This is my sister.

35 Student's Book p31, Act. 2

1 This is my brother.
2 This is my dad.
3 This is my grandpa.
4 This is my sister.

30 Workbook p31, Act. 1

1 This is my dad.
2 This is my brother.
3 This is my sister.
4 This is my grandma.
5 This is my grandpa.
6 This is my mom.

36 Student's Book p32, Act. 1

Two, or three, or four,
Or five, or six, or more.
What is a family?
Listen to me.

This is mom and me.
This is mom and me.
This is a family.
A nice family.

This is dad and me.
This is dad and me.
This is a family.
A nice family.

(Repeat chorus)

A mom, a dad, and me.
A sister and a brother,
This is a family.
A nice family.

A mom, a dad, and me.
A sister and a brother.
A grandpa and a grandma.
A nice family.

Two, or three, or four,
Or five, or six, or more.
This is a family.
A nice family.

31 Workbook p32, Act. 1

See above for script.

38 Student's Book p33, Act. 1

1 Is this your sister?
Yes, it is. She's two!
2 Is this your dad?
No, it isn't. This is my grandpa.
3 Is this your dad?
Yes!
4 Is this your mom?
Yes, it's my mom.
5 Is this your grandma?
Yes. It is.
6 And is this your brother?
Yes, that's right!

Student's Book p33, Act. 2

Paul: Hey, Penny. Hey, Penny.
Is this your mom?
Penny: No, it isn't.
This is my sister. My sister.
Penny's Brother: Hey, Penny. Hey, Penny.
I'm not your sister. I'm your brother. Your brother.
Penny: Ah, OK. This is my brother.
My brother.
Paul: Hey, Penny. Hey, Penny.
Is this your sister?
Penny: Yes, it is. This is my sister.
My sister.

32 Workbook p33, Act. 1

1 Is this your mom?
No, it isn't. This is my grandma.
2 Is this your brother?
Yes, it is.
3 Is this your brother?
No, it isn't. It's my sister.
4 Is this your grandpa?
Yes, it's my grandpa.
5 Is this your dad?
Yes. It is.
6 Is this your sister?
Hahaha. No, it isn't. It's my mom.

39 Student's Book pp34–35, Act. 1

1 **Misty:** Look!
Whisper: A squirrel.
2 **Whisper:** Hello. What's your name?
Squirrel: I'm Sammy. Hello.
3 **Squirrel:** Look! Nuts!
Whisper: Wow. How many do you have?
Squirrel: Ten!
4 **Squirrel:** For you!
Whisper: Thank you.
5 **Squirrel 2:** Hello.
Squirrel: This is my sister, Jumpy.
Whisper: Hello.
6 **Misty:** Look, Whisper!
7 **Whisper:** Is this your brother?
Squirrel: No, it's my grandma.
8 **Whisper:** Your grandma is cool!

33 Workbook p34, Act. 1

1 **Misty:** Look!
Whisper: A squirrel.
2 **Whisper:** Hello. What's your name?
Squirrel: I'm Rocky. Hello.
3 **Rocky:** Look! Nuts!
Whisper: Wow. How many do you have?
Squirrel: Ten!
4 **Rocky:** For you!
Whisper: Thank you.

Student's Book p36

What is an animal family?
Look at the dogs. Woof! Woof!
Look at their babies!
The cat is a mother. Meow!
Look at all of her babies!
Is this a chicken? Yes, it is! Cluck! Cluck! Cluck! Cluck!
The chicken has black and yellow babies.
Is this a chicken? No, it isn't. It's a baby duck! Quack! Quack!
The baby duck has lots of brothers and sisters!
What is an animal family?
Let's find out more!

40 Student's Book p36, Act. 1

1 chicken 2 dog 3 duck 4 cat

34 Workbook p36, Act. 1

This is the chicken. Color it orange.
Look. This is the cat. Color it blue.
And there's the dog. Color it red.
And what's this? It's a duck. Color it green.

35 Workbook p37, Act. 3

Start at the blue house. Go to the cat family. They are so lovely, aren't they? Now go to the duck family. OK, and now go to the dog family. Oh, look. Three little puppies. And now go to the family of chickens. There are four little chicks.

41 Student's Book p38, Act. 1

Close your eyes. Imagine there's a new baby in the family.
Is it a baby dog?
Is it a baby cat?
Or is it a baby duck?
Or is it a new brother or sister for you?
There's a new baby in the family.
Now open your eyes and draw the new baby.

36 Workbook p38, Act. 1

Look at the baby cat. Color it orange.
Look at the baby dog. Color it red.
Look at the baby duck. Color it yellow.
Look at the baby chicken. Color it blue.
And now look at the baby. Color it green.

42 Student's Book p39, Act. 1

mom dad
grandpa sister
brother grandma

43 Student's Book p39, Act. 2

Girl: Look. This is my mom.
Narrator: Red.
Girl: Look. This is my dad.
Narrator: Blue.
Man: Is this your grandma?
Girl: Yes! This is my grandma.
Narrator: Yellow.
Girl: This is my sister.
Narrator: Pink.
Man: Is this your grandpa?
Girl: Yes, it is.
Narrator: Green.
Man: Is this your brother?
Girl: Yes! This is my brother.
Narrator: Orange.

4 At the Zoo

44 Student's Book p40, Act. 1

Whisper: Look at all the animals!
Misty: Let's see the lions. Come on, Whisper.
Now say the words:

fish	lion
parrot	big
zebra	small

45 Student's Book p40, Act. 2

It's a lion.
It's big. It's big.
It's a fish.
It's small. It's small.
It's a zebra.
It's black and white
It's a parrot.
It's red and blue.

37 Workbook p40, Act. 1

1 a parrot	**3** a lion
2 a fish	**4** a zebra

46 47 Student's Book p41, Acts. 1 and 2

1 It's a big lion.
2 It's a black and white zebra.
3 It's a small fish.
4 It's a small lion.
5 It's a big fish.
6 It's a green parrot.

38 Workbook p41, Act. 1

1 It's a small zebra.
2 It's a small lion.
3 It's a big zebra.
4 It's a big lion.
5 It's a small fish.
6 It's a blue and red parrot.

48 Student's Book p42, Act. 1

Can see the lion in the zoo?
It's a big, yellow lion looking at you.
Can you see the zebra in the zoo?
It's a black and white zebra looking at you.
Looking at you.

Where are the animals in the zoo?
Can you find them?
Can you find them?
Where are the animals in the zoo?
They're looking at you!
They're looking at you!

Can you see the fish in the zoo?
It's a small, red fish looking at you.
Can you see the parrot in the zoo?
It's a green and red parrot looking at you.

(Repeat chorus x2)

39 Workbook p42, Act. 2

See above for script.

50 Student's Book p43, Act. 1

1 What's your favorite animal?
My favorite animal is a lion.
2 What's your favorite animal?
A parrot.
3 What's your favorite animal?
My favorite animal is a fish. A big, yellow fish.
4 What's your favorite animal?
A zebra!

Student's Book p43, Act. 2

Penny: Look! Look! At my book!
It's a fish. A big fish.
Paul: Oh, no! It's a shark. It's a shark. A white shark.
Penny Oh, no! No, thank you!
Paul: What's your favorite animal?
Penny: A penguin, of course!
A black and white penguin – like you!
Paul: Oh, really? Thank you!

40 Workbook p43, Act. 1

1 What's your favorite animal?
My favorite animal is a lion.
2 What's your favorite animal?
A parrot.
3 What's your favorite animal?
My favorite animal is a fish. A small, orange fish.
4 What's your favorite animal?
A zebra!

41 Workbook p43, Act. 2

What's your favorite color?
My favorite color? Mmm. It's green.
What's your favorite number?
It's one.

51 Student's Book pp44–45, Act. 1

1 **Misty:** Look, Whisper! It's a big lion.
Whisper: Yes, it's really big!
2 **Whisper:** Hi, I'm Whisper.
Lion: Hello, I'm Henry.
3 **Whisper:** Hi! How many stripes do you have?
Zebra: I don't know.
4 **Whisper:** Hi! I'm Whisper. What's your name?
Fish: Hi, I'm Tom.
5 **Whisper:** Wow! Look at that small fish.
Fish: Yes, it is small. It's my sister.
6 **Whisper:** Oh … I'm sorry, Misty. Come with me.
7 **Parrot:** Hello. What's your name?
Misty: I'm Misty.
8 **Misty:** My favorite animal is a parrot!

42 Workbook p44, Act. 1

1 **Misty:** Look, Whisper! It's a big lion.
Whisper: Yes, it's really big!
2 **Whisper:** Hi, I'm Whisper.
Lion: Hello, I'm Henry.
3 **Whisper:** Hi! How many stripes do you have?
Zebra: I don't know.
4 **Whisper:** Hi! I'm Whisper. What's your name?
Fish: Hi, I'm Tom.

43 Workbook p44, Act. 2

1 **Whisper:** Wow! Look at that small fish.
Fish: Yes, it's small. It's my sister.
2 **Whisper:** Oh … I'm sorry, Misty. Come with me.

Student's Book p46

What is an animal habitat?
Where do these animals live?
Look at the pond!
The frog lives in the pond.
The fish lives in the pond, too.
Look at the big tree!
The small monkey lives in the big tree!
The parrot lives in the tree, too!
Look at the grassland.
The giraffe, the zebra, and the lion live on the grassland.
What is an animal habitat?
Let's find out more!

52 Student's Book p46, Act. 1

1 monkey 2 frog 3 tree 4 pond 5 grassland

44 Workbook p46, Act. 1

Look at the frog. Color it blue.
Look at the monkey. Color it orange.
Look at the tree. Color it red.
Look at the pond. Color it green.
Look at the grassland. Color it yellow.

53 Student's Book p48, Act. 1

1 Let's go into the jungle.
2 Look! Can you see the parrot?
3 There it is! It's green and red.
4 Listen. What's that?!
5 Oh, no! It's a big lion!
6 Ruuuun!!

45 Workbook p48, Act. 1

1 Let's go into the jungle.
2 What can you see?
3 There! I can see a monkey. Wow!
4 Listen! What's that?!
5 It's a parrot. It's red, yellow, and blue.

54 Student's Book p49, Act. 1

parrot
lion
zebra
big fish
small fish

55 Student's Book p49, Act. 2

1 My favorite animal is a zebra. A black and white zebra.
2 My favorite animal is a fish.
3 My favorite animal is a big lion.
4 My favorite animal is a parrot.

5 My Food

56 Student's Book p50, Act. 1

Whisper: Mmm. Lots of food.
Misty: Yes, we have oranges, tomatoes, pears, milk, chocolate, and cupcakes.
Now say the words:

milk
cupcakes
oranges
tomatoes
chocolate
pears

57 Student's Book p50, Act. 2

Oranges,
Tomatoes,
Cupcakes, and chocolate.
Cupcakes, and chocolate.
Milk and pears.
Lots of food
For us to share.

58 59 Student's Book p51, Acts. 1 and 2

1 Yum! I like oranges.
2 Mmm. I like pears.
3 I don't like tomatoes. Yuck!
4 Ugh! I don't like milk.
5 I like chocolate. Yummy!
6 Ugh! I don't like cupcakes.

46 Workbook p51, Act. 1

Tom: I like pears.
Ruby: I like pears.
Tom: I like tomatoes.
Ruby: I don't like tomatoes.
Tom: I don't like milk.
Ruby: I like milk.

60 Student's Book p52, Act. 1

I don't like cupcakes.
Yes, it's true.
But I like oranges.
And I like you.
I like you.
I like you.

I don't like pears.
Yes, it's true.
But I like tomatoes.
And I like you.
I like you.
I like you.
I like you.
I like you.

I don't like milk.
Yes, it's true.
But I like chocolate.
And I like you.
I like you.
I like you.

47 Workbook p52, Act. 1

See above for script.

62 Student's Book p53, Act. 1

Do you like blue?
Yes, I do.
Do you like pink?
Yes, I do. I like pink.
Do you like yellow?
No, I don't. I don't like yellow.
Do you like red?
No, I don't.
Do you like orange?
Yes, I do. Orange is my favorite.
Do you like green?
No, I don't.

Student's Book p53, Act. 2

Paul: Do you like cake?
Penny: Yes, I do. I like cake.
Paul: Do you like pears?
Penny: No, I don't. I don't like pears.
Paul: Do you like chocolate?
Penny: Yes, I do. I really like chocolate. How about you?
Paul: Um.

48 Workbook p53, Act. 1

1 Do you like cupcakes, Eve?
Yes, I do.
2 Do you like pears, Eve?
Yes, I do.
3 Do you like oranges, Eve?
No, I don't.
4 Do you like tomatoes, Eve?
No, I don't.
5 Do you like chocolate, Eve?
Yes, I do.
6 Do you like milk, Eve?
No, I don't.

63 Student's Book pp54–55, Act. 1

1 **Misty:** Four cupcakes. Two for me and two for you.
Whisper: Thank you. I like cupcakes.
2 **Whisper:** Milk?
Misty: Yes, please.
3 **Whisper:** How many cupcakes do you have?
Misty: Four.
Whisper: No, You have three cupcakes.
5 **Misty:** And now I have two cupcakes!
Whisper: What? But …
7 **Whisper:** Sammy! It's you! That's not OK.
Sammy: Sorry.
Whisper: Come with me.
8 **Misty:** Cupcakes for Whisper, me, and our new friend!
Sammy and Whisper: Thank you!

Student's Book p56

Where do fruit and vegetables come from?
Where does our food come from?
Potatoes and carrots are vegetables.
Potatoes come from the ground.
Carrots come from the ground, too!
Do you like carrots? I do!
Pears, oranges, and bananas are fruit.
Bananas grow on trees.
Pears and oranges grow on trees, too!
Where do fruit and vegetables come from?
Let's find out more!

64 Student's Book p46, Act. 1

1 potatoes 2 carrots 3 bananas 4 ground

65 Student's Book p58, Act. 1

Close your eyes. Imagine a party. A party with lots of food.
Lots and lots of food. Mmmm.
There are cupcakes and oranges and chocolate and milk.
And there are lots of other things, too.
All the food you like is on this table.
All of your favorite food.
Take a plate. Now put the food on the plate.
Now open your eyes and draw your favorite food on your plate.

6 My Town

66 Student's Book p60, Act. 1

Misty: Where's the toy store?
Whisper: Hmm. I don't know.
Now say the words:

bus stop	movie theater	toy store
school	hospital	park

67 Student's Book p60, Act. 2

Movie theater, toy store, hospital, bus stop.
Through the park.
This is cool.
This is my way to school.

49 Workbook p60, Act. 1

1 bus stop
2 hospital
3 school
4 toy store
5 movie theater
6 park

68 Student's Book p61, Act. 1

Hi, I'm Will. In my town, there's a movie theater. There's a park. There are two schools.
Hi. My name's Flo. In my town, there's a park. There's a school. There are three bus stops.
Hello. My name's Tom. In my town, there's a school, a park, and a movie theater. And there's a hospital.
Hi. I'm Lola. In my town, there's a hospital and a park. There are two toy stores.

69 Student's Book p61, Act. 2

Will: There's a movie theater.
Tom: There's a school, a park, and a movie theater.
Lola: There are two toy stores.
Flo: There are three bus stops.

50 Workbook p61, Act. 1

Hi, I'm Ava. Look at the picture of my town. There's a park. There's a toy store. There are two schools, and there is a movie theater.
Color Ava's map yellow.
Hi. My name's Bob. Look at the picture of my town. There's a park.

There's a school. There are two toy stores.
Color Bob's map blue.
Hello. My name's Mia. Look at the picture of my town. There's a park. There's a toy store, and there's a movie theater.
Color Mia's map red.
Hi, I'm Nick. Look at the picture of my town. There's a park, a hospital, and two schools.
Color Nick's map green.

70 Student's Book p62, Act. 1

My town.
It's a really cool town.
Let's look at a map.
My town.
There are people all around.

There's a school.
There are three stores.
There's a hospital.
There are five bus stops.
(Repeat verse)

(Repeat chorus)

There's a park.
It's where I play.
There's a movie theater.
Let's go there today.
(Repeat verse)

(Repeat chorus)

51 Workbook p62, Act. 1

See above for script.

72 Student's Book p63, Act. 1

Where's the park?
It's there.

Where's the toy store?
It's over there.

Where's the bus stop?
It's there.

Where's the movie theater?
It's over there.

Student's Book p63, Act. 2

Penny: Where's the park?
Penguin 2: There's a park. There's a park. It's there.
Penny: Thank you!
Penny: Where's the movie theater?
Penguin 3: There are two movie theaters. There's one over there.
Penny: Thank you! ... Ahhhh.

73 Student's Book pp64–65, Act. 1

1 **Misty:** There's the movie theater.
Whisper: But where's the toy store?
2 **Misty:** Where are we?
Whisper: I have an idea!
3 **Whisper:** Excuse me. Where's the toy store?
Pigeon: Come with me.
4 **Pigeon:** Look! It's here.
Whisper: Thank you. Watch out!
5 **Pigeon:** Ouch.
Whisper: Oh, no!
6 **Whisper:** Stay here.
7 **Whisper:** Here you go.
Pigeon: Oh. Thank you.
8 **Pigeon:** Perfect!

52 Workbook p64, Act. 1

1 **Misty:** There's the movie theater.
Whisper: But where's the toy store?
2 **Misty:** Where are we?
Whisper: I have an idea!
3 **Whisper:** Excuse me. Where's the toy store?
Pigeon: Come with me.
4 **Pigeon:** Look! It's here.
Whisper: Thank you. Watch out!

Student's Book p66

What is a map of a town?
What is in this town?
Let's look at a map.
There's a movie theater in this town.
Is there a sports center in this town?
Yes, there is.
Is there a café in this town? Yes!
There are two cafés in this town!
Where's the market? It's here! Look at all the vegetables!
Where's the playground? It's here! It's my favorite place in town!
Wheeee!
What is a map of a town?
Let's find out more!

74 Student's Book p66, Act. 1

1 market
2 café
3 playground
4 sports center
5 hospital
6 movie theater

54 Workbook p67, Act. 3

1 Go to the school.
2 Go to the movie theater.
3 Go to the hospital.
4 Go to the park.
5 Go to the bus stop.
6 Go to the toy store.

75 Student's Book p68, Act. 1

1 You're at the playground.
2 You're at the movie theater. *Shhh!*
3 You're at home.
4 You're at school. *Hello, Class.*
5 You're in the toy store. *Wow!*
6 You're in bed. *Zzzzzzzzz.*

55 Workbook p68, Act. 1

You're in the hospital. Ahhh. Color it red.
You're in the park. Yeah. Color it blue.
You're in the café. Color it green.
You're at the sports center. Color it orange.
You're at the market. Color it yellow.
You're in bed. Color it pink.

7 Jobs

76 Student's Book p70, Act. 1

Misty: He's a police officer.
Whisper: And she's a doctor.
Now say the words:

teacher	gardener	vet
firefighter	police officer	doctor

77 Student's Book p70, Act. 2

Look! A teacher, a police officer, a doctor, a vet, a firefighter, and a gardener.

78 79 Student's Book p71, Acts. 1 and 2

1 He's a teacher.
2 He's a police officer.
3 She's a doctor.
4 He's a vet.
5 She's a firefighter.
6 She's a gardener.

56 Workbook p71, Act. 1

1 He's a gardener.
2 She's a doctor.
3 She's a firefighter.
4 He's a police officer.
5 He's a teacher.
6 She's a vet.

80 Student's Book p72, Act. 1

He's a teacher.
A teacher?
Say hello.
Hello.
He's a police officer.
A police officer?
Say hello.
Hi.
She's a vet.
A vet?
Say hello.
Hello.
And now …
And now?
It's time to go.
Oh. Goodbye.

All the different jobs that people do.
Helping me and helping you.

She's a doctor.
A doctor?
Say hello.
Hello.
He's a firefighter.
A firefighter?
Say hello.
Hi.
She's a gardener.
A gardener?
Say hello.
Hello.
Hi.
And now it's time to go.
Oh. Bye-bye.

(Repeat chorus)

Thank you.

57 Workbook p72, Act. 1

See above for script.

82 Student's Book p73, Act. 1

1 Is he a doctor?
No, he isn't. He's a gardener.
2 Is she a teacher?
Yes, she is.
3 Is he a firefighter?
No, he isn't. He's a police officer.
4 Is she a vet?
No, she isn't. She's a firefighter.

Student's Book p73, Act. 2

Friend: Is he your dad?
Penny: Yes, he is.
Friend: Is he a firefighter?
Penny: No, he isn't. He's a gardener.
Friend: Is she your mom?
Penny: Yes, she is.
Friend: Is she a doctor?
Penny: No, she isn't. She's a gardener, too.

58 Workbook p73, Act. 1

1 Is she a teacher?
No, she isn't. She's a gardener.
2 Is he a police officer?
Yes, he is.
3 Is she a vet?
No, she isn't. She's a doctor.

83 Student's Book pp74–75, Act. 1

1 **Teacher:** What's his job?
Whisper: He's a police officer.
2 **Teacher:** Stop it.
3 **Teacher:** What's her job?
Misty: She's a doctor.
4 **Misty:** Ouch!
Teacher: Oh, no. Now stay here.
5 **Teacher:** What's her job?
Whisper: She's a gardener.
6 **Whisper:** Look! I have lots of potatoes.
Teacher: That's great!
7 **Teacher:** And what's my job?
Whisper: You're a police officer *and* a doctor …
Misty: And you're a gardener …
Whisper: And …
8 **Whisper and Misty:** A teacher!

Student's Book p76

Which jobs are inside, and which are outside?
Where do they work? Inside or outside?
What's his job?
He's a farmer. He's outside.
What's her job?
She's a dentist. She's inside.
Open your mouth!
What's his job?
He's a salesclerk. He's inside.
This vet is outside. This vet is inside!
This teacher is inside. This teacher is outside!
Which jobs are inside, and which are outside?
Let's find out more!

84 Student's Book p76, Act. 1

1 farmer
2 salesclerk
3 dentist
4 inside
5 outside

85 Student's Book p78, Act. 1

Close your eyes. Imagine. What's your job?
Are you inside? Or are you outside?
Are you a doctor? Are you a farmer?
Are you a gardener Or a teacher? Are you a firefighter?
Are you a dentist? A window cleaner or a vet?
What are you? Choose a job.
Now draw your job.

8 My Clothes

86 Student's Book p80, Act. 1

Misty: I don't want to wear my coat today!
Now say the words:

hat
coat
scarf
sweater
boots
gloves
T-shirt
jeans

87 Student's Book p80, Act. 2

Jeans and T-shirt.
A coat and sweater.
Gloves and my boots.
A scarf and hat.
How cool is that!

88 Student's Book p81, Act. 1

1 Find me. I'm wearing jeans and my boots.
2 Find me. I'm wearing a sweater and a hat.
3 Find me. I'm wearing my coat and a hat.
4 Find me. I'm wearing jeans and a T-shirt.

89 Student's Book p81, Act. 2

1 I'm wearing jeans and my boots.
2 I'm wearing a sweater and a hat.
3 I'm wearing my coat and a hat.
4 I'm wearing jeans and a T-shirt.

59 Workbook p81, Act. 1

1 I'm wearing a hat.
2 I'm wearing a scarf.
3 I'm wearing boots.
4 I'm wearing a sweater.

90 Student's Book p82, Act. 1

It's cold! It's cold!
What can I do?
Put on more clothes.
That's good for you!
(Repeat)

I'm wearing my jeans,
My T-shirt, and sweater.
Now I'm wearing my hat.
Oh, that's much better.

(Repeat chorus)

Now I'm wearing my coat.
And I'm wearing my boots.
And I'm wearing my scarf.
Oh, look! That's so cute!

(Repeat chorus)

60 Workbook p82, Act. 1

See above for script.

92 Student's Book p83, Act. 1

So, what's Fran wearing?
She's wearing a green sweater.
A green sweater. Ah, OK. Here it is.

Is Will wearing a sweater?
No, he isn't. He's wearing a blue coat.
OK. A blue coat.

Is Fran wearing a scarf?
Yes, she's wearing an orange scarf.
OK. It's here. And is she wearing a hat?
No, she isn't wearing a hat.

Is Will wearing a hat?
Yes, he's wearing an orange hat.
OK. An orange hat.

Is Fran wearing boots?
Yes, she is. Blue boots.
Thanks.

And is Will wearing a scarf?
No, he isn't.
OK. Is he wearing red boots?
Yes, he is. He's wearing red boots.

Student's Book p83, Act. 2

Woman: Look at Paul.
Is he wearing a coat?
Children: No, he isn't. No, he isn't.
Woman: Is he wearing a scarf?
Children: No, he isn't. No, he isn't.
Woman: Is he wearing a hat?
Children: Yes, he is. Yes, he is.
Woman: Look at Penny.
Is she wearing a coat?
Children: Yes, she is. Yes, she is.
Woman: Is she wearing a scarf?
Children: Yes, she is. Yes, she is.

Woman: Is she wearing a hat?
Children: Yes, she is. Yes, she is.
Paul: Oh, Penny. Penny, stop!
Oh, Penny. Penny, stop!
Penny: Weeee! . . . Look! I'm wearing my hat!

61 Workbook p83, Act. 1

1 Is he wearing a hat?
2 Is she wearing gloves?
3 Is he wearing boots?
4 Is she wearing a T-shirt?
5 Is he wearing jeans?
6 Is she wearing a scarf?

93 Student's Book pp84–85, Act. 1

1 **Mom:** Is that you, Misty?
2 **Mom:** What are you wearing?
Misty: Uh, jeans and my red T-shirt.
3 **Mom:** It's cold. Put on a sweater.
Misty: OK, Mom.
4 **Misty:** I'm wearing my sweater now!
Mom: Good. But put on your boots and a scarf.
5 **Misty:** OK. I'm wearing my boots and my scarf.
6 **Mom:** OK. But put on your coat and your hat, please.
Misty: Oh, Mom!
7 **Mom:** Misty?
Misty: I'm wearing my hat and coat now. Bye!
8 **Misty:** Oh, no. I'm hot now!

62 Workbook p84, Act. 2

1 **Mom:** What are you wearing?
2 **Misty:** Uh, jeans and my red T-shirt.
3 **Mom:** It's cold. Put on a sweater.
4 **Misty:** I'm wearing my sweater now!
Misty: Oh, no. I'm hot now!

Student's Book p86

How are clothes different?
Clothes are soft . . . and clothes are hard.
Look at this sweater. It's soft.
Look at this hat. It's hard.
This belt is soft. This belt is hard.
It's hot! He's wearing sunglasses.
Is he wearing boots? No, he isn't.
It's cold! She's wearing a hat, a scarf, gloves, boots, and a sweater.
Is she wearing a T-shirt? No, she isn't! She's wearing a coat.
How are clothes different?
Let's find out more!

94 Student's Book p86, Act. 1

1 soft
2 hard
3 cold
4 hot
5 belt
6 sunglasses

95 Student's Book p88, Act. 1

1 Put on your sweater.
2 Put on your scarf.
3 Put on your coat.
4 Put on your gloves and your hat.
5 Look in the mirror.
6 Say, "Cool!"

63 Workbook p88, Act. 1

Put on your sweater. Color it green.
Put on your scarf. Color it red.
Put on your coat. Color it orange.
Put on your gloves and your hat. Color it blue.
Look in the mirror. Color it yellow.

96 Student's Book p89, Act. 2

Hi, I'm Tim. I'm wearing a green sweater, a yellow scarf, and jeans.
Hi. My name's Kate. I'm wearing a red coat, a yellow scarf, and an orange hat.
This is Sally.
Is she wearing a green coat?
Yes, she is.
Is she wearing a blue hat? No, she isn't. It's orange.

9 My Hobbies

97 Student's Book p90, Act. 1

Misty: Swim club is for me.
Whisper: Dance club is for me.
Misty: Ooh! Soccer club!
Whisper: Mmm. Yes!
Now say the words:
play soccer | paint a picture | read
run | swim | dance

98 Student's Book p90, Act. 2

Read and paint.
Let's have fun!
Swim and dance.
Let's have fun!
Play soccer.
Run, run, run!!

99 Student's Book p91, Act. 1

1 Look. I'm running.
2 Look at me. I'm painting.
3 Look. I'm swimming.
4 Look at me. I'm dancing.
5 Look. I'm playing soccer.
6 Look. I'm reading a book.

100 Student's Book p91, Act. 2

I'm reading a book.
I'm painting.
I'm dancing.
I'm swimming.
I'm running.
I'm playing soccer.

101 Student's Book p92, Act. 1

Play and fun.
Fun and play.
All together.
Play today.

(Repeat chorus)

I'm reading.
I'm having fun.
I'm swimming.
I'm having fun.
I'm dancing.
I'm having fun.
Come on. Come on.
Come on, everyone!

(Repeat chorus)

I'm playing soccer.
I'm having fun.
I'm painting.
I'm having fun.
I'm running.
I'm having fun.
Come on. Come on.
Come on, everyone!

(Repeat chorus x2)

64 Workbook p92, Act. 1

See above for script.

103 Student's Book p93, Act. 1

1 Are you swimming?
Yes, I am.
2 Are you reading?
No, I'm not. I'm painting.
3 Are you running?
No, I'm not. I'm playing soccer.
4 Are you reading?
Yes, I am.
5 Are you dancing?
Yes, I am.
6 Are you running?
Yes, I am.

Student's Book p93, Act. 2

Penny: Look at me!
I'm swimming. Look, Paul, look! I'm swimming.
Penny: Look at me!
I'm running. Look, Paul, look! I'm running.
Penny: Are you running?
Paul: No! No, I'm not.
Penny: Are you dancing?
Paul: Yes! Yes, I am.

65 Workbook p93, Act. 1

1 Are you playing soccer?
Yes, I am.
2 Are you painting a picture?
No, I'm not.
3 Are you running?
No, I'm not.
4 Are you swimming?
Yes, I am.
5 Are you dancing?
No, I'm not.
6 Are you reading.
Yes, I am.

104 Student's Book pp94–95, Act. 1

1 **Misty:** Soccer Club is in here.
Whisper: Great!
2 **Whisper:** Let's play a game! Guess what I'm doing?
3 **Misty:** Uh, OK. Are you dancing?
Whisper: No, I'm not!
4 **Misty:** Are you swimming?
Whisper: Yes! I'm swimming!
5 **Misty:** OK. My turn!
6 **Whisper:** Where are you, Misty?
7 **Misty:** Guess, Whisper! Guess!
8 **Whisper:** Ow!
Misty: I'm sorry, Whisper! Are you OK?
Whisper: Yes, I'm OK.

66 Workbook p94, Act. 1

1 **Misty:** Soccer Club is in here.
Whisper: Great!
2 **Whisper:** Let's play a game! Guess what I'm doing?
3 **Misty:** Uh, OK. Are you dancing?
Whisper: No, I'm not!
4 **Misty:** Are you swimming?
Whisper: Yes! I'm swimming!

67 Workbook p94, Act. 2

1 **Whisper:** Let's play a game! Guess what I'm doing?
2 **Misty:** Are you swimming?
3 **Misty:** OK. My turn!
4 **Whisper:** Where are you, Misty?

Student's Book p96

How do we make a bar chart?
Let's make a tally chart.
How many children are reading?
One, two, three, four, five, six.
Let's make a bar chart about hobbies!
How many children like computer games?
One, two.
Three children like swimming.
Four children like movies.
And two children like dancing.
Look at the bar chart!
How do we make a bar chart?
Let's find out more!

105 Student's Book p96, Act. 1

1 bar chart
2 tally chart
3 computer games
4 movies

106 Student's Book p98, Act. 1

Close your eyes. Imagine you're with your friends.
How many of you are there? Are you a small group of children? Or are you a big group of children?
It's a beautiful day. What are you doing?
Are you swimming? Or reading? Or are you running around? What are your friends doing?
Dancing? Painting? Playing soccer?
Now open your eyes and draw what you and your friends are doing.